D.J. VELLA

MY LIFE WITH
THE KID

D.J. Vella

MY LIFE WITH THE KID
Copyright © 2025 by D.J. Vella. All rights reserved.

Stratus Publishing
contact@stratuspublishing.com

The characters and events portrayed in this book are fictitious. Any similarity to real persons, living or dead, is coincidental and not intended by the author.

No part of this book may be reproduced, or stored in a retrieval system, or transmitted in any form or by any means, electronic, mechanical, photocopying, recording, or otherwise, without express written permission of the publisher.

ISBN-13: 979-8-9997594-1-2

Book cover designed by Lance Hancock Design
Editor: Sara DeGonia | DeGoniaEditing.com
Printed in the United States of America

My Life with the Kid

D.J. Vella

My Life with the Kid

To my late mother and father—whose quiet strength and unwavering love taught me that even in the darkest chapters, there's always a reason to keep turning the page. Their memory is stitched into every line of this story.

And to my grandfather—whose life was a tapestry of hard truths and unforgettable tales. His stories didn't just inspire this novel; they gave it its pulse. In every moment of danger, longing, and redemption, his legacy lives on.

D.J. Vella

CHAPTER ONE
WALDORF ASTORIA, NYC

The air buzzed with quiet anticipation—low murmurs, clinking glasses, the soft hum of jazz drifting through the space—as we stepped into the grand ballroom of the Waldorf Astoria Hotel.

My wife, Amy, and I moved toward the check-in table, scanning the seating chart for our assignment. Table 17. A prime spot, just behind the first row of tables that lined the dance floor.

I glanced around, my eyes quickly landing on familiar faces—friends, acquaintances, and a few old adversaries—their presence stirring echoes of past encounters. The night promised intrigue.

As we approached our table, I spotted Natalie sitting alone, her posture relaxed yet watchful. The moment her eyes met mine, she sprang to her feet, her voice rising with surprise. "I can't believe it! How are you? I've been so looking forward to seeing you guys."

I smiled, taking in the warmth in her expression. "I'm great.

With so many familiar faces here, it feels like we've stepped back in time."

She nodded, a wistful smile curving her lips. "The only thing missing is the Kid."

I held her gaze for a beat before replying with quiet certainty. "Give it time."

As Amy and Natalie exchanged a warm embrace, I eased into my seat, facing the dance floor. The chair to my right remained open for Amy, while Natalie took her place beside her—a familiar presence I had known for most of my life. An accomplished singer with striking features, she stood at five foot three, her enviable figure effortlessly drawing attention. I couldn't ignore the absence of her husband, a man I had only met on a few occasions, but I decided against asking where he was.

As more guests arrived, the space around our table filled with an eclectic mix of personalities. To Natalie's right sat a couple I didn't recognize, their conversation low but animated. Farther down the line sat my cousin Joanne and her friend Olivia—two faces my wife and I both knew well. Having recently separated from her husband, Joanne had chosen to bring Olivia along for company, a choice that felt fitting for the occasion.

To my left, one seat remained empty, waiting for its intended occupant. Beyond it sat another couple, also unfamiliar to me. But it was the woman, Annette, who immediately caught my attention. Her short blonde hair framed striking blue eyes, and she carried herself with an effortless grace—a refined sweetness that set her apart. Elegantly dressed and youthful in appearance, Annette exuded a quiet charm, one that I didn't yet know would leave its mark on the evening. As it turned out, she was a distant cousin of the man we had gathered to celebrate—though I didn't know it then—a connection that would unfold in ways I couldn't anticipate.

After the introductions, my wife, Natalie, Joanne, Olivia, and I launched into reminiscing about the good old days. We had shared a history that stretched back to our teenage years in Los

Angeles during the late 1970s—a time full of unforgettable moments. As the room steadily filled with guests, I noticed more and more familiar faces among the crowd.

People frequently stopped by our table to greet one of us, and it wasn't long before our little corner of the room became a hub of activity. It wouldn't have been surprising if the other guests at our table started thinking we were celebrities, given the sheer number of visitors and the attention we received. Of course, Natalie truly carried some star power thanks to her successful singing and acting career. But beyond that, we all shared a unique connection to someone who had profoundly impacted our lives—a bond that brought with it a certain air of importance.

Table 16, just to our left, was filled with a mix of current and former members of La Cosa Nostra from Los Angeles. I recognized most of them, and they certainly recognized me as well. At six feet three and 230 pounds, I wasn't exactly someone who blended into the background. At forty-eight years young, I was no longer looking for any trouble, but I would never turn my back on it if it came my way.

To the left of Table 16 sat Table 15, where members of some of the Five Families from New York were gathered. The atmosphere around those tables carried an undeniable weight, a reminder of old alliances and reputations that could never truly fade.

James Mallarino, the renowned heartthrob singer of the 1960s, occupied Table 7—situated right in front of ours, off the dance floor. His fame was tied not only to his own iconic career but also to his close connection with Paul Vicarro, the legendary singer and actor who defined an era in Hollywood. Though Paul was no longer with us, his influence remained deeply woven into all our lives. Jimmy shared the table with his wife, Elizabeth (Beth), family members from Philadelphia, and several pop singers of his generation. The table was large, mirroring his significant legacy. The event celebrated Jimmy's achievement; the NY Actors Guild had named him Favorite Actor of the

1960s—a well-deserved honor. This gathering was nothing short of extraordinary, as every notable figure in Jimmy's orbit seemed in attendance.

As we chatted, I leaned toward Amy to whisper something, but a loud voice from my left cut through the conversation. Turning, I saw a man from Table 16 towering over Annette, his tone sharp and aggressive as he barked, "You shouldn't be here."

His words were loud enough to draw attention, and he grabbed her left arm, pulling her up from her chair and drawing her close to emphasize his point.

"I want you to leave, and leave now," he demanded.

Annette's face froze in fear. I glanced at the man she had been sitting with, hoping he'd step in, but he remained motionless, paralyzed by uncertainty. It was clear he wouldn't act.

I stood up, my voice firm as I said, "What the hell is wrong with you? Let her go."

His response came immediate and hostile: "Mind your business and shut the fuck up."

Not exactly the kind of words I responded very favorably to.

I knew he was connected to someone at Table 16, and though I had walked away from that life, I understood the potential consequences of intervening. Still, there was no way I could stand by and watch him intimidate and manhandle her. As I moved toward him, he released her, bracing himself for what was coming. Before things could escalate, several men from Table 16 quickly stepped in, forming a barrier between us. Vic, a captain in the Poporri family, seated at Table 16, approached and demanded we stop.

"Philly, you should know better," he said, his tone carrying both authority and familiarity.

"What would you have me do?" I shot back. "Watch this moron smack the girl around?"

Vic sighed, brushing it off. "He's had a few drinks. Just leave it alone."

I nodded, agreeing to de-escalate, though the tension lingered. Vic turned to the man, who I learned was named Mitch, and ordered him back to their table. Mitch, a hot-headed associate in his early forties with a build that screamed overconfidence, reluctantly obeyed. He carried himself as if untouchable, but it was clear his invincibility would soon be tested.

I settled back into my seat as my wife Amy, Natalie, Joanne, Olivia, and I resumed our lively conversation. Suddenly, a wave of murmurs rippled through the room, and I caught the phrase "I don't believe it" echoing around us. Turning to my right, I saw him—"the Kid"—walking in, accompanied by JJ, who was practically a fixture at his side these days.

It had been two years since I'd last seen him, as I'd been out of the country, though we spoke on the phone all the time. As he entered, the room seemed to come alive. People flocked to him, shaking his hand, greeting him warmly, and wrapping him in hugs.

My cousin Joanne, with a knowing tone, muttered, "Of course she has her arms around him."

The "she" in question was a woman clinging to him as he made his way through the crowd. His reputation with the ladies was legendary, and, from experience, I could confirm it was well-earned.

The Kid eventually reached Table 7, where Jimmy, his family, and friends were seated. Before he could settle in, Joanne sprang to her feet, exclaiming, "Kid!"

He turned, his face lighting up. "Oh my God, I don't believe it." Making his way over to us, he added, "I had no idea you guys were flying in to be here. I only found out yesterday that I'd even make it." He explained that he'd spent the past two weeks in Tokyo, working on a deal, and had only just returned.

Greeting Joanne, Olivia, and Natalie with hugs and kisses, he finally turned to Amy and me.

"You two, get over here," he said with a grin, pulling us into a warm embrace. "It's so good to have you guys home. I wish I could have been there when you got in."

I smiled. "It's good to be back."

"We have so much to catch up on and go over," the Kid said. "Tokyo was great; I had some very interesting meetings. You guys feel like learning Japanese? Just kidding."

We both laughed.

After our warm reunion, the Kid's gaze wandered over to Annette.

"Oh, my goodness, Annette, how are you? I haven't seen you in forever."

Annette's response was barely audible—a soft "hi" as she kept her eyes low.

I couldn't help but blurt out, "You know her?"

"Yeah," he replied casually, "she's Jimmy's cousin. Why?"

I looked to see where Jimmy was, but he wasn't around. I shook my head. "If I'd known she was connected to you or Jimmy, I would've handled it differently."

At that, the Kid's friendly demeanor shifted to one of concern. "Handled what? What are you talking about?" he asked, furrowing his brow.

"Damn, Kid," I muttered. "I wish I'd known that earlier."

Clearly puzzled now, he leaned in. "Philly, what's going on? What happened?"

I took a deep breath and laid it all out for him: how Mitch had stormed over to our table, grabbed Annette, and threatened her right in front of everyone. As I recounted the incident, the Kid's expression grew darker with each word—the warmth of our reunion quickly replaced by a simmering anger. I couldn't help but notice that everyone at Table 16 had become visibly uneasy; their eyes flitted nervously between us, as if they shared our disquiet.

"Who was it?" the Kid finally demanded.

I gestured toward Mitch, who was leaning casually against a concrete column just steps from their table.

"Let me handle it," I offered, ready to step in.

But the Kid shook his head quickly and firmly. "No, we're not looking for trouble tonight," he said calmly. "You and JJ stay here; I'll go talk to him."

There it was—a quiet resolve replacing the shock. The Kid's protective instincts had taken over, and despite the unsettling circumstances, he wouldn't let things escalate further tonight.

Turning to Annette, his tone softened. "Are you okay?" he asked.

She managed a tearful "yes," though her eyes still glistened with uncertainty.

Sensing her discomfort, he probed further. "Do you know who he is?"

Annette hesitated before replying, explaining that she had seen him a few times years ago, back when her ex-husband was still in the picture. Her ex-husband had moved to LA and became associated with the Poporri family before landing in prison on a five-to-eight-year sentence for armed robbery.

I noticed the Kid taking off his sport jacket and watch, clearly preparing for a serious conversation. At forty-eight, he still carried himself with the strength and poise of a younger man, his presence commanding attention. As he walked over, the room seemed to still—everyone at Tables 16 and 15 looked up, silently watching the interaction unfold. Despite the tension, no one made a move or said a word.

JJ and I instinctively positioned ourselves a few feet away from the Kid, flanking him on his right and left sides, ready to step in if needed. When the Kid approached Mitch, the atmosphere grew heavier.

Mitch, oblivious to who the Kid was or the significance of his presence, sneered. "What the fuck do you want?"

"I'm just a guy who wants to explain something to you," the Kid calmly replied.

Mitch, still defiant, said, "Yeah? What's that?"

At that moment, we saw the Kid's left fist plunge into Mitch's throat, forcing him to grab his throat with both hands. The Kid kicked him square in the balls so hard that we saw Mitch's eyes about to bulge out of his head. The Kid snap-kicked him in the right knee, and he went down. It all took no more than ten seconds.

The room grew quieter as the exchange unfolded, with people standing nearby, including me, JJ, Jimmy, Vic, and a few of Vic's men.

Vic eventually stepped forward, his voice cutting through the tension, "Jimmy"—who was back from his disappearance—"stop this."

It was clear that only a select few could influence the Kid in moments like this—Jimmy being one of them. Their bond, forged over decades, was unshakable. Jimmy had been like an older brother to the Kid, guiding him since they'd first met when the Kid was just seven years old. That connection was something no one could break.

Jimmy stepped in. "Kid, stop. That's enough. I think he's got the message."

The room's tension seemed to ease as two of Vic's men moved to assist Mitch, who was visibly hurt and unsteady on his feet.

The Kid turned toward Mitch, fixing him with a sharp glare. "Hey, tough guy, don't you want to know what I was going to tell you?"

Mitch appeared in a lot of pain, his knee probably broken, but he looked at the Kid.

"You're not as tough as you think you are," the Kid said, looking at the two guys holding Mitch up. "Get him out of my sight."

Vic nodded to his guys, and they immediately did just that. The Kid looked at Vic, Vic looked back, and they both nodded. It was over, and everyone returned to their tables.

"I'll be back," the Kid said, and he headed over to Jimmy's table.

As if the evening hadn't taken such a dramatic turn, he greeted everyone at Table 7 with his usual charm, mingling effortlessly and leaving the tense moment behind.

We all took our seats again, and a pretty, wide-eyed woman in her thirties—Claire, who'd previously introduced herself—pushed her wine glass aside. "I've never seen anything like that!" Her cheeks were flushed, her tone somewhere between awe and disbelief.

I chuckled. "That was nothing. You should've seen him back in his prime."

Graham, a lean man in a slate-gray suit seated at our table—also someone I'd just met—leaned forward, his voice low but clear. "Would you mind telling us about it? Sounds like there's a good story there."

I paused for a moment, reflecting on the countless memories I'd shared with the Kid over the years. "Sure, if you're interested."

The table seemed to collectively nod in the affirmative. So, I prepared to take them back in time, weaving together the stories that defined him, me, and those unforgettable younger days.

CHAPTER TWO
THE KID MOVES TO LA

*E*veryone at the table listened in anticipation of what I was going to say, so I cleared my throat and began.

Let me start with the Kid's real name, Dominic Argianno.

Dominic was the kind of kid who could be your closest ally—or your deadliest foe—depending on who you were. In the late '70s and early '80s, few dared mess with him. And even now, as you've just witnessed, that indomitable presence hasn't faded one bit.

I paused, recalling the first time we crossed paths.

I met Dominic back in 1975. We were both fifteen years old. I walked into our usual hangout—the Malibu Grill in LA—and there was this new kid, hanging out like he was sizing up the place. The Grill was the spot back then for teenagers who thought they were somebody in LA. We were a tough crowd, all of us between fifteen and twenty-five, dreaming about how we'd become the next "made guy." We idolized the movie *The Godfather*—but we still blasted the Beach Boys, the Four Seasons, and, of course, Vicarro's music. Vicarro was just on another level.

Dominic was a young face, new to the scene. Ralph—"Fat Man," we called him, though never to his face—was one of the older guys, probably in his late thirties. He ran the Grill for the Poporri family and was a tough son of a bitch. When I realized Fat Man knew Dominic, I figured he must be all right. Still, I didn't know much about him at that point.

Then one day, Rocco stopped by the Grill. When Rocco showed up, everyone took notice—he wasn't just any guy. He was a captain in the Poporri family and one of Paul Vicarro's closest men. And if you knew anything about LA back then, you knew Paul had all the clout. Rocco didn't come around for idle chatter, so when I saw him talking to Dominic, I knew this Kid had connections. Rocco's presence alone made everyone stop and pay attention.

I leaned back, letting the memories wash over me.

Paulo Vicarro—Paul—was a name you couldn't ignore. He was a famous singer of his time, a true legend. But what made him fascinating wasn't just his talent—it was the entourage of "made guys" that always surrounded him. Paul was the nephew of Carlo Poporri—Pop—head of the powerful Poporri family in LA. It was a strange mix: Hollywood glamour and the kind of loyalty that made you realize he was no ordinary celebrity.

As Dominic and I got to know each other, I remember asking him one day, "How do you know Rocco?"

Without hesitation, he replied, "He's part of the family." That single sentence hit me like a ton of bricks. No matter how tough I thought I was, I knew better than to mess with someone connected to Rocco. Rocco had a reputation that preceded him—he was as ruthless as they came. As a captain in the Poporri family, his name alone carried enough weight to make most people think twice. Few dared to challenge him, and I wasn't about to be one of them.

Dominic's connection to someone like Rocco made it clear that this kid wasn't just anyone. I once saw Rocco beat two guys half to death because he thought they were making jokes about Paul. Some of the other stories I heard about Rocco were even worse—like guys who crossed Rocco and were never seen again.

The Poporri family held sway over organized crime in California, with deep ties to the Barbieri family in New York. At the helm was Pop, who wielded significant power but answered only to Lorenzo Barbieri—the *capo di tutti capi* in New York. Their bond ran deep, rooted in their shared birthplace of Licata, Sicily. This connection solidified their alliance and ensured that Pop's authority was rarely challenged. It was a dynamic that shaped the landscape of organized crime in LA during their reign.

As time went on, Dominic and I started talking more, and before long, we were hanging out regularly. He was a good kid—easy to talk to, with a natural charm that drew people in. Over the course of a year, our friendship grew stronger, and we became inseparable. We'd spend our days swapping stories and chasing girls, and let me tell you, even at sixteen, Dominic always had girls around him. He had that effortless magnetism that set him apart.

One day, two new guys started showing up at the Grill. A few of the older guys seemed to know them, but it was clear from the start that these two were trouble. They carried themselves with an air of intimidation, and it didn't take long for them to start throwing their weight around. They'd boss people around, and most either complied, stopped coming to the Grill altogether, or ended up regretting it.

The leader of the pair was a guy named Mikey. He was built like a tank—a bodybuilder and a former Golden Gloves boxer. Tough as nails, with a temper to match, Mikey was the kind of guy who'd rather throw a punch than have a conversation. His hands were fast, no doubt about it, but as I'd later find out, there was someone whose hands would become even quicker. But that's a story for later.

CHAPTER THREE
THE KID GETS A NICKNAME

One day at the Grill, Mikey was sitting at a table with two of his guys, eating and chatting. He called out to Dominic, who was sitting with me at the counter, and demanded that he bring him some mustard. I saw the look on Dominic's face—he wasn't used to being ordered around like that. It was clear Mikey didn't know who Dominic was connected to, or he would have thought twice about it.

Dominic hesitated for a moment but then got up and brought the yellow mustard over to Mikey's table. When he handed it to him, Mikey stood up and said, "What the fuck, are you stupid? Don't you know by now I like the spicy brown mustard? You are a fucking moron," as he lifted Dominic by his shirt off the ground and pulled him in close.

Again, Dominic said nothing.

Mikey said, "Do you hear me, loser?"

No response.

Mikey was twenty-five. Dominic was sixteen. But Mikey

didn't care. He smacked Dominic so hard I thought he'd knocked some of his teeth out. Dominic went down, and Mikey walked over and kicked him in the gut. "Next time, you get me what I want."

Everyone there just watched without saying a word. Dominic got up, limping and bleeding from the mouth as he started to walk away. I went to help him, but Mikey said to me, "Leave him the fuck alone or I'll lay you out next."

I froze. I didn't know what to do. Dominic was my friend, but at the same time, I didn't want to get my face kicked in.

Dominic looked at me and said, "It's okay, Philly. I'll be okay," as he started to limp home alone.

It wasn't until later that I understood the full extent of Dominic's background. He lived in Paul's house, surrounded by Paul's family members, and was treated as part of the family. What truly surprised me was learning about Dominic's grandfather and his significant ties to the Barbieri family in New York. His grandfather had been a trusted captain for Lorenzo Barbieri, the head of the family, and often traveled to California on behalf of Lorenzo's business interests. Through these trips, he formed a close friendship with Paul—a connection that would shape Dominic's life.

Dominic's grandfather had begun bringing him along on these California trips ever since he was barely seven years old. As he grew older, Dominic's participation was limited to school holidays—as restricted by his mother—but nothing could break the bond between them. Being his grandfather's only grandson, their relationship proved as steadfast as it was rare.

When Dominic turned fifteen, his ties to California deepened as he moved to California to live full-time in Paul's house. He attended school with the rest of us and began to make a new life for himself, still looking forward to his grandfather's visits.

His grandfather, a man who not only navigated the treacherous maze of organized crime but also carefully laid the groundwork for Dominic's potential role within the family, had indelibly marked his destiny. Those early experiences ran deep, defining Dominic in ways I hadn't yet understood at the time.

So that day, Dominic walked into Paul's house bleeding from the mouth and looking beat up, and Paul saw him and said, "What the hell happened to you?"

"I'll be okay," Dominic said.

Paul was insistent that Dominic tell him what had happened. Let me also mention that Rocco was like part of the family as well, and although Rocco worked for Paul and took orders from him, he was still part of the Poporri family.

More importantly, Rocco liked Dominic and thought of him like a little brother.

Finally, with enough nagging, Dominic agreed to tell Paul what had happened, but he wanted Paul's promise that Paul would do nothing. Dominic insisted that he wanted to handle this himself, in his own way, in his own time. Paul apparently agreed, so Dominic told him what happened and who beat him up.

Later, Dominic told me, "As soon as I told them what happened, Rocco immediately blurted out, 'I'm going to kill that prick.'"

"Uncle Paul, you gave me your word," Dominic said.

Paul said, "Okay, are you sure? I can have Rocco fix this."

Dominic said, "No."

Paul looked at Rocco and said, "Let this pass."

"But Paul—" Rocco said.

Paul immediately cut him off, responding, "Let it go."

Rocco nodded his head yes.

The room hung on my every word, as I set the stage for how Dominic became "the Kid."

About two hours after the altercation with Dominic, I'm still hanging out at the Grill with a bunch of guys, including Mikey. Suddenly a black Cadillac rips around the corner, pulls up, and out comes Rocco, Johnny—another made guy—and two other guys I didn't know. Everyone froze, because when these guys came around, you stood up and listened, even Mikey.

It was a warm day, but for some reason, one of the two guys sitting in the back of the car that I didn't know was wearing a trench coat. I found out why as they were leaving. Rocco immediately walked right up to Mikey and grabbed him by the throat. I was standing three feet away from Mikey, so I heard what was said.

"I have been instructed not to kill you," Rocco said. "That Kid you smacked around before has more balls than you'll ever have. If it weren't for him, you would be in the fucking ground right now. So, let me explain something that even a moron like you can understand."

Rocco is squeezing his throat so tight as he is talking that Mikey is starting to turn blue. "That Kid is very special to me, and when someone fucks with him, they are fucking with me. You so much as look at him cross-eyed again, I don't care who tells me what not to do, I will beat you so badly you will beg me to put two fucking bullets in your head, do you understand me?"

Mikey quickly nodded yes as best he could, with complete fear all over his face. Rocco let go, and Mikey took a big breath.

"I'm sorry. I didn't know," Mikey said.

"You know now."

As the four of them turned and walked back to the car, I noticed the guy with the trench coat slipping a sawed-off semi-automatic shotgun out from under his trench coat as he got in the car. Everyone at the Grill realized how close Mikey came to not breathing.

And that's how Dominic got his nickname "the Kid." Rarely did anyone ever call him Dominic after that day. The name just stuck.

After they left, everyone sat stunned. We all knew that no one was to touch this kid under any circumstances unless you wanted to deal with Rocco and his crew. I knew at that moment: this kid was going places. I just felt it. He could have had Mikey killed but decided not to.

That night, I headed over to Paul's house to check in on the Kid. The moment I walked in, I saw Rocco, his demeanor cold and distant. It was clear he wasn't in a friendly mood. Rocco was the kind of guy whose approval mattered—a man you absolutely wanted to stay on the good side of.

When I made it upstairs to the Kid's room, we started to chat. He looked thoughtful, almost contemplative. Then he shared something that left me stunned.

"Paul told me," he began, "he spoke to my grandfather, and they decided if I want to learn how to handle things myself, I'm going to need some special training."

I asked what he meant by that, curiosity taking over, and he hesitated for a moment before continuing. "No one is supposed to know," he said, lowering his voice. "Please don't repeat it."

I could feel the weight of what he was about to say and hesitated myself, realizing the responsibility of knowing something so secretive. But the Kid trusted me enough to tell me anyway.

Paul had orchestrated something extraordinary—something most people couldn't even imagine. Through quiet influence and the kind of leverage that only decades in the shadows could earn, he secured the Kid a place in a covert, ultra-classified CIA field program hidden deep in Southern Nevada. This wasn't your standard-issue training at "the Farm," where typical agency recruits learned tradecraft. This was something altogether different—more intense, more selective, and far more secretive.

It was a program whispered about in the corridors of Langley, reserved for a handful of elite operatives being groomed for off-the-books operations. Admission wasn't just about skill—it required a sponsor with serious clout in the agency. Paul knew the right people to make it happen. He cashed in old favors, navigated back channels, and pulled strings buried so deep in the intelligence community they practically hummed with static.

This wasn't about survival in back alleys or handling neighborhood threats. The lessons here would be different—sharp, calculated, designed for a world where mistakes were fatal and the line between predator and prey blurred in the shadows. Paul and the Kid's grandfather knew exactly what they were setting in motion. And when the Kid stepped into that training facility, he wouldn't just be walking into another phase of his life—he'd be walking into something far more intense, far more defining, far more life-changing.

CHAPTER FOUR
CIA TRAINING

The Kid was only sixteen when he left, a teenager stepping into a world most could hardly imagine. The year at the Grill without the Kid felt strange—like a void in the rhythm of our group. I'd heard whispers that he'd been back once or twice on leave, but he never came around, nor did he call. I found myself wondering whether he was intentionally keeping his distance or if it was part of the strict discipline his training demanded. There were moments of doubt, wondering if he'd moved on from me and the guys altogether.

Life went on, and I focused on my own goals, hitting the gym regularly and getting bigger. But when I finally saw the Kid the following summer, at seventeen, it was as though I was looking at someone entirely new. The transformation was undeniable.

He carried himself differently—more confident, more deliberate in his actions. You could see it in his eyes, in the way he sized up a situation with quiet strength.

His demeanor was unshakeable, and it was obvious he'd grown tougher, both mentally and physically.

He had started to build muscle—a sign that whatever he'd been through that year had left him stronger in every sense. The Kid wasn't just back; he had evolved into someone who felt larger than life.

It was clear that whatever training he'd undergone had shaped him into the person everyone now knew as "the Kid."

When the Kid came by the Grill, he greeted me warmly, giving me a big hello, and we shared a firm hug. Everyone else chimed in with greetings, except for Mikey, who sat there with a cautious expression, unsure of how to react. While the Kid didn't acknowledge Mikey directly, he made no effort to avoid his gaze either. The tension between them hung in the air, unspoken but palpable. After some small talk, the Kid turned to me and said, "Let's go get some lunch." I understood right away that he wasn't interested in sticking around the Grill to eat, so we left together.

Once we were alone, I took the opportunity to ask him how things were going and what the training had been like. His answer, delivered with both candor and quiet pride, offered me a rare glimpse into a world that was reshaping him.

"Let me tell you," he began, "the training is intense and extremely difficult, but I'm learning a lot. I put in twelve to fourteen hours a day, every day. It's not all physical, but most of it is. I've got a private tutor keeping me on top of my schoolwork, though I'm not sure that part is going too well," he admitted with a faint grin.

He leaned in, eyes glinting with a mix of intensity and pride as he laid out the details of his training. "They're not just teaching me hand-to-hand combat—we're mastering everything, from knives and batons to handguns and long rifles. But the real backbone of the program is Japanese Kenpo."

He paused, letting the significance of his words sink in.

"Kenpo isn't purely about brute force," he explained, his eyes glinting. "It's about balance—a blend of offense and defense that flows naturally. We practice rapid-fire combinations: punches, kicks, elbows, and knees, all chained together so that you can overwhelm an opponent before he has a chance to react. The throat—one of the most exposed, vulnerable points on the human body—is where I set my sights. Every day, without fail, I train my strikes to land there with precision. It's not about brutality; it's about efficiency. One clean shot, and it's over. I don't just practice the motion—I study the anatomy, the timing, the fear it provokes. Because in a real fight, hesitation is the enemy, and the throat is the shortcut to silence."

His voice softened a fraction as he continued. "And it's not just about striking. We learn to block and parry dynamically—not by stiff, static shields but by redirecting an attacker's force, turning their momentum into an opening for our own counterattack."

He shifted slightly, as though moving naturally into another part of the lesson. "A key part of Kenpo is the art of moving fluidly, effortlessly shifting between defense and offense. Every technique is honed for efficiency—every motion calculated to conserve energy and maximize impact. It's all about understanding body mechanics, the right angles, and using leverage to my advantage."

Then his tone grew even more measured, hinting at a deeper philosophy. "Beyond the physical techniques, Kenpo teaches us situational awareness. We learn to read an environment, to evaluate a threat in mere seconds, and decide whether to counter, evade, or neutralize an aggressor. And the stress drills—they mimic real-life encounters, forcing us to think and act quickly under pressure."

He leaned back, a confident calm settling over him. "In short, Kenpo is about training ourselves to react instantly and decisively, no matter what comes our way. It's not simply a martial art—it's our lifeline."

"I spend two hours every day, one hour when I wake up and another before bed, working on stretching and building speed. The Kenpo training is no joke; it's really intense. When I started, they measured the speed and range of my punches and kicks. Just last week, they checked again, and I'm up 300 percent from when I started."

His tone grew more reflective. "There's a psychological element too—something I never really expected. It's all about keeping calm under pressure and mastering your mind. Every sparring session leaves me with more aches, bruises, and scars than I ever thought possible. But strangely enough, I'm not afraid of the bruises anymore. I'm even looking forward to the next training session in two weeks."

As I listened, I could see how much he'd grown—not just physically but mentally. The Kid had become someone entirely different, someone shaped by rigorous discipline and the challenges he'd faced head-on. It was clear this was just the beginning for him.

When he was finished, I joked, "Are you ready to kick Mikey's ass yet?"

The Kid's laugh was infectious as he replied, "No, not yet, but I'm sure as hell getting there. You'll know when I'm ready. He'll know too." His confidence was unmistakable, and it was clear he had his own timeline for everything.

During his two weeks back, my cousin Joanne couldn't hide her excitement whenever he was around. She'd always been crazy about him, and with just a week left before he had to leave, they finally started seeing each other. From that point on, I didn't see much of him—he spent most of the next week with her, and I couldn't blame him. When it was time for him to leave, he gave me a casual, "I'll see you soon," before heading off again.

True to form, the Kid kept his distance, and I wouldn't see him for another six months, until one of his weekend trips back—a reminder that in his world, he was always moving forward, forever evolving.

Paul's two daughters were older than the Kid, but the bond they shared was genuine—they all got along seamlessly, like family. Paul's connections, however, were what truly set him apart. The story goes that in 1947, when Paul met the infamous Giovanni "Silk" Vitelli in Cuba, the Kid's grandfather was by his side. That moment, they say, marked a turning point for Paul, solidifying his influence with the family and earning him the respect of those in power.

Despite not being a made man himself, Paul's relationships ran deep. His web of connections was so vast and intertwined with powerful figures that it gave him an almost mythical status. People assumed he was part of the mob because his authority and influence spoke volumes—even without an official title. I guess being Pop's nephew didn't hurt. It made his position unique, straddling the line between two worlds, yet firmly commanding respect in both. Something the Kid would look to emulate in the future.

By the time the Kid was eighteen, his time at the intense training school was nearing its end, though he still returned occasionally for short stints to refine his skills. His dedication to staying sharp didn't waver—he trained daily at a local gym. When he was back in LA, I joined him, making it part of my routine too. He began teaching me hand-to-hand techniques I'd never even heard of growing up on the streets. The methods he shared gave me a true sense of confidence and fearlessness I hadn't experienced before.

The Kid was spending almost all his time in LA by then, and our bond deepened. We were practically inseparable, sharing not just workouts but countless conversations and laughs. As I grew closer to him, I also found myself welcomed into Paul's world. I started developing a better relationship with Paul's family and got to know Rocco and Johnny on a different level. Rocco, who had always been a figure of quiet intimidation, began to warm up to me. There was something about those occasional smiles of his—they felt like rare, hard-earned moments of approval. Over time, I found myself able to relax in his presence, which was no small feat given his reputation. Life during those days felt like it was shifting, as if I were stepping into a world much larger than I had imagined.

It all felt surreal, attending a "graduation" unlike anything I'd ever imagined. Jimmy's call had been intriguing enough, but once we arrived at the supposed steel-fabricating complex in Nevada, it became clear this was no ordinary event. Paul's private plane had brought us there in style, but the setting—a hidden CIA training facility—set the tone for something extraordinary. The ceremony itself was understated, nothing like a traditional graduation. There was no cap and gown, no speeches, no crowd—just the Kid, Paul, Rocco, Johnny, Jimmy, and me, seated silently around a boxing ring. The atmosphere was charged, though quiet, as if everyone understood the significance of what was about to take place.

It wasn't long before we learned that this "graduation" required the Kid to pass one final test. The "master," who had personally overseen the Kid's training, stepped into the ring to set the stage. He was an older gentleman, his movements deliberate and composed. He reminded me of the master from the TV show *Kung Fu*—wise, skilled, and commanding respect without speaking a single word. A fifth-degree martial artist with decades of experience, he was a figure that inspired both reverence and curiosity.

The tension in the room rose as three men entered the ring, all looking physically fit, fully equipped with protective gear—gloves, body pads, and headgear. The challenge was clear: the Kid would have to hold his own against these three men for a full minute. It sounded simple enough, but the setup made it clear that this was no small feat.

The rules for the bout were clear: once any one of the three opponents hit the canvas, they were immediately ruled out and barred from launching further attacks.

When the master signaled for the Kid to enter, there he came. At five foot eleven and 170 pounds, the Kid was in peak condition. His V-shaped frame was all muscle, lean and powerful, with not an ounce of fat on him. His arms—measuring a solid fifteen inches—were a testament to his training dedication. He looked every bit the part of someone who'd spent the last two years forging himself into a disciplined and formidable force. This was it—the culmination of everything he'd been working toward. All eyes were on him as he stepped into the ring, prepared to prove that his training had made him unshakable. The challenge ahead was clear, but there was no doubt in my mind that the Kid was ready for it.

The master rang the bell, signaling the start of the Kid's final test, and what followed was nothing short of astonishing. The Kid was off the ground at the sound of the bell— he must have been five feet in the air, swirling with a kick to the head that knocked the first guy down to the canvas. At the same time, one of the other guys leapt up in the air, trying to kick the Kid in the head, but the Kid somehow moved, and punched him in the balls with his fist from below.

I could not believe the speed. It was hard to follow. The guy went straight down and hit the canvas hard. The third guy stood in front of the Kid, and it was a kick and four punches before he was on the canvas too. All three guys were now lying on the canvas. The Kid moved with such speed and precision that it was almost impossible to follow his actions. He displayed an incredible combination of agility and control, effortlessly engaging with his opponents in a way that left everyone watching in awe.

Within moments, the Kid had demonstrated the full extent of his training, neutralizing the challenges presented by the exercise with remarkable efficiency. His movements were fluid, calculated, and masterful—every action executed with a purpose. By the time the master rang the bell again, the demonstration had ended, and the Kid walked over to check on the other participants, ensuring they were fine. They all stood, shook hands, and exchanged respectful bows.

The master addressed us, his voice filled with pride. "In all the years I have taught, Dominic is the absolute best and fastest I have ever trained. No one in the history of this program has ever completed the final exam with such skill and precision and done so in thirty seconds."

His words affirmed what we all knew: the Kid was ready for whatever came next.

The master addressed him with a respect that reflected the gravity of the moment. "Dominic," he began, "you are the very best I have ever trained. Your dedication and skill are unmatched, and if you continue to work hard and refine your craft, no one will ever get the better of you."

He paused; his voice steady as he shared a deeper truth. "But there is something you must understand. In this world, skill alone doesn't always command respect. Because of your demeanor and appearance, those who do not know you will not fear you because they are not aware of your ability. They may mistake your quiet confidence for weakness and challenge you, unaware of your true abilities."

The master's words to the Kid resonated deeply, carrying a mix of wisdom, encouragement, and caution.

The master's tone softened, conveying a genuine care for the Kid. "I know the life you were born into, and I know the people who surround you. You have a good heart—a good soul. Never let anyone take that away from you. Use your skills for good, not for evil. To prevent many altercations that will obviously come before you, at some point, you must demonstrate what you are capable of, just as you did tonight in the ring. Then people will fear you, and you won't always have to prove your ability again and again.

"When the situation calls for it, and only then, pick out the biggest, meanest, toughest individual and let everyone see you beat him like they have never seen an individual beaten before. After that, you will no longer have to prove anything to anyone. But make sure that person deserves the beating you give him."

The sincerity in his words hung in the air, leaving a mark not just on the Kid, but on everyone present. It was advice born of experience, a reminder to balance strength with purpose, and to wield power with responsibility. It was the kind of guidance that hinted at the challenges ahead while reinforcing the character needed to face them. Those words would set the stage for everything that was to come. The exchange between the Kid and the master felt like a perfect conclusion to the chapter.

When the master bowed and wished him well, the Kid returned the gesture with respect but couldn't help showing his appreciation by throwing his arms around him and saying, "Thank you." The warmth of the moment was genuine, and it said a lot about how much the Kid valued the guidance and mentorship he'd received.

As we all left, the mood lightened. Everyone started playfully teasing the Kid about hugging the master, though it was clear they admired the connection the two shared. The plane ride back to LA felt celebratory—an air of accomplishment and camaraderie as we reflected on the Kid's incredible journey.

We capped off the night with dinner at the Brown Derby in a private room, away from the bustle. The laughter, good food, and stories made it one of those evenings you never forget—a celebration of not just the Kid's achievements but the bond we'd all built along the way. It truly felt like the beginning of something great.

Joanne looked at me in awe. "I always thought the CIA thing was just a rumor," she said. "Are you saying he actually went there? For two years? How did I not know that?"

I smiled and said, "Because it was a secret back then."

CHAPTER FIVE
STANDING ON HIS OWN

The Kid's determination to carve his own path was something I always admired. Despite Paul's generous offers to set him up with something more comfortable or lucrative, the Kid stood firm. "No," he'd say, "I want to make it on my own." That sense of independence defined him, even if it meant taking on tough, physical jobs like loading boxes onto trailer trucks.

I never fully understood why he didn't immediately step into his grandfather's shadow. There was no rebellion in him, no defiance—just a quiet resistance, as if something unseen was gently steering him elsewhere. Maybe it was the quiet strength in the master's teachings, or the grounding presence of his mother's unwavering love and dreams for him. Whatever it was, it shaped him in subtle, powerful ways.

I found myself drawn into his current, sensing his journey was meant to be different. And though I couldn't yet name it, I was certain his true path would reveal itself in time—like a story unfolding in low, reverent tones, meant only for those patient enough to listen.

It wasn't glamorous work—backbreaking at times—but the Kid's mindset made it worthwhile. I used to nudge him, tossing out ideas like setting up bookmakers or putting money out on the street, thinking it would be an easier and more profitable route. But he'd just shake his head and smile. "Let's try playing it straight," he'd say, with that unshakable belief in doing things the right way.

Those days at the loading docks weren't just about earning a few bucks. They were a testament to the Kid's character—his drive, his discipline, and his refusal to take shortcuts. It was as if every box he loaded was another step toward proving he could stand on his own, no matter how tough the road. That ended rather quickly when Jake got in his face.

Jake was the type of boss who seemed to thrive on barking orders, pushing buttons, and making sure everyone knew he was in charge. He wasn't small either—a big guy in his early twenties with a presence that commanded attention, whether you wanted to give it or not. The other workers had warned us about him, saying he always singled someone out to ride hard, shifting his focus from one person to the next every day. It seemed like a calculated way to keep everyone on edge and working as fast as possible, probably because his paycheck depended on our efficiency.

Jake never picked on me. Maybe it was my size—something about me must've given him pause. But one Tuesday, he turned his sights on the Kid. From the moment we hit the ground that morning, Jake was on him, throwing out snide commands and barking corrections like, "Pick it up," or, "Stop slouching." It was relentless. The Kid stayed calm, steady as ever, absorbing it all with that quiet composure he was known for. But you could see it—Jake wasn't just pushing buttons; he was looking for a confrontation.

Midway through the day, Jake finally crossed a line. "Either you pick it up," he snapped, stepping in close, "or I'll smack you silly."

The Kid didn't flinch. He met Jake's glare, voice low but unwavering. "You can bark all you want," he said, "but if you try to put your hands on me, it will be something you will regret for a very long time."

Everyone stopped lifting boxes and watched. I guess Jake felt he had to do something, or no one would respect him again. He went to either punch or smack the Kid in the face. This was the first time I saw the Kid in action outside of the graduation. Jake swung; it was priceless. The Kid blocked and threw a punch, then a kick, and I saw a tooth and blood spew from Jake's face. The Kid worked on the body with two or three punches, Jake was on the floor, and it was over.

The Kid bent down to Jake lying on the floor. "Do you know where the social club off Malibu Boulevard in the Italian section is?"

Jake, looking slightly uncertain but ultimately nodded, acknowledging that he did.

The Kid continued in his composed tone. "You're going to pay me and Philly for the whole week. Deliver our week's pay to the club. If you fail to deliver, I'll be back, and I can promise you the next conversation will be far less pleasant than this one. Clear?"

Jake, clearly shaken, nodded once more.

Without missing a beat, the Kid turned to me and said, "Let's go. We're done here."

And just like that, we left.

As we were leaving, I said to the Kid, "Did you break any ribs in making your point?"

"One, maybe two," he said, "but I'm not sure I should have done that. Remember what the master said to me. Jake is no one except an asshole."

"Not to worry," I said. "I have a feeling there will be more assholes in your future."

We laughed and went to lunch.

That Friday night at the club felt like a turning point—like we'd just closed the final page of one chapter and were cracking open the first lines of the next. When Jake walked in and handed over the envelope, there was a weight to it, a quiet sense of finality. No more boxes. No more shadowing other men's missions. I saw it in the Kid's eyes—he was already two steps ahead, thinking about the road forward.

After Jake left, the Kid turned to me with a small smirk. "All right, Philly, we're done loading boxes. Let me talk to my grandfather—we'll start putting some money on the street."

That night, the Kid went home and called his grandfather. As always, the conversation was direct, no small talk.

His grandfather's first question cut straight to it: "Are you ready to come back to New York and work with me?"

There was a pause. The Kid took a breath.

"If I came back and worked with you, it would crush my mother. I won't do that to her."

His grandfather didn't argue—he understood all too well. His daughter had never accepted the life he chose. She'd built her world as far from it as she could, and the Kid's respect for that ran deep. After a quiet moment, his grandfather said, "All right, I'll speak to Pop and Paul. I'm sure it won't be a problem."

True to his word, the old man made the calls. Strings were pulled. Doors opened. A few days later, his grandfather called and explained the terms: the Kid wouldn't be officially part of the Poporri family, but with his grandfather's blessing, he'd be allowed to operate under their protection in LA. He'd need to kick up to one of Pop's captains—standard arrangement—but he'd be independent.

Paul, ever loyal and always watching out for the Kid, stepped in with an offer before anyone asked. He'd back the Kid financially, front the capital for his street operation.

When his grandfather heard that, he nodded in approval. "That's a good man," he said. "He believes in you. Don't let him down."

Paul had two daughters he adored, but no sons. I think that ever since the Kid moved in with him, Paul began to see him as the son he never had. From arranging the CIA training to standing by him through thick and thin—he did everything a father would do.

Just like that, the wheels were in motion. Quietly. Efficiently. The Kid wasn't in the life—but he wasn't entirely out of it either. Not yet.

With Paul's backing and his grandfather's blessing, we started loaning money—carefully, methodically, and always with an eye for opportunity. Before long, we crossed paths with a bookmaker who needed protection. The arrangement came naturally, and just like that, we found ourselves taking a slice of his action.

It was the start of something bigger, a venture that combined the Kid's calculated approach and my drive to make our mark. Those days were filled with possibility, like we were laying down the foundation for a future that was just beginning to take shape.

The arrangement with one of Pop's captains kept things smooth for us. By kicking up a piece of the earnings, we avoided any interference from the Poporri family.

It seemed like word had traveled quickly that we were not only handling our business but also aligned with the Kid's grandfather and Paul—both of whose reputations carried weight.

That alone gave us enough breathing room to operate without problems.

The money started rolling in steadily, though it wasn't anything to write home about at first. There were moments when we had to apply a little pressure to those who were late with payments—nothing too dramatic but enough to remind them of who they were dealing with.

I'll never forget the first time we lent a thousand dollars to Bill, a guy who ran with a tough crowd but clearly didn't understand the rules of the game.

The payment was due on Friday, but when Friday came, Bill was nowhere to be found.

I immediately said, "Let's go pay Bill a visit."

The Kid, calm as ever, said, "Let's give him until Monday. If he doesn't show, we'll pay him a visit."

It seemed the Kid was always going out of his way to avoid confrontation.

Monday came and went, and still no sign of Bill. That evening, the Kid turned to me and said, "Let's go take a ride."

It was early in the evening when we pulled up to the bar Bill liked to frequent. The place was buzzing with about twenty people, all nursing drinks and chatting away. The Kid scanned the room and spotted Bill at the bar, deep in conversation with two of his guys.

I was ready to jump in, fists flying, just waiting for the Kid's nod. But the Kid had his own plan.

As soon as Bill saw us, he stammered, "I know I'm late, but I had a few issues."

Before he could finish his excuse, the Kid moved like lightning—spinning and kicking Bill square in the teeth. In the same fluid motion, he snapped the leg of one of Bill's guys standing next to him. The third guy froze as the Kid turned to him and said, "It's your choice."

The guy shook his head no, backing up a step, clearly deciding he wanted no part of this.

The scene was chaotic—Bill was slumped on the bar, blood dripping from his mouth, while his buddy writhed in pain, clutching his broken leg.

The Kid leaned in and said to Bill, "Tomorrow, you'll drop off what you owed last Friday. Plus, the vig for this week is now double. And I expect another payment this coming Friday. Miss one payment, and you'll be walking on stumps. Am I clear?"

Bill, trembling, managed to choke out, "Absolutely."

As we walked out, I couldn't help but ask, "Why didn't you let me take one of them out?"

The Kid smirked and replied, "Honestly, I figured if I

handled it and they were just watching you, they'd be more afraid of what you might do because of your size. Plus, I needed the exercise."

We both laughed, but the message had been sent loud and clear.

After that, we rarely had issues with late payments. Still, I couldn't shake the feeling that we were laying the foundation for something bigger—maybe even paving the way for the Kid to get made one day. But life has a funny way of upending expectations on their head, and I was way off on that one.

After six months of grinding, we finally squared up the $100,000 loan with Paul. When the Kid tried to hand over more as a gesture of gratitude, Paul wouldn't hear of it.

"Absolutely not," he said, firm but with a hint of pride. "Now you're on your own."

It was a defining moment—a quiet acknowledgment that the Kid had reached a new chapter, one where he would need to stand on his own.

A few days later, the Kid got a call from his grandfather. He didn't say much—just one sentence, simple and weighty. "Dominic," he said, his voice gravelly with age and meaning, "I'm proud of you."

That was it. No long speech. No elaboration. But those four words carried the weight of a lifetime.

Later, the Kid told me about the call. He said it was so fulfilling, deeper than he expected. Hearing those words from the man he'd looked up to his whole life filled him with a quiet, lasting pride. For all the paths he didn't take, for all the ones he chose instead, that call was a sign he'd done something right.

"It meant everything," he said. "I'll never forget it."

About a month later, it was a Friday night around 10:00 p.m., and we were sitting at a quiet table in a restaurant, finishing dinner before heading out to the clubs. The mood was light, laughter floating between bites and drinks.

Then Rocco walked in.

His eyes scanned the room until they landed on us. He made a beeline straight to our table.

He didn't sit. He just stood there, serious, his face etched with something heavy.

"Kid," he said, voice low and grim, "we need to go back to the house."

The Kid looked up, sensing something was off. "What's going on, Rocco?"

Rocco hesitated, his mouth moving before the words could form. "It's—your grandfather," he finally said. "He's gone."

The Kid froze. For a moment, it looked like time itself paused around him. His expression shifted slowly—from confusion to disbelief, and then to something raw and painful.

We were on our feet in seconds, leaving my car behind in the parking lot and piling into Rocco's with Johnny driving. The silence in that car felt like a weight pressing on all of us.

On the drive, the Kid turned to Rocco, seated in the passenger seat. "Give me the details. Now."

Rocco shifted uncomfortably. "Paul wants to tell you himself."

That didn't sit well.

The Kid's voice erupted with more rage than I'd ever heard from him. "Tell me the fucking details now, Rocco. I'm not waiting."

Rocco sighed, almost like it hurt to say it. "He was shot. Your grandfather. He was having dinner with one of the Romano family captains. The Romano family's in the middle of a war—small, but deadly. That's all I know. Two shooters. Everyone at the table went down."

We pulled into the driveway minutes later. Paul was already there, waiting by the front door. His face was lined with grief, and when the Kid stepped out of the car, Paul met him with open arms. They embraced like father and son.

Inside, without delay, the Kid asked, "Do we know more than what Rocco told me? Dinner with a Romano captain? What else?"

Paul glanced at Rocco, but the Kid cut him off. "Don't look at him. I forced it out of him."

Paul nodded solemnly. "I got the call from Lorenzo about an hour ago. Your grandfather was having dinner with a Romano captain—someone he trusted. But that captain's family is neck deep in a civil war. Two shooters hit them mid-meal. Your grandfather's two guys went down, along with three others. We don't know yet who ordered it or who pulled the triggers. But we'll find out."

The Kid was quiet for a moment. "Paul, I need to get back to New York."

Paul didn't hesitate. "Take my plane. It's fueled and ready. I'll have a car waiting for you when you land."

The Kid nodded his thanks, embraced Paul again, and went upstairs to pack a bag.

Paul turned to me. "Philly, fly with him. Just in case."

"Absolutely," I said without blinking.

But when the Kid came back down with a small suitcase, he looked at both of us and said, "I'm going alone."

Paul frowned. "Your mother will worry more if you're alone."

"That's exactly why Philly can't come," the Kid said. "If he's with me, she'll think I'm going to do something she doesn't want me to do. I'll be fine. I'll see you all when I get back."

Paul nodded and said, "Be safe—I will see you in a few days."

Rocco and I drove him to the airport. After he boarded, Rocco took me back to the restaurant to pick up my car.

Paul pulled me aside before I left and said, "Handle things until he gets back. I'll be in New York for the funeral."

The Kid stayed in New York for almost three weeks. While he was gone, I kept our LA operation humming—quiet, clean, controlled.

When he finally returned, we sat down at a small restaurant, tucked in a quiet corner booth. No crowds. No noise. Just the two of us.

Over dinner, he told me what happened in New York.

"After the funeral," he told me quietly, "my mom and I sat

together on the couch. She turned to me, her eyes filled with that tired kind of sadness that only comes from years of silent hoping—and quiet fearing. She said, 'Please, Dominic. Don't follow in your grandfather's footsteps. And don't avenge his death. That was the life he chose. I always knew it would end this way.'

"She paused, then added, 'Be like your father. He was a good man, Dominic. A man with a kind heart, full of quiet strength. He loved you deeply and wanted more for you than the life your grandfather lived. He respected him—but he didn't want that life for you. He wanted you to live freely. To be happy. Fulfilled.' "

He looked down for a second, like the weight of her words still sat heavy on his chest.

"I told her I would," he said. "And I meant it—at least as far as she needed to know."

He didn't say a single word about what we were building in LA.

The following week, Lorenzo sent for him.

"We sat at the kitchen table in Lorenzo's Brooklyn home," the Kid said. "He poured coffee. No guards. No formality. Then he asked me flat out: 'Do you want to join the family?' "

That wasn't how it usually worked. No invitations. No recruiting. You had to come to them. But this was different—because of the Kid's grandfather. Because of the respect he'd earned. Because of what Lorenzo already knew about the Kid and what he was doing in LA.

"I told him," the Kid continued, " 'I can't thank you enough for the offer, privilege, and the respect for my grandfather. I know how close he was to you. But I have to go back to LA. It would destroy my mother if I stayed here and followed in his footsteps. All the men in her life are gone—except me.' I couldn't do that to her."

Lorenzo understood. He nodded slowly and said, "Your grandfather was the closest family I ever had. I trusted him with my life."

Then the Kid asked, "We don't know who the shooters were?"

Lorenzo gave him a crooked smile. "I thought you didn't want to get involved."

"I don't," the Kid said. "But knowing they paid for what they did will help me sleep better."

"They were part of an internal Romano war," Lorenzo explained. "We don't usually interfere with that, as you know. But because it was your grandfather? I'll find out. And when I do, you'll know. And if you ever need anything—anything—you come to me. In the meantime, Paul's watching over you."

The Kid finished his story, leaned back, and looked me dead in the eyes. "When I find out who the shooters were and who ordered it, they're all gone."

I nodded. "Just say the word," I told him. "And we'll make it happen."

CHAPTER SIX
POP'S ADMIRATION

The Kid's sense of justice was always unwavering, especially when it came to how men treated women. One night, while we were at a nightclub chatting with some girls, it was clear the Kid couldn't ignore what was happening at the bar.

Vinny Rasco, or "Munch," a made man in the Cattaneo family, was doing what he did best—pushing himself on girls who wanted no part of him. Munch wasn't exactly blessed in the looks department, but what truly turned most girls away was his lack of polish—sloppy habits, an absence of class, and a bad attitude that seemed to repel rather than attract. The Kid had no tolerance for guys like him, and I could see it in his eyes as he watched the scene unfold.

The two girls at the bar stood out—not for flashy outfits or loud personalities but for their understated elegance. They carried themselves with class and dressed conservatively yet sophisticated, a stark contrast to the typical crowd. It was obvious they weren't there for the usual party scene, and that made Munch's behavior even more out of place.

When the Kid excused himself and started walking toward the bar, I knew he wasn't going to let it slide. I followed close behind, bracing myself for what might happen next.

The Kid approached Munch with a calm demeanor, greeting him casually. "Hey Munch, how are you?" he said, his tone friendly but deliberate. Munch barely acknowledged him, clearly annoyed at the interruption.

"I see you met my friend," the Kid said. "I've been looking for her."

Munch, skeptical, shot back, "No, you haven't. I saw you over there talking with those other girls."

Without missing a beat, the Kid replied, "Why don't we go to the other side of the bar, and I'll buy you a drink?" His approach was smooth, attempting to defuse the tension without escalating the situation. It was classic the Kid—calm, confident, and always in control.

The tension in the air thickened as Munch dismissed the Kid with a smug wave of arrogance. "Fuck you. Get out of my way, little boy. I'm talking to this girl, and she wants a real man," he sneered, ignoring every clear signal that the girl wanted nothing to do with him.

Calm but resolute, the Kid stood his ground. "She obviously doesn't want to talk to you. You've been all over her, and she's been pushing you away. Why don't you just leave her alone?"

Munch's expression darkened as he stepped closer, clearly attempting to intimidate. "Fuck you, do you know who you're talking to?" he demanded, as if his status alone was enough to silence anyone who dared challenge him. In most cases it might have, but with the Kid, it was different.

Munch grabbed the girl by the arm and started pulling her closer to him. The Kid stepped aside and moved the other girl out of the way as he said to Munch, "Let her go."

"Get the fuck away from us," Munch said. "We want to be alone."

At that moment, I know what's going to happen next, so I have my eyes on the two guys standing behind Munch, because I know they will look to intervene. Before I could blink, and as Munch is holding this girl with one arm, the Kid hits him in the side with a left, and Munch immediately lets go of the girl. As soon as he let go of the girl, the next three or four punches were brutally quick.

You look down, and there's Munch lying on the floor, blood coming out of his mouth and two teeth lying next to him. At that moment, I decked one of the guys—I broke a few ribs with a left. The other guy froze. The Kid looked at the guy left standing and said, "You have two choices. You can either help them up and take them to a hospital, or you can be stupid, in which case you will be lying next to them. Only, we won't be so charitable with you." I figured we were going to have to deck him, but he decided to choose option one.

After it was over, and those guys had left, both girls turned to the Kid and said, "Thank you." I couldn't help but think, *What about me?* But that was how it always went. He had a way of drawing all the attention, whether he meant to or not.

The Kid, always calm and composed, suggested to the girls, "It might be best if you both head out. I'm not sure if any of Munch's friends are planning on showing up, and it's better to be safe." They nodded in agreement, clearly relieved to have the situation defused.

Just before heading out, the girl who had been on the receiving end of Munch's unwanted attention stopped and asked, "What's your name?"

Without hesitation, the Kid replied, "Everyone calls me the Kid." She smiled warmly and said, "I'm MaryAnn. It's a pleasure to meet you, Kid. I don't know what we would've done if you hadn't stepped in. That guy really had me on edge. Is there a number where I can reach you, just in case I run into those guys again?"

He nodded and said, "Sure, here's my number—call me if you have any trouble with them." He handed her a napkin with his number, and she tucked it away carefully before walking out with her friend.

Moments like these reminded me of how effortlessly the Kid handled even the toughest situations. It was just who he was.

About three hours later, one of the barmaids answered a phone call and waved the phone at the Kid, calling out that it was for him. He casually strolled over from where he'd been standing a few feet away, talking to someone. I was leaning against the bar when she handed him the receiver, and I couldn't help but hear as he answered.

"Hello. But, Paul, yes, yes, Paul, yes, okay, we'll be there," he said with a serious tone before hanging up.

I gave him a look and said, "That didn't sound good."

He shook his head slightly. "It wasn't. We've got a sit-down at Pop's house at 5:00 a.m."

I said, "We?"

The Kid nodded. "Yeah, we. You were invited too."

I couldn't help but roll my eyes a bit. "Perfect. Just how I wanted to end my night. Would it be too much to ask that you stop rescuing random girls?"

The Kid laughed, and soon enough, so did I. At least humor made the situation feel a little less heavy, even if it was shaping up to be a long night.

On the way to Pop's house, I said, "I don't like this, Kid. You put your hands on a made guy. Not only that, you hurt him pretty bad."

"Don't worry," the Kid said. "Pop is old school. He'll understand—or at least I hope so."

His attempt at reassurance didn't exactly ease my nerves. "That's comforting," I muttered sarcastically.

Pop's house was something else—grand and imposing, with an air of tradition that made it feel like we'd stepped into a Sicilian estate. One of Pop's men patted us down before leading us to the dining room. The room itself was impressive, dominated by a large rectangular wooden table that seemed to anchor the space.

At the head of the table sat Pop, his presence commanding without effort. To his right was Paul, with Johnny and Rocco standing behind him like sentinels. On Pop's left was Salvatore, the boss of a smaller crime family in LA, the Cattaneo family. Despite his title as Don, Salvatore didn't carry the same weight or influence as Pop. Next to Salvatore sat Anthony, a captain in the Cattaneo family, and beside him was his brother Munch—a made man in the Cattaneo family—bandaged and bruised, a visible reminder of the Kid's earlier encounter.

Munch's injuries were extensive, including bandages around his chest from the two broken ribs the Kid gave him, bandages on his nose, which was broken, and wire in his jaw, which was also broken. It was hard for him to talk, but I had to give him credit, he did try. Behind Munch stood the two guys who had been with him at the club. One of them was nursing a few broken ribs, courtesy of my left hook.

The room also had a handful of Pop's men, standing off to the side, their presence adding to the gravity of the situation. It was clear this wasn't just a casual meeting—it was a moment that could shift everything.

Pop set the tone of the sit-down with calm authority. "We are here to settle a dispute between Munch and the Kid." His directness added weight to the room. He then turned to Anthony, asking him to present his grievance on behalf of his brother.

Anthony didn't hold back. He began with an assertive demand for satisfaction, describing what he called an "unprovoked and brutal attack" on his brother, a made man in the Cattaneo family, by the Kid. By the rules we live by, Anthony argued, such actions warranted severe consequences. The Kid must go. While the Kid wasn't formally part of any family, Anthony emphasized that he knew Munch's status and had still raised his hands to him. He continued, describing how his brother had been "merely talking to a girl at the bar" when, according to Anthony, the Kid became jealous and attacked for no reason. To strengthen his claim, Anthony motioned to the two men standing behind Munch, stating that they could verify his story.

The room remained silent throughout Anthony's account—there was no space for arguments or interruptions at a sit-down like this. Respect for the process and the speakers was paramount, no matter how heated the subject. The Kid, seated across from Anthony with me beside him, held his composure and didn't utter a word. He understood the rules of these meetings all too well—a knowledge passed down from his late grandfather, whose influence and wisdom had shaped him profoundly. Since his grandfather's passing a year earlier, Paul had naturally stepped into the role of guide and protector, offering the Kid a sense of continuity and support in navigating this world. The scene was heavy with unspoken tension, every detail of the room and the people within it contributing to the gravity of the situation.

Pop turned to the Kid and asked, "What is your side to this grievance, Kid?"

The room fell silent as the Kid began recounting the events in detail, his voice steady and deliberate. He painted a clear picture of what had happened, leaving no room for ambiguity.

Munch, unable to contain himself, blurted out, "That's a lie!"

But Pop's raised hand and stern look silenced him immediately.

Munch quickly apologized, "I'm sorry, Pop," and sat back, his frustration evident but restrained.

The Kid continued, unfazed by the interruption. He spoke with conviction. "Pop, although I am not a formal member of this family, I understand the rules we all live by. I would never disrespect you, the rules, or the members of the families, but I was taught from an early age that we protect women and children. We don't abuse or mistreat them. Yes, I knew he was a made member of the Cattaneo family, but I had no choice. Munch wouldn't stop harassing this girl.

"I tried to get him to walk away with me and leave her alone, but he refused. It wasn't until he grabbed her and became physical with her that I intervened. I know I would do it all over again if the same situation arose. I am willing to face whatever consequences you decide."

Hearing those words, my stomach dropped. I was convinced we were both dead.

The Kid, however, wasn't finished. "Furthermore," he added, "it's evidence of my respect for you, the rules, and the fact that Munch is a member of the Cattaneo family that he is able to sit here with us."

Pop, intrigued, interjected. "I'm not quite sure I understand what you mean."

The Kid clarified, his tone unwavering, "If it weren't for my respect for you and the families, he wouldn't be able to sit or stand."

At that moment, I thought he'd gone too far. My heart sank, and even Paul's expression betrayed a flicker of concern. It felt like the room held its breath, waiting for Pop's reaction.

Pop, ever composed, finally spoke. "Well, it sounds like we have two totally different stories of the same event here."

Before anyone could process his words, Anthony jumped in again, his voice sharp. "It doesn't matter! He struck a made man. That cannot go unpunished."

The tension in the room was palpable, every word carrying the weight of what might come next.

Pop again raised his hand, to Anthony this time, and continued. "I've listened to your side, Anthony, on behalf of your brother, and I've listened to the Kid's side. Now let me tell you my side."

He recounted the story of his granddaughter, who had come home visibly shaken the night before after an evening out with a friend for drinks. "Since she doesn't live in California—and was merely in town visiting for the week—I doubt anyone would be familiar with her."

Pop described how she told him about a man who had accosted her at a bar—a "low-life scumbag," as she put it—and the stranger who stepped in to help her.

According to her, the stranger had tried everything to avoid a fight, urging the man to leave her alone. But when the man refused and became physically aggressive with her, the stranger intervened, protecting her and leaving the aggressor on the floor bleeding. Pop continued, saying he'd asked his granddaughter for the names of both men involved. She didn't know the name of the man who had accosted her, but she thought he was called "Much" or something. But she clearly remembered the other stranger's words: "Everyone calls me the Kid."

The room fell into a stunned silence. The Kid and I were floored, but relief washed over us. Paul's expression softened—a subtle sigh of relief visible on his face. Across the table, however, the tension was palpable. Sweat glistened on the brows of those who had been pushing for punishment, their confidence visibly shaken by Pop's revelation. It was a moment that turned the tide, leaving everyone to reconsider the weight of their arguments.

Pop continued. "Would you two gentlemen"—Pop was looking at the two guys standing behind Munch—"like to verify which one of these stories is correct?"

These guys knew that Pop knew the truth, and if they lied to Pop and backed Munch, they wouldn't live to see the sun come up in the morning. If they went against Munch, they might be dead anyway, but at least they had a chance. They decided to answer truthfully. They both agreed that Pop's granddaughter's story was correct.

Munch, visibly struggling to form words, finally managed to say, "I'm sorry, Pop. I had no idea she was your granddaughter." His tone was apologetic, but it was clear the weight of the situation had hit him hard.

Pop, ever composed, raised his hand, signaling for silence. "I understand," he replied simply.

As the room absorbed his words, Pop continued, his voice carrying unmistakable authority. "Let it be clear that from this day forward, this Kid is with me. Anyone who has trouble with him has trouble with me. I hope I make myself clear."

The declaration left no room for ambiguity. The tension in the room dissipated, replaced by the undeniable recognition of Pop's decision. It was a moment that marked a new chapter, not just for the Kid but for everyone present. Then, with firm finality, he said, "This sit-down is over."

The atmosphere shifted as everyone rose from their seats, acknowledging Pop's authority with silent nods. As we made our way out, the Kid paused to express his gratitude, saying, "Thank you."

Pop, in his composed manner, replied, "No, thank you." It was a subtle exchange, but it carried profound meaning—a mutual respect cemented in that moment.

As the doors closed behind us, Salvatore, Don of the Cattaneo family, remained behind, evidently for a private conversation with Pop. The rest of us departed, and what followed after was shrouded in mystery. Whatever was discussed, it led to an undeniable outcome—within a week, Munch was never seen again. His absence spoke volumes, and word spread quickly. The whispers were clear: the Kid was officially with Pop now.

That alignment with Pop marked the beginning of a profound transformation. The Kid's standing shifted entirely, and everything around us began to change in ways we couldn't have anticipated. People started to treat the Kid differently. It felt like the dawn of a new era—one that carried both opportunity and weight.

Two months later, Giovanni's was the destination—a lively Italian restaurant and club that drew everyone from made guys to movie stars. It had been a while since we'd been there, but the Kid's suggestion to grab a bite before hitting the clubs sounded perfect. When we arrived, the place was packed, and the maître d' informed us there were no tables available.

The Kid, ever resourceful, spotted Jimmy at a big booth with his wife and another couple. Without hesitation, he said, "Come on, let's go squeeze in there." The maître d' didn't stop us as we made our way over.

Jimmy welcomed us warmly, and after exchanging pleasantries, the Kid asked, "Is there room for us?" They all squeezed in and invited us to join, and soon we were seated, ordering drinks and dinner.

After dinner, I noticed some familiar faces at the bar—girls we knew. I motioned to the Kid, and he agreed, "Let's go say hello."

We thanked Jimmy and his group for letting us crash their table, and we headed to the bar. As we approached, the Kid accidentally bumped into someone.

The guy, clearly looking for trouble, snapped, "Watch who the fuck you're bumping into, jerkoff."

I expected the Kid to respond quickly, but instead, he calmly said, "I'm sorry."

That alone surprised me, but the guy wasn't done. "You better be sorry, asshole," he added, trying to provoke him further.

The Kid didn't take the bait. He simply glanced at me and nodded no—a silent signal to let it go. We moved on and started chatting with the girls, leaving the tension behind. It was classic Kid—knowing when to stand his ground and when to walk away.

The scene at Jimmy's table quickly turned into a spectacle. The loud, self-important voice cut through the noise of Giovanni's, and when we turned, there was Gregory Santoro—"Gregory Muscles"—standing there, posturing like he owned the place. His reputation was more bark than bite, but in his mind, he was king of his turf, especially at the gym we frequented. We had never had any issues with him, but we also kept our distance, exchanging the occasional hello and goodbye when we worked out.

We made our way to the table just as Jimmy was starting to rise from the booth. The Kid immediately stepped in front of him, catching everyone off guard, including me. "Jimmy, what are you doing? Do you know how tough this guy is?" he said, his voice calm but deliberate. For a moment, I was completely confused, wondering what game the Kid was playing.

Greg, however, took the bait, nodding along smugly, as if basking in praise.

Gregory Muscles' sidekick, Marty—"the Lion," though nobody could figure out why they called him that—stood off to the side, radiating misplaced confidence. Marty fancied himself a martial arts expert, always showing off his moves at the gym, much to everyone's quiet amusement.

The Kid turned to Jimmy again. "Jimmy, what happened?" he asked.

Before Jimmy could answer, Beth, his wife, interjected angrily, "He insulted me, and then it escalated!"

The Kid nodded, his expression shifting slightly. "Beth, he insulted you?" he repeated, letting the words hang in the air. "He doesn't realize how close we are. Nor does he realize Jimmy is my brother. One more thing he doesn't realize yet."

The Kid then turned toward Greg and Marty, his focus sharp. He locked eyes with Marty and said coolly, "You're in quite a bit of trouble—more than you realize."

The air in the room grew tense as people began backing away, clearing the space in front of Jimmy's table. The open area, usually a dance floor after midnight, became the stage for whatever was about to happen.

The Kid glanced at me and made a subtle motion, silently assigning Muscles to me. I couldn't help but smirk. It wasn't often that I got the green light, and the prospect genuinely thrilled me. Greg and Marty, for all their bravado, looked frozen in place, their earlier confidence replaced by uncertainty. The Kid's composure and calculated words had already shifted the power dynamic entirely.

The Kid's tone was sharp and deliberate as he addressed Marty, cutting through the tension in the room like a knife. "You can either let this drop and walk out of here, or I'll give you one swing or one kick, and after that, it's not going to end well for you," he warned, his words calm but laced with unmistakable authority.

Marty froze, his confidence faltering as he tried to process the situation. He didn't move, clearly caught between his bravado and the reality of what was unfolding. The Kid, unwavering, leaned in slightly. "This is your only chance to walk out of here. I strongly suggest you take it."

The silence in the room grew heavier, the air thick with anticipation of Marty's next move. It was yet another example of the Kid's ability to take control of a moment, leaving no room for confusion about the outcome.

Marty appeared too embarrassed to back down, so he lunged at the Kid and swung wildly. He missed. The Kid ducked and responded by striking Marty in the throat with a powerful left fist. Marty doubled over, clutching his throat with both hands. Before Greg could react, I landed a solid right hook to his stomach, lifting him off the ground—I could feel something break.

At the same time, the Kid delivered a snap kick to Marty, resulting in a compound fracture of his right knee. It was chaotic. Marty collapsed to the floor. As soon as Greg moved again, I hit him with another devastating right punch, splitting his jaw and knocking him out. The whole thing took no more than twenty seconds.

The Kid then turned to the onlookers and pointed at the jerk who had given him a hard time at the bar, beckoning him over. When he approached, the Kid grabbed him by the collar and demanded, "Get your friends and take these two losers out of my sight."

There was no room for argument or discussion; he made it clear that the guy was no one of importance at that moment. As his crew removed Marty and Greg, the maître d' had the busboys come out to clean up the mess. Within ten minutes, everything was back to normal.

From that day on, whenever we returned to Giovanni's, we never had to wait for a table again.

This was just the beginning. The years the Kid and I spent together forged a bond that grew stronger with time. We were inseparable, and though his mastery of calm and control often defused situations, there were moments when conflicts couldn't be avoided—especially with guys who didn't know us or who underestimated the Kid's quiet demeanor. Those encounters rarely ended well for them.

CHAPTER SEVEN
THE KID MEETS ALPHONSE

One night remains etched in memory—a moment when we realized the Kid wasn't just skilled at dishing it out but could also take a punch with remarkable resilience. We were at a club, hanging out and chatting, when a heated argument broke out between the son of a made guy and another man. The disagreement spilled outside, and as luck would have it, the Kid and I were standing near the exit talking to some girls.

That's when Ciro, the son of a made guy in the Cattaneo family, approached us to explain what was going on. As he was talking with us, out of nowhere, this big bruiser blindsided the Kid with a vicious punch to the jaw that hit so hard it lifted him off the ground.

None of us saw it coming—not me, not Ciro—and the Kid went down, part of a tooth chipped and knocked loose. It was the only time I'd ever seen him hit like that, and it was shocking to witness.

Ciro reacted instantly, grabbing the bruiser and shouting,

"What the fuck are you doing? It's not him—he's one of us!"

The bruiser had mistaken the Kid for the troublemaker hassling Ciro.

The tension was thick, and I hesitated, aware of the rules—especially with made men involved. You never lay your hands on a made guy, or his family, unless you were ready to deal with the consequences. The Kid, of course, was the exception, as he'd demonstrated once before.

The Kid sprang to his feet and immediately launched into the air, delivering a kick to the bruiser's face. The man staggered back, slamming against the wall near where we stood. The Kid then followed up with a few more punches, and down he went. Ciro and I had to intervene, pulling him back because I feared the Kid might actually go too far in front of the crowd of about twenty people watching us.

As he struggled against us, the Kid shouted at Ciro, "Get your hands off me, or I'll lay you out next to this piece of shit! Who the hell is he anyway? He blindsides me—he's fucking dead!" He tried to go back for another shot, but I held him back.

"Kid, you have to stop," I said, tightening my grip. I didn't know who the guy was, but I had a gut feeling he was someone important.

Eventually, the Kid relented, leaving the guy motionless on the floor. The crowd stayed silent, the tension hanging thick in the air. Turning to Ciro, the Kid said coldly, "When he wakes up, tell him he's dead."

Ciro held up his hands, trying to deescalate. "Kid, I apologize. This is a big misunderstanding. That's Alphonse from New York. He's Joey Doves's son. He doesn't know who you are either."

The Kid stared at him, then shook his head in disbelief. "Unbelievable."

The Kid's reaction was unlike anything I'd seen before. Walking back into the club, the packed bar seemed to amplify his frustration.

Without hesitation, he grabbed a guy by the shirt, pulled him away from the bar, and said, "Get the fuck out of my way."

It was a side of him I hadn't witnessed before, but considering the sucker punch he'd just taken, it wasn't surprising. The guy didn't argue—he moved quickly, and so did a few others, clearing space for us at the bar.

The Kid ordered a scotch on the rocks, his jaw visibly clenched. Turning to me, he muttered, "My jaw is killing me. That prick caught me good."

I couldn't help but respond with a smirk. "Looking at the state you left him in, I think he'd trade for a broken tooth."

That broke the tension, and we both burst out laughing.

After a few minutes, the Kid started to relax, his composure returning. He spotted the guy he'd pulled away from the bar earlier and called him over. To my surprise, he apologized, saying, "I'm sorry I did that." Then, in true Kid fashion, he turned to the bartender and said, "Whatever this guy is drinking tonight is on me."

The bartender nodded. "Absolutely."

It was a small gesture, but it spoke volumes about the Kid's character—always balancing strength with respect. Moments like these were what made him unforgettable.

The next morning brought another call from one of Pop's captains. He reached out, saying, "The old man wants to see you and Philly today."

The Kid responded simply, "Okay, we'll be there this afternoon."

On the drive over, the Kid swung by to pick me up and filled me in. My reaction was immediate—"Not again," I muttered, half in jest but fully knowing that meetings at Pop's house always carried weight.

"Thank you, by the way," the Kid said. "It's a good thing you stopped me when you did last night. I wanted to hurt him really bad. That would have made today's meeting a lot more difficult."

I just nodded and smiled.

Pop greeted us in the kitchen, where we all sat down at the table. Without wasting time, he got straight to it. "I heard about what happened last night. Do you know who that guy was that you beat pretty good?" he asked.

The Kid, calm as ever, replied, "Yes, he was the guy who sucker punched me and broke my tooth."

Pop smiled faintly, and then the gravity of the situation became clear. "His name is Alphonse. He's not made, but he is the son of Joey Doves in New York."

Joey Doves—acting head of the Battista family, one of the infamous five families—was a name that carried undeniable weight.

Pop continued. "I spoke with Joey this morning. I assured him I'd speak with you and that this incident is over. He agreed that his son has a hot temper, as do you, and his son had no right to strike you like that. But his son didn't know you were with me. It's been settled as a misunderstanding. Now, I want your word that it's over."

The Kid leaned back slightly, his trademark humor shining through as he quipped, "Does that mean I can't kill him?"

Pop fixed him with a serious stare, and after a beat, the Kid laughed, nodded, and said, "Of course you have my word."

What stood out most was Pop's ability to turn even the most volatile situations into calm resolutions. Joey Doves's involvement, the weight of both families, and Pop's declaration sealed the matter. Of course, little did anyone know, twenty years later, the Kid would cross paths with Alphonse once again, and their reunion would prove to be anything but ordinary.

Over the next year, the Kid's shift in priorities became impossible to ignore. While everyone expected him to climb deeper into the Poporri family's ranks, he seemed to be pulling away instead. Our loan-sharking operation and the bookies under us ran smoothly, thanks to the Kid's reputation and connections. Nobody dared to interfere. Most believed it was just a matter of time before he got made—I did too. But the Kid had other plans, and I couldn't have been more wrong about his trajectory.

When I suggested expanding our operations—letting some of the guys handle the scores they pitched our way in return for the Kid's backing—he shut it down every time. He maintained a clear boundary, and nothing was ever allowed to cross it.

That line became even clearer when Sammy the Pill floated the idea of selling drugs. The Kid's reaction was explosive. He grabbed Sammy by the throat, his voice sharp and unwavering: "If I ever find out you sold one pill or one joint using our name, I'll hang you by your balls myself. Do you understand?"

Sammy's immediate, panicked, "Yes, yes," left no room for argument. Everyone in our crew knew drugs were officially off the table.

Later, the Kid pulled me aside, his tone calmer but resolute. "Lose Sammy," he said.

I hesitated, asking, "Lose him, lose him?"

He clarified. "No, I just don't want him hanging around with us anymore. Make it clear. This guy is trouble, and if we let him stick around, one day he'll bite us in the ass."

I followed through a few days later, telling Sammy to stay away if he wanted to keep breathing. He got the message. After that, we'd only see him occasionally—at a club or a restaurant. He was always polite, offering a quick hello, but he never lingered or tried to reconnect. Eventually, he faded from sight entirely, and years passed without a trace of him.

The Kid's decisions during that time revealed a lot about his values and his vision for the future. He wasn't interested in shortcuts or reckless moves, and he wasn't afraid to make tough calls to protect what we'd built. The Kid's shift was becoming more and more apparent, and it seemed like he was wrestling with two opposing forces—the legacy of his grandfather and the wishes of his mother and father. His actions spoke volumes, though. Instead of chasing power or status within the Poporri family, he started focusing on helping others, stepping in for strangers and protecting the innocent. It was a side of him that contrasted sharply with his tough exterior, but it made sense. Beneath all that grit, he had a heart that couldn't ignore what was right.

It was confusing to watch him navigate those crossroads, especially when everyone assumed he'd follow his grandfather's path and get made. But the Kid was never one to take the easy or expected route. His struggle to choose between the two roads—one paved with tradition and the other with his own values—was a defining moment. Time, as they say, would tell.

CHAPTER EIGHT
A NEW MOB CONNECTION

One sunny morning after our usual few hours at the gym, we decided to escape the routine and head to the beach with a few girls. The salty air felt invigorating as we loaded our gear into the car, anticipation of relaxation fueling our laughter along the drive.

When we arrived, we wandered along the shoreline, searching for the perfect spot to lay our blankets. About ten feet from where we planned to settle, we noticed a woman setting up two kids on a blanket on the sand. She crouched down beside the boy and said in a gentle tone, "Listen to your sister, and I'll be back in a few hours." With that, she walked away, leaving the kids free to explore their little slice of the beach.

The kids settled in and turned on their small radio. Just as we began arranging our blankets—our chosen sanctuary only a stone's throw away—the soft hum of music joined the murmur of the sea. The kids seemed content, lost in the simple pleasure of chatting and listening to their favorite songs. The peace, however, was soon interrupted by the approach of a man whose presence carried an unfamiliar weight. The scene, a tapestry of routine summer bliss and quiet moments, suddenly shifted as that man drew closer, setting the stage for something unexpected to unfold on the sands that day.

He was intimidating, dressed in Levi dungarees with a motorcycle chain hanging off his pants, heavy riding boots, a cutoff T-shirt, and tattoos covering his arms. His long hair was tied in a braid, and a beard added to his rough appearance. Standing back on the concrete walkway, a group of his friends loomed, observing the scene. We later learned they were part of a small tough motorcycle gang, with this man—called "Braid" for his braided ponytail—leading the pack.

Braid walked up to the young boy and sneered. "Why don't you go get me a soda while I sit and talk with your sweet friend here?"

The boy, looking scared out of his mind, stammered, "That's my sister."

Undeterred, Braid turned his attention to the girl, saying, "Come on, sweet thing. You're coming with me. I'll show you a good time. Your little brother can find his own way home."

I don't know what would have happened next if we hadn't been there, but the Kid didn't hesitate. He was already on his feet, walking toward them. Kneeling beside the kids, he said warmly, "How are my favorite cousins doing?"

The siblings were too scared to respond, unsure what was happening.

Then, the Kid looked up at Braid and asked, "Is this guy bothering you?"

Again, silence from the kids—fear was etched on their faces.

Braid scoffed and spat back, "Who the fuck do you think you are? How about I call my boys down here, and we kick your ass—and that big goon too," He pointed at me, as I stood nearby but hadn't yet moved.

The Kid stood up slowly, calm but ready. "I hope you have more than just those four jerkoffs standing back there," he said coolly, nodding toward Braid's gang. "Because five of you definitely won't be enough."

The shift in power was immediate; Braid hesitated, startled by the Kid's confidence. But he waved for his crew to come down, signaling them to join him. They started approaching, clearly trying to intimidate us.

The Kid turned to me and said simply, "Take the biggest one. I'll handle the rest." It was a moment of pure clarity—he was ready, and so was I.

At that moment, just before they reached us, the Kid moved with precision and force, landing a devastating strike to Braid's throat. The impact left him gasping for air, but the Kid wasn't done. He followed up with a swift kick to the groin, doubling Braid over before smashing his face into his knee with brutal efficiency. The sound of bone snapping echoed as the Kid delivered a final kick to Braid's knee, leaving him crumpled on the ground, unable to move. Blood and teeth scattered across the sand, and the chaos sent everyone nearby scrambling for safety—including the young siblings who had been at the center of it all. Braid was out cold, leaving four more opponents to deal with.

The first guy to charge met the Kid's foot midair, a perfectly executed kick that sent him sprawling to the ground, clutching his face. Meanwhile, the largest of the group came straight for me as I placed myself in his path. He swung wildly, but I sidestepped with ease and countered with a powerful left hook to his gut, breaking a few ribs, I'm sure. As he doubled over, I followed up with a right hook that cracked his jaw. He hit the sand hard and stayed there, groaning in pain.

The last two men froze, their confidence shattered. The Kid turned to them, his voice calm but laced with menace. "You've got two options," he said. "Pick up these assholes and leave or end up lying right next to them." The choice was clear—they scrambled to gather their fallen friends, eager to escape.

As they struggled to drag Braid away, the Kid stepped forward, grabbing him by his braided hair. His voice dropped to a low growl, each word deliberate. "Do you know who I am? They call me the Kid. I'm not hard to find. If I ever see you again, it'll be your last. Clear?"

Braid, blood dripping from his face, managed a weak nod. The Kid's involvement didn't just end the confrontation—it left a lasting impression.

When he turned back to check on the young siblings, his calm and reassuring presence was exactly what they needed. They said, "Thank you, mister."

"Don't mention it," he said. "Enjoy the rest of your day, and forget this ever happened." The weight of his words carried comfort and closure.

The girl, the older sibling, probably sixteen, still shaken but curious, asked his name. His understated reply, "They call me the Kid," was enough to leave an indelible mark—a quiet moment of strength and protection that would stay with them long after the chaos had passed.

The day moved on as if nothing extraordinary had happened, but the evening brought a surprising twist. We were at Paul's house when the phone rang. Rocco answered and walked over to Paul to whisper who it was. The intrigue was immediate. Paul's exchange on the phone, which turned from polite surprise to genuine appreciation, set the tone.

When he hung up, he came back into the living room and shared the details with us.

"That was Fabrizio Venti—the Don of Louisiana. He wanted to personally express thanks to you boys for protecting his grandchildren today at the beach. His daughter happens to be here on vacation with her children."

Paul's reaction—"You boys never cease to amaze me"—said it all. "Fabrizio said to tell you he is in your debt. If you ever need anything, he's a phone call away. One more thing—he said not to worry about Braid coming to look for you."

We both burst out laughing, and I said, "Who would have thought."

CHAPTER NINE
LOYALTY

One night at a local club, amidst a haze of cigarette smoke and pulsing music, the Kid and I were nursing our drinks at the bar when one of our guys came over, urgency written on his face. He asked to speak with the Kid. Without missing a beat, the Kid simply nodded and said, "What's up?"

This was Vito "Long Legs" Bruzzi, a nickname that hinted at his gangly figure—but beneath that facade was a genuinely decent guy, someone who, despite dreaming of being made one day, had always followed my orders without a trace of hesitation.

Vito's eyes were heavy with worry as he explained he was in deep trouble. His sister Charlotte, ensnared by a relentless drug addiction, had siphoned off every penny he had as he tried hopelessly to support her. He'd attempted to force the dealers to stop supplying her, but his efforts fell on deaf ears, leaving him drowning in debt.

Desperation drove him into the arms of a shylock, and now the pressure to repay—or suffer dire consequences—was suffocating him. With palpable shame, Vito admitted he'd made a monumental mistake by not coming to us first, his pride and embarrassment keeping him silent until there was no other choice.

The Kid leaned in, his tone cool and measured as he asked, "Who's your sister's dealer and who's the shy?"

The moment he spoke, I knew we were about to stand up for Vito—this was the Kid in action. If you were with us and had even a scrap of decency, he wouldn't let you drown.

Vito exhaled a weary sigh before admitting, "This nobody dealer named Monkey, and the shy is Alexander the Moose." As fate would have it, Alexander was not made but was associated with the Poporri family—a family in which the Kid held considerable influence.

The Kid's silent nod said it all: "Let's see what we can do."

Soon, the four of us—me, the Kid, Vito, and one of our muscle guys—clambered into a car and sped off into the night toward the bar where Alexander plied his trade. We strode in with purpose, making a beeline for the bartender.

The Kid's voice cut through the din as he ordered, "Tell Alexander the Kid is here to see him." A quick phone call later, Alexander emerged from the shadows.

"Hey Kid, nice to see you," Alexander said, his greeting curt and measured, his glance flicking briefly over Vito as he began piecing together the reason for our arrival. The Kid wasted no time. "Alexander, I understand one of my guys borrowed money from you, and you're applying pressure." For an excruciating moment, they locked eyes. Then the Kid pressed, "What does he owe you?"

Alexander grunted, "A lot."

"How much?" the Kid demanded, his tone unyielding.

"30K, including the vig," Alexander finally admitted, the words heavy with reluctance.

The Kid's thin smile barely shifted his steely resolve. "And how much did he borrow?"

"What does that matter?" Alexander snapped, defensiveness flaring—until, under the Kid's unblinking gaze, he lowered his voice to a whisper, "10K."

"And how long ago?"

"Six months," came the measured reply.

"And how much has he paid?"

"2K."

With the numbers etched in the charged atmosphere, the Kid laid out his plan with deliberate calm: "Here's what I'll do. I'm going to give you 20K tomorrow and call it even."

Alexander's eyes widened in disbelief. "That's a big discount. I've never done that before."

"This is a one-time offer. Accept it, or deal with the consequences. Your choice," the Kid said, his tone decisive and laden with finality.

Under that unyielding stare, Alexander relented. "Sure, Kid, as a favor to you." It was clear that Alexander didn't want to test the Kid or have him as an enemy.

"The money will be here tomorrow. Let's go," the Kid replied, and just like that, we turned on our heels and left the bar, the weight of our decision hanging in the smoky air.

Back in the car, Vito asked, "How can I thank you, Kid?"

"You can't," the Kid snapped. "You're on my shit list for not coming to us first."

Ashamed, Vito muttered, "I'm sorry, Kid. It won't happen again."

The Kid shook his head. "Now, where's this Monkey low-life drug dealer?"

We drove to a run-down dive bar—the kind of place where Monkey hung out.

The moment we stepped in, all eyes turned our way. After a brief nod from Vito, the Kid asked, "Who's Monkey?"

Vito pointed him out.

Approaching Monkey, who hardly appeared intimidating at all, the mood in the bar turned tense. The Kid's dislike for anyone selling drugs ran deep. Without warning, the Kid landed a solid punch on Monkey. A few more savage blows followed, leaving Monkey reeling in serious pain. As two of his friends lunged to intervene, they quickly backed off when they saw mine and one of my guy's .45s pointed squarely at them.

The Kid shoved Monkey against the bar, took out a .45 from his back waistband and pressed the barrel of the gun into his mouth. In a voice loud enough for every patron to hear, he warned, "Anyone who sells drugs to Charlotte will have to deal with me. Am I fucking clear?"

The gravity of his words sank in immediately. With that, the Kid dropped Monkey, who crumpled to the floor.

We stepped out of the bar into a cool night, the tension still crackling in the air. Vito never did manage to clear his debt entirely, yet his loyalty to the Kid—and later to me after I was made—remained unyielding, a silent vow in our brutal world. That night sent ripples through the streets. Charlotte, Vito's sickly sister, found herself shunned by most dealers, their hands trembling at the thought of dealing with someone under the Kid's shadow.

That night wasn't just another chapter in our business; it was a stark lesson in loyalty, respect, and the unforgiving realities we all had to face.

In the weeks that followed, Vito scraped together every dollar he could to get Charlotte into rehab—a desperate gamble fueled by the faint hope of redemption. But it wasn't enough. He came to us, asking for another $5K to cover the costs. When I told the Kid about Vito's request, I didn't sugarcoat it: "You know we're probably never seeing this money again."

The Kid nodded, his expression in agreement, before saying simply, "Give it to him."

That decision wasn't about the money—it was about loyalty, about standing by someone who had always been there for us. A few years later, I crossed paths with Charlotte again. She was clean, her transformation quiet but profound, a rare glimmer of hope in the chaos of our lives. That moment reminded me that sometimes, even in our world, the right choice can lead to something good.

CHAPTER TEN
PHILLY'S GODFATHER

*E*namored by the stories he was hearing, Graham, one of those at our table paying close attention to my stories, edged closer, eyes bright with anticipation and the kind of reverence reserved for campfire legends, asked, "Did the Kid ever kill anyone?"

I smiled, paused for a moment, and said, "That's not an easy question to answer. Depends on your definition of killing someone."

The table got quiet.

"We weren't murderers," I continued. "We were tough, sure—but we lived in a world with rules. And in that world, breaking those rules could carry serious consequences. Grave ones. The Kid never looked for violence, but he never ran from it either. He always protected himself—and the people he loved or cared about."

I leaned back, let that sit for a beat, then said, "Let me tell you a story. You can decide for yourself."

My godfather's seventieth birthday party turned into a memorable evening, highlighting both his values and the Kid's ability to step up in tense, emotional situations. While I initially saw the party as a family obligation, bringing the Kid along was the perfect excuse to leave early—though, as it turned out, his presence made all the difference.

On the drive over with my cousin Joanne, I explained to the Kid the kind of man my godfather was—hardworking, kind, and nothing like the godfathers in our world. He had always wanted the best for me, pushing me toward education and a legitimate path. The Kid's response—"He sounds like a wonderful man"—showed his respect before even meeting him.

At the party, the Kid quickly fit in, greeting family members he knew and meeting others for the first time. When I introduced him to my godfather, something seemed off. My godfather wasn't his usual self, and when I asked what was wrong, he requested to speak with me alone. Leaving the Kid with Joanne, who clearly enjoyed having the Kid's full attention, I followed him into his study.

He confided in me about a disturbing situation involving his daughter, Sara, and her abusive boyfriend, Juan Ricardo, also known as "Aces." Despite my godfather's success in the clothing business and his clean, respectable lifestyle, he was now being threatened by this punk. Aces had struck Sara more than once and warned her not to involve anyone—not even her own father.

She'd tried to end it, but Aces wasn't having it.

Sara was a really nice girl. How she ended up with a lowlife like him was beyond me.

My godfather was perplexed—unsure of how to proceed. He wanted Aces out of the picture and away from his daughter, but fear and legitimacy kept him frozen. Aces had already warned that he'd kill him if he tried to intervene. So now my godfather didn't know what to do. Knowing my life path, my godfather insisted I stay out of it.

Still, I wanted the Kid's input. I went out and asked him to join us in the study. Joanne wasn't pleased—I'd interrupted her chat with the Kid—but she held her tongue. Inside the study, my godfather told the whole story again, adding some additional details. When emotions took over, his English broke into bursts of Italian. The Kid, fluent from childhood thanks to his grandparents, followed every word without missing a beat.

When my godfather asked whether he should involve the police, the Kid responded thoughtfully: "Signore Sporano, what is the name of this Puerto Rican boy?"

As soon as the question left the Kid's mouth, I knew Aces was in trouble.

"Juan Ricardo," my godfather answered, "but they call him Aces. He lives in the Watts section of LA."

The Kid suggested a quieter approach: "I know a few police detectives from Watts. Why don't you let me see what they advise before you make any official moves?"

My godfather's face lit up, clearly relieved to have a potential solution. The Kid's respectful reply in Italian, with a Sicilian dialect—"Ogni compare di Philly è compare miu" (Any godfather to Philly is a godfather to me)—only deepened the trust in the room. The three of us returned to the party, but the wheels were already turning in my mind.

About an hour later, the Kid and I left the party, leaving my cousin Joanne to catch a ride home with another family member.

As we drove back, the Kid said, "I can trust you want to handle this?"

Without hesitation, I replied, "Absolutely." That moment solidified the Kid's unwavering loyalty—not just to me but to anyone in need.

"What are you thinking?" I asked. "Because I think we should just find him, and I'll put two bullets in his head."

"That sounds like a simple solution," the Kid said, "but how do we track down this degenerate lowlife in the Watts area?" He paused for a moment, then added, "I've got an idea. Let's head to the drug center."

He asked if I had any extra pieces in the car, since he knew I always had mine under my front seat.

"There's a .45 under your seat."

He reached under the passenger seat and found the weapon; I had made a special case for both seats. After checking that it was loaded, he tucked it under his right leg. We drove to the part of town known for drug deals, stopping at a corner in front of a candy store we knew was the headquarters for the local drug kingpin.

We waited until one of the street dealers approached our car. The Kid rolled down the window, holding the .45 below the sill so it wouldn't be visible.

"What are you guys looking to score?" the dealer asked.

The Kid replied, "I want to talk to Leroy."

"There's no Leroy here," the dealer said. "You wanna score?"

The Kid shot back, "Listen, go inside and tell Leroy the Kid wants to talk to him."

The dealer stared at the Kid, taken aback.

"If you don't go inside now, and we drive away and Leroy finds out we were here, they'll be picking pieces of you off the street."

The guy looked stunned but eventually turned and walked into the store. About two minutes later, he came back out, looking shaken.

"Leroy's in the back," he said.

As we got out of the car, the Kid slipped the .45 into the waistband on his hip under his shirt, telling the dealer, "Watch the car."

The dealer nodded; we knew nobody would dare touch the car.

We cautiously entered the candy store, and everything seemed fine. When we reached the back room, Leroy emerged from behind a large old wooden desk.

With a grin, he said, "Kid, Philly, how are you guys?"

"Fine," we both replied.

"What can I do you for?" Leroy asked.

"I have a problem you might be able to help me with," the Kid said.

"Anything you need, Kid."

About a year earlier, Leroy had been busted for drugs and lost a significant shipment to the cops. While the Kid had little love for drug dealers, he respected Leroy's younger brother, who was a clean, straight-A student, uninvolved in the drug world. Leroy's partner was Pete Falcone, nicknamed Viper, a made guy from the Cattaneo family who was furious about the lost drugs and wanted to send a message by targeting Leroy's little brother. The Kid heard about it and stood up to Viper to defend an innocent Kid he didn't even know—that was just how he was.

The Kid and I sat down with Viper and two of his guys at his favorite lunch spot.

Without preamble, the Kid said, "Viper, this isn't really my business, but we both know drugs are frowned upon in our world. I don't care how you earn your money, but when you're planning on hurting an innocent kid who's trying to do the right thing—and who has nothing to do with your business—that's a bridge too far for me. I'm asking you to leave him alone. He had nothing to do with you losing your drugs to the cops. How you handle Leroy—that's on you."

Viper leaned back and, with a dismissive tone, replied, "I don't know why it matters to you; he's just some black drug dealer's brother."

The Kid's eyes narrowed as he shot back, "As I said, he's innocent. He doesn't deserve to pay for the sins of his brother."

Eventually, Viper backed down and agreed to leave Leroy's brother out of it.

When Leroy found out, he made a special trip to thank the Kid, and I was there. The Kid explained he didn't do it for Leroy, whom he despised for his craft, but for his little brother, because he was innocent. Leroy said he was in the Kid's debt.

Anything he ever needed, he just had to ask.

"Do you know a degenerate called Aces?" the Kid asked.

"Sure, I know him," Leroy said. "He's part of that crazy Puerto Rican crew. What's he done?"

"Something he shouldn't have. I need this problem to go away."

Leroy nodded. "Say no more. You boys have a good evening, and consider your problem handled."

The Kid thanked him and shook his hand.

About a week later, my godfather called. "Philly, you're not going to believe this, but there was a gunfight last night between drug dealers in the Watts section, and Aces is dead. You can tell the Kid he doesn't need to talk to his detective friends."

I acted surprised. "Wow, really? That's good news, godfather. I'll tell him."

My godfather never asked for details, and I never volunteered. I had a strong sense he knew more than he let on, but it was never mentioned again.

CHAPTER ELEVEN
A HEART NOT IN CRIME

Though deeply respected and fully capable within the world of crime, the Kid's heart was never truly in it. While the life offered power, money, and connections, his quiet detachment spoke volumes. His strength, loyalty, and skill made him an undeniable force, but beneath it all, he wrestled with something deeper, a pull toward a different path. The allure of becoming "made" or climbing higher in the criminal hierarchy simply didn't captivate him.

On the other hand, the draw of that life—the tradition, prestige, the edge of danger—held a strong appeal to others around him, including me. Yet, even surrounded by those immersed in the life, the Kid seemed to walk his own road, guided by an inner compass that set him apart. His struggle revealed a tension between the world he inherited and the world he envisioned, hinting at a heart that valued justice and loyalty above power or status.

One afternoon, the Kid pulled me aside with a look I hadn't seen on him before—serious, contemplative. No swagger, no front. Just honesty.

"Philly," he said, "I know you've always wanted more than just putting money on the street and running a couple books. We keep getting approached—guys bringing us deals, scores, things they want us to back. I've always shut them down. But lately, I've been thinking . . . I need to take a different road."

He paused, like he was trying to measure each word before it left his mouth. "I don't want to hold you back, but it's time I did something different. Either you come with me, and we try to make money the old-fashioned way—smart, clean, even legit— or we go our separate ways. No matter what, we're still brothers. I'll always have your back. But this gangster stuff? It's not for me anymore."

There was no judgment in his voice. Just resolve.

He looked away for a moment, then added, softer this time, "I know my grandfather loved me. I never questioned that. And I understand why he lived the life he did. Back then, with Lorenzo, things were different. They didn't have a lot of choices. The streets were the only ladder they could climb. Being in the life meant survival—and sometimes, success. I admired that. For a long time, I thought that was my path too. Thought it was in my blood. But now . . . I'm not so sure. Maybe there's another way. A better one. I don't know what it looks like yet—but I know I need to try."

I didn't need time to think it over. I looked him in the eye and said, "Then I'm with you. Let's give your way a shot."

He blinked, almost surprised. "Really?" he said. "I didn't expect that. But . . . I'm glad."

And in that moment, the old world we knew started to fade behind us, and something new—uncertain, but ours—was maybe just beginning to take shape.

A week later, the Kid had a plan. He told me about the conversation he had with Paul, asking him to set up a meeting with Pop.

Soon, the three of them were gathered at Pop's house, where the Kid got straight to the point.

"I'm torn," he began, his voice low but steady. "I grew up in this life, and I love many of the people in it. Without you, Pop—and you, Paul—I wouldn't be where I am today. But I know I want something different. I'm not entirely sure what that looks like yet, but I want to earn and build something the legitimate way. I know it may have been my grandfather's dream, but I don't want to get made. I need you to help me walk away from what Philly and I built on the street, giving me the chance to start over."

After a moment of silence, Pop leaned forward and replied, "Kid, I'm proud of you. Your inner strength, the willingness to always help others, and the clarity of your direction astound me. Just like my granddaughter MaryAnn, who I am happy lives in a legitimate world, I understand and am happy for you to do the same. If this is where you want to go, then you can walk away. I will give you a fair deal on your street money: one of my captains will take over your shylock operation and the bookies you've been backing, and you'll receive 25 percent of the profits each month for the next year. In addition, he will gradually return your initial investment. And if you ever change your mind, I'll always be here for you."

They all stood—the Kid embraced Pop and Paul, murmuring, "You both have given me more than I deserve."

That meeting marked a turning point—a carefully structured deal that would keep us financially afloat as we began to step away from our old life and move into an entirely new chapter.

Two weeks later, the Kid came to me with an idea: going into the private sanitation business. Though it was unfamiliar territory, the promise of making money was enough for him to get on board. The Kid explained that we'd need to meet with Marino, a businessman who would lay out the details. Clearly,

Paul's influence was behind this opportunity, as things like this didn't just happen out of the blue. When we arrived at Marino's office, it was bustling and professional, a stark contrast to the grittier environments the Kid and I were used to.

After being directed by the receptionist, we entered a polished office where Marino and his partner Joe conducted business. Marino, a savvy entrepreneur, wasted no time outlining their proposal. They would front the money to purchase a garbage route that included an older truck—functional but in need of upgrades. The deal offered equal partnerships, with each party holding 25 percent. Marino and Joe would recoup their initial investment as profits grew. The proposition seemed legitimate and promising.

Grateful for the opportunity, I wanted to thank Paul personally. When we went back to the Kid's house, Paul was home, so I thanked him.

His advice was straightforward: "Keep your nose clean, and stay out of trouble."

The garbage business was a turning point—and the Kid got his first real taste of how the legit world played the game. We worked hard, expanding the operation and adding a second truck as profits grew.

Marino, despite his lack of formal education, became a mentor to the Kid. His diverse background—ranging from garbage collection to movie production to retail manufacturing and sales—made him an invaluable source of insight.

Marino's partner, Joe, was a quieter presence, speaking only when necessary, but Marino himself took an active interest in nurturing the Kid's potential. Over time, Marino even brought the Kid into certain meetings with other businesspeople.

One such meeting, where I was also present, was with a producer pitching a Broadway play—only he wanted to launch it in Los Angeles.

Despite an impressive presentation, Marino's pragmatism was evident when he asked the producer how much he was putting up. The producer admitted he wasn't putting up any of the $500,000 required, and Marino immediately declined the deal.

His reasoning was simple: "When someone puts nothing up, they have nothing to lose."

The lesson stuck with the Kid, reshaping how he viewed business and risk. As we left the meeting, he turned to me and said, "Wow, what a great lesson."

Like me, he initially thought it was fair—the guy had the idea, all he needed was money. But Marino had seen right through it, explaining to the Kid that money is a very valuable tool. Without it, no business, no matter how great the idea, can succeed. And now, the Kid understood: having the idea wasn't enough. From that day on, he started thinking differently about how deals really worked.

Through this journey, the Kid absorbed invaluable lessons from Marino, cementing his shift away from his past life and into legitimate ventures. It became clear that the connections through Paul had opened this door, but it was the Kid's determination and growing passion for business that truly helped him succeed.

One night, Marino's wife's birthday party brought everyone to a high-end LA club called the Penthouse. Despite its misleading name—situated on ground level—the place exuded sophistication. After the party in a private room began to wind down, Marino's wife suggested moving to the bar for a nightcap. About ten others decided to tag along.

The Kid and I were standing about fifteen feet away, chatting, when we heard Marino raise his voice. "Behave, that's my wife," he said loudly, standing protectively beside his striking younger wife.

Two men were in front of Marino, and before they could blink, the Kid and I were standing by his side.

One of the men turned to Marino and sneered, "Do you know who I am, old man?"

Without missing a beat, Marino replied, "No, but if you keep this up, you're going to find out who I am."

At that moment, the Kid stepped in with his signature calm. "Marino, why don't you finish your drink at the bar with your beautiful wife? I'll buy these gentlemen a drink."

The man scoffed. "I don't need your drink."

The Kid, undeterred, responded, "Funny, you said you were someone important. I know most important people in LA, and yet, I don't know you."

The tension escalated as the man shot back, "I'm with Anthony of the Cattaneo family. Does that ring a bell?"

The Kid's expression didn't flinch. "You mean Anthony, who used to have a brother Munch, who I beat to a pulp one night when he opened his mouth to me?"

The man's bravado instantly shattered. His face went pale, his voice trembling. "Are you the Kid?"

"You do know me," the Kid replied, a sharp edge in his voice.

The man stammered out an apology, his fear palpable.

Meanwhile, I stood beside the other guy, ready to act on a single cue. The man turned to Marino, his tone desperate. "Please accept my apologies. This was a misunderstanding."

Marino just looked at him without acknowledgement.

The Kid wasn't done. He gestured for the guy and his friend to follow him to the end of the bar, toward an open area.

I stayed close behind, laser-focused on the second guy. When the Kid suggested taking the conversation outside, the guy hesitated, confused.

"Why do we need to go outside to talk?"

The Kid's tone shifted, firm and commanding. "I'm sorry. I didn't realize that sounded like a suggestion. Let me put it differently—either you walk outside, or you'll be carried out."

That was enough. Both men reluctantly agreed, visibly shaken. Once outside, they barely took a moment before turning and sprinting down the block, disappearing into the night.

The Kid and I shared a laugh at their panicked retreat and strolled back inside.

Marino, visibly relieved, thanked us.

The Kid dismissed it with a wave, saying, "It was nothing. Let's have a drink."

By Monday, it was back to business as usual, but the events of that night reaffirmed the Kid's ability to command respect and defuse situations with a mix of calm authority and calculated intimidation. Moments like that only added to his legend.

Many times, when we needed to make a point with someone, the Kid would suggest that I handle it. My size alone often kept people from arguing; the intimidation factor was enough to get the message across. People usually weren't keen on challenging me when I stood in front of them. But when it came to actual fighting, I always felt confident having the Kid watching my back. He was quick, precise, and fearless. If the Kid went on his own and the people involved didn't know who he was, it usually took a few kicks or punches before they realized they should start paying attention. Once they understood who he was and what he represented, things often ended before they truly began.

However, those dynamics would change in the coming years, as his reputation grew and the need for physical confrontation became less frequent. The way we handled situations evolved, shaped by the lessons we learned and the presence the Kid commanded over time.

By 1981, we had both just turned twenty-one, and life felt like it was falling into place. Money was coming in steadily, and our business—modest by some standards—was thriving for a couple of kids who'd started with nothing. Girls were always around, the laughter was constant, and for a while, it felt like there wasn't much else to ask for.

The Kid, however, made one thing clear whenever someone brought up the idea of settling down. "I'm not ready for that," he'd say with a grin. "I like being free."

And free he stayed, as anytime a girl tried to pin him down, he'd instinctively pull back. He had a way of balancing being magnetic and unattainable, a combination that seemed to keep girls intrigued.

At the time, we were frequenting a club called the Loft. It was the place to be in LA. Movie stars, singers, made guys, wannabes—all sorts of people crammed into the scene. Some were genuine somebodies, while others were just trying to fake it, typical wannabes. They usually stood in line the longest to get in. Even the most stunning girls in LA often found themselves waiting over an hour to pass the velvet rope.

For us, though, things were different. The door bouncers let us in without hesitation—no waiting in line, no hassle. To be clear, they weren't exactly rolling out the red carpet for us yet. But something about the way the Kid carried himself, and the energy around us, made it clear that "yet" wouldn't stay a question mark for long.

Entering the Loft was always an experience. The layout immediately set the tone for the night. From the street, you walked through two big black glass doors onto the platform area that overlooked the entire club. Seven or eight steps led down to the main floor, and from that vantage point, everything was in view—the sprawling main bar straight ahead, the buzzing dance floor to the right, and just beyond that, the exclusive VIP section.

The VIP section was something else. Elevated by two steps, it stood apart from the rest of the club. It even had its own private bar and a certain air of exclusivity, often reserved for movie stars, made guys, and the elite of LA's nightlife.

A three-foot black wrought iron fence surrounded it, giving just enough visibility to create the illusion of privacy while still reminding everyone on the main floor it was there.

From ground level, the fence reached about four and a half feet off the ground, adding to the sense of separation.

Despite its allure, we rarely found ourselves in the VIP area. It was quieter, more subdued—not where the real action was. The energy and, more importantly, the female attention were always centered around the main bar. That's where we preferred to stay, soaking in the excitement of the Loft and the vibrant crowd that filled it. Getting into the VIP section required passing the ever-watchful bouncer stationed there, but for us, the main bar was where the night truly came alive.

CHAPTER TWELVE
THE LOFT & THE BEAST

One night at the Loft, the Kid caught the attention of Stephanie, a stunning girl who seemed to glide through the room with effortless grace. She looked like she had stepped straight out of *Playboy*—beautiful, classy, and approachable. Everyone in the place either knew her or wanted to, but Stephanie had a reputation for being selective, rarely dating despite the endless stream of admirers vying for her time.

We were standing at the bar when Stephanie walked in. I couldn't help but comment, "God, is she gorgeous?"

The Kid looked up and agreed, "She sure is."

As she passed by, she greeted us with a casual "hi," and the Kid immediately seized the moment.

"Stephanie, would you like a drink?"

She stopped, smiled, and said, "Sure."

The three of us chatted for a while, but it was clear where her attention was focused. Recognizing the spark, I excused myself, saying, "I'm going to walk around," and leaving them to continue their conversation.

Later, I saw the Kid at the bar talking with one of the guys, but Stephanie was nowhere in sight. Curious, I asked, "What happened to Stephanie?"

He shrugged and said, "She had to leave."

I couldn't resist teasing him. "Wow, the Kid strikes out."

He grinned and replied, "Easy, big guy. I'm going out with her tomorrow night."

That was the beginning of what turned into a brief relationship.

Over the next few weeks, the Kid saw Stephanie a couple of times during the week and on Saturdays. She seemed to have her sights set on something more serious, and after about a month, I figured she had him locked down. But one Saturday night, as I was hanging out at the Loft with some friends, including my cousin Joanne, the Kid walked in alone, just past midnight.

Surprised, I asked, "What the hell are you doing here? I thought you were with Stephanie."

He shook his head and said, "Nah, that's over."

When I asked what happened, he made a gesture mimicking a noose around his neck, signaling that things had gotten too serious for his liking.

"I told her I just wanted to keep it simple," the Kid said. "Nothing heavy, nothing serious. She said she understood, until it became clear she didn't. So I went over to her house and ended it."

That was who he was—always straightforward, always direct. I asked how she reacted.

"Not well," he admitted, "but such is life."

As we were talking, Joanne walked over and greeted the Kid with a big hug, saying, "How are you?"

He hugged her back, replying, "Fine, gorgeous. How are you?"

Just then, I spotted Stephanie entering the club. Turning to the Kid, I said, "Kid, turn around. Look."

He did, and there she was, standing on the platform, clearly seeing Joanne still close to him. Even though it was just a friendly hug, everyone knew Joanne had a soft spot for the Kid. It was the kind of timing that could only happen in a place like the Loft.

Stephanie stormed down from the platform, her anger palpable, and marched straight over to the Kid. "So, this is what you left me for?" she demanded, her voice sharp and cutting.

Joanne, caught off guard, started to respond, "Hey, wait a minute—" but I quickly stepped in, pulling her aside to avoid escalating the situation.

The Kid, calm and composed, looked at Stephanie and said, "Stephanie, what are you talking about?" He explained that their relationship was over and that he was simply hanging out with friends.

Stephanie, clearly upset, shot back, "I can't believe you don't want to be with me. Half the guys in this place would wait in line to be with me."

Without missing a beat, the Kid replied with a touch of attitude, "I don't wait in lines."

Her frustration boiled over, and she swung her right arm, aiming to slap him. But the Kid's reflexes were too quick. He caught her arm mid-swing with his left hand. "Stop," he said firmly.

Undeterred, she immediately swung her left arm, but he caught that one too, this time with his right hand. Holding both her arms, he looked at her and said calmly, "Stephanie, please stop. This is silly."

She pulled back, and the Kid let her go. Her face flushed with anger, she spat out, "Fuck you, Kid," before storming away.

I couldn't help but quip, "That went well."

The Kid just smiled, brushing it off as if nothing had happened.

We stayed at the bar, talking and enjoying the night. The Kid was seated to my right, and I had a clear view of the end of the bar behind him. About an hour later, I noticed Stephanie standing at the far end of the bar, Armando's arm draped around her shoulders. Armando was a muscle-bound wannabe with the Cattaneo family, a guy who spent his days working out and his nights collecting debts for one of the made guys. He was there with his crew of misfits, all of whom thought they were untouchable, backing down only to made men.

Armando caught my eye, clearly aware that I'd seen him with Stephanie. He knew about her brief relationship with the Kid, and jealousy was written all over his face. Stephanie, knowing full well how much the Kid detested guys like Armando, seemed to be playing into it.

Armando raised his glass in a mocking salute, signaling for me to tell the Kid to turn around.

I leaned over and said, "Look behind you." The Kid turned, saw Armando with his arm around Stephanie, and watched as Armando raised his glass with a smug grin.

The Kid nodded once, then turned back to me, looking unfazed, but down deep I knew he was fuming—just as I was.

"Let's go over there and beat the shit out of all of them," I said, ready to act.

The Kid shook his head. "No," he said firmly.

I pressed him. "Are you going to let him get away with that?"

It was an insult, plain and simple—a way for Armando to say, "She's with me now, and you're an asshole."

The Kid, however, had already thought it through. "If we go over there and I beat the piss out of him, Stephanie is going to think I'm jealous and that I did it because of her. I damn well don't want her to think that, because after how she acted tonight, I don't care what she does or who she does it with."

I knew he was right. That's exactly what she—and everyone else—would have thought.

The Kid added, "Don't worry, Armando's not going anywhere. There will be another day, another time, and then I'll deal with it."

He was calm, but I could tell he was pissed. He hated having to let it slide, but he knew it wasn't the right moment. As much as I wanted to act, I trusted his judgment. The Kid always played the long game.

About half an hour later, we heard loud voices coming from the VIP section. Both of us glanced over and spotted Anthony and his crew from the Cattaneo family. Among them was JoJo Malone, known as "the Beast," who served as a mechanic for the family. He earned his nickname due to his brutal nature, causing pain and suffering without a shred of mercy. He was undoubtedly someone to be feared. Many viewed him as a psychotic killer, so much so that even the "made" members of Anthony's crew were wary of him. Very few dared to speak out of line around the Beast; everyone understood that if you crossed him, you either had to kill him or be prepared to constantly look over your shoulder. I had heard tales about him that sent chills down my spine.

The loud voice we heard was the Beast shouting at a cocktail waitress named Cathy, a sweet and charming mother of a six-year-old girl. I couldn't fathom what she could have possibly done to provoke him, but with the Beast, it didn't take much.

As we watched, the Kid turned to me and said, "If he lays a hand on her, I'm going up there to split him open."

"Kid, please, no—not him," I said. "Anyone else, but not him. Their whole crew is there, and let's be honest, they are not fans of ours. Let's wait until we have more backup—at least Rocco or Johnny."

The Kid insisted. "Just watch my back with those other idiots."

I couldn't help but worry. I'd seen the Kid fight many times; he was incredible. I watched him take out three trained assassins during his graduation. But those guys weren't the Beast. Very few people frightened me like he did, and I had serious doubts about the Kid taking him on alone. I pleaded with him again, insisting this was madness.

Just then, the Beast slapped Cathy and sent her crashing to the ground. Cathy was approximately five feet three inches tall and weighed about a hundred and ten pounds, while the Beast towered at six foot four and weighed around two hundred eighty pounds.

The moment Cathy hit the floor, the Kid sprang into action. Instead of passing the bouncer on the bottom step, he leapt over the iron fence, four and a half feet off the ground, and performed a spinning kick that connected with the Beast's jaw. I watched as teeth flew from the Beast's mouth, likely due to weak gums—there were quite a few.

The Beast, still on his feet, staggered back, slamming against the bar, shaking his head as he glared at the Kid, declaring, "I'm going to kill you."

As everyone cleared out of the way, the Kid stood his ground, clearly hoping the Beast would charge, and charge he did. As the Beast lunged toward him, the Kid landed a punch right in the middle of the Beast's throat, cracking his Adam's apple. Blood began to seep from the side of the Beast's neck. Then the Kid followed up with a powerful kick to the groin, lifting himself off the ground to add force and hitting the Beast hard.

The next thirty seconds unfolded as a brutal assault. I lost count of how many punches and kicks the Kid landed, but by the end, the Beast was left with a shattered Adam's apple, a broken nose, jaw, and cheekbone, two fractured ribs, a split kneecap, and a broken elbow.

No one in the club moved; everyone stood frozen in awe. Even the music cut off, and the lights were turned on.

It was a stunning display.

When the Kid finally finished with the Beast, he walked over to Anthony, eye to eye, and said, "I meant no disrespect to you, but you know he deserved it."

Anthony nodded but didn't say a word, likely partly agreeing with the Kid, but maybe not wanting to face a lengthy conversation with the Kid later at Pop's house again.

At that moment, everyone in the club—and soon everyone everywhere—learned what the Kid had done to the Beast. From that night on, I never doubted his strength or his courage again.

Everything would change after this night, but the evening was still far from over.

The Kid turned to me and said, "Let's go," as we made our way down the steps of the VIP section. Everyone parted to let us through. At first, I thought we were leaving, but the Kid had different plans. Instead of heading toward the exit, he veered right, heading straight for Armando and his crew at the edge of the main bar. They had just witnessed the chaos, and the tension was palpable; everyone in the Loft had seen it unfold.

Armando stood at the end of the bar beside Stephanie, dressed in a suit with his collar open and half the buttons on his shirt undone to reveal his muscular chest. A thick gold chain hung around his neck. As the Kid approached, the fear on Armando's face—and that of his crew—was unmistakable. After what they had just seen, and with not a single made member of the Cattaneo crew having stepped in, they understood they were in deep trouble. The Kid had taken down the Beast, and the Cattaneo family had done nothing to stop it.

The Kid walked right up to Armando and taunted, "Did you enjoy saluting me earlier?"

To which Armando nervously replied, "I didn't mean anything by it; I was just being friendly!" His expression, especially with Stephanie standing right next to him, was priceless.

At that moment, I positioned myself next to the biggest guy in Armando's crew. I figured it was the perfect chance to make a statement. I launched a powerful left hook into his gut that lifted him off the ground. I followed up with a right to the gut and then another right to his jaw, and he went down hard.

The Kid turned to me, grinning. "Philly, you think he got the message?"

"I think so, but let's send a few more messages," I said, glancing at some of the other guys in Armando's crew, who were now taking a few cautious steps back and standing frozen.

The Kid put his right arm around the back of Armando's neck, turning him around so they could both face the bar and talk privately. "The next time you insult me, it'll be the last thing you do," he warned before slamming Armando's face into the bar. Blood exploded everywhere, even splattering on Stephanie. Armando's nose was broken, and his face was drenched in blood.

Turning to Stephanie, the Kid said, "Tell your new boyfriend he can have you." With that, he looked at me and said, "I'm hungry; let's go grab some breakfast." We strolled out of the club, knowing things would never be the same again.

Two weeks later, the Beast was discharged from the hospital. As he began rehab, he started making threats. Some folks overheard him declare that the Kid better watch out, because once he healed, he was going to kill him.

When we caught wind of this, the Kid simply said, "He can try, but he better not miss. Because next time, he won't need a hospital; he'll need an undertaker."

We never got the chance to test that theory. Just a week after his threats became known, the Beast was found dead in the back of a Cadillac, two bullets in the back of his head.

The origin of the hit remained a mystery. My guess was that Pop or maybe even the Cattaneo family had ordered it. They must've known that if the Beast targeted the Kid, they would have to answer to Pop themselves. In any case, we no longer had to worry about the Beast or look over our shoulders for him again.

Those were golden years, when everything seemed to align perfectly. The respect we commanded was undeniable—people gave us space, and even "made guys" knew better than to create unnecessary tension. By steering clear of their businesses, we inadvertently kept the peace, allowing us to move freely through the nightlife and beyond.

The next year truly felt like living in a dream. The attention we received from stunning women was unending. Every night out was its own spectacle, filled with laughter, excitement, and moments that felt larger than life.

The Loft and other hot spots welcomed us like VIPs—no

lines, no waiting, no hassles. Restaurants with the best reputations always had a table for us.

Meanwhile, the hard work we put into the business paid off. It grew steadily, which meant more disposable cash to enjoy everything we wanted and more. The freedom, the confidence, and the sheer energy of those nights made it feel like nothing could disrupt that rhythm. It's no wonder those memories stand out as some of the best times—unforgettable moments of youth and ambition, wrapped in the glow of a life lived fully.

Telling these stories had everyone at our table listening intently. The music playing in the background—no one even left their seats for a break.

Natalie chimed in, "I have a few stories about the Kid too."

My cousin Joanne added, "I have a few as well," and the rest urged, "Tell us more."

CHAPTER THIRTEEN
NATALIE

*N*atalie leaned over and said, "Philly, remember when you and the Kid helped my son Bryan when he was getting bullied by Fang's son at school?"
I smiled and replied, "Oh, wow—I sure do. How could I forget that?"
And with that, she began by saying, "Let me give some color first."

I've known the Kid since he was about seven years old. I was five years older than him, so he always seemed like this cute, sweet little Kid to me.
I spent a lot of time with him since I used to hang out with Paul's youngest daughter, Peggy—she was my age.
In many ways, Paul adopted me into his family, especially because I never really knew my own dad. As we grew up, the Kid was like a little brother to me.
I never saw him as a man until one night, when he was

nineteen. Suddenly, we were at a family party, and the Kid was leaning against an outdoor bar set up for the party. He turned and I looked at him, and the way he looked back at me made me realize what all those other girls had seen in him for years.

One thing led to another, and before long, we became more than just friends.

She paused, her eyes growing distant with old memories.

I got pregnant at seventeen and then married Bryan's father—a man who turned out to be nothing but a loser. By the time I was nineteen, we were divorced. He was both physically and mentally abusive. I remember when I finally told him I wanted a divorce; he hit me and told me it wasn't going to happen. I felt so lost and didn't know what to do.

Peggy, knowing what was happening, urged me to come over to the house one night. When I arrived, Paul was there, and when he saw the bruise on my face, he said, "Natalie, tell me what's going on." I told him everything.

He reassured me and promised that my husband wouldn't hurt me anymore, and he would agree to the divorce. Later, I learned he'd sent Rocco and Johnny over to handle the situation. I hadn't seen my husband for over two weeks, until one day he showed up at the house. He knocked on the door and announced that he'd decided to let me have full custody of Bryan, would sign all the necessary papers, and that he'd never bother me again. I suppose the fact that he was in such a sorry state—sporting a cast on one arm and one leg, looking like he'd been run over by a train—made him relent. And once the divorce was finalized, I never saw or heard from him again.

When the Kid was nineteen, I was twenty-four, and little Bryan was nearly seven.

When I first began dating the Kid, he told me he wasn't looking for anything serious—and at first, I agreed. But before long, I found myself hopelessly in love. He had this unexplainable chemistry that captured me completely. I used to say, 'You've never been kissed until you've stood in the dark with the Kid.' "

Cousin Joanne piped in with a chuckle, "Isn't that the truth?" and soon the whole table joined in laughter.
Then Natalie's voice softened further.

But when I realized I was in love with him, I couldn't help but try to hold onto him, and eventually it all blew up in my face. I remember one argument—about two months into our relationship—when I gave him a hard time about going out with his friends, knowing exactly what that meant. He stormed out in anger. Fueled by my frustration, I decided to go out on my own.

I called one of my girlfriends, and we ended up at a club called Gazebo in LA, around 1:00 a.m. There we sat at the bar with some guy who kept boasting about his toughness and his crew's loyalty. I wasn't impressed and couldn't wait to get away from him.

Just then, my girlfriend nudged me and said, "Look who just walked in."

I turned to see the Kid entering with Philly and a couple of other guys. He didn't usually frequent Gazebo, so someone must have tipped him off.

Spotting me, he walked over and softly asked, "Can we talk?"

I felt a surge of warmth and almost threw my arms around him, but I managed to say, "There's nothing to talk about."

With a playful glint in his eye, he turned to the guy I'd been chatting with and declared, "You're in my chair."

The tough guy, caught off guard like a deer in headlights, stammered, "I'm sorry, I was just saving the seat for you."

As he hurried off, I couldn't help but burst out laughing—and the Kid laughed too. I teased him, "Is there anyone who isn't afraid of you?" And our laughter filled the space, smoothing away the tension of the earlier fight.

We spent the rest of that night making up, and I was like putty in his hands—I just couldn't help myself. Even after our relationship eventually ended, I carried that heartbreak with me. Every time I ran into the Kid afterward, which was often more than I ever wished, his ever-sweet demeanor only deepened the pain of remembering what once was.

As Natalie finished that story, the energy at our table shifted into a reflective silence for a few of us, in our own memories of the Kid—a man who had touched all our lives in ways both profound and unforgettable.
After a moment, Natalie continued.

Two years passed, and my son Bryan had just celebrated his ninth birthday. One Friday afternoon, Bryan came home from school looking upset, a bruise visible on his face.

"What happened, Bryan?" I asked, but he refused to speak. Instead, he rushed to his room, declaring he would never return to school. I felt a wave of distress wash over me, unsure of how to help.

After a bit of persistent prodding, Bryan eventually emerged from his room and opened up. He explained that Fang's son, William, had bullied and humiliated him in front of his classmates. Bryan was terrified because William had warned him that he was going to beat him up on Monday.

Fang was a famous English rock star, and his son was big, a year older than Bryan, spoiled, and took karate lessons, making him intimidating to most kids in his grade. To top it off, he always had a bodyguard around and rode to school in a limo, accustomed to getting whatever he wanted.

After calming Bryan down somewhat, he still insisted he wouldn't be going to school on Monday. So I knew I had to act. I contemplated calling Peggy and asking her father, Paul, to speak to Bryan, but that didn't feel like the right solution. Bryan idolized the Kid, who treated him like a little brother. But could I really call the Kid after two years of silence? I poured myself a glass of wine and mulled it over. Finally, reminding myself that this was about my son, I decided to put my pride aside. I was sure the Kid would help if he could.

At 10:00 p.m., I dialed Paul's house, hoping to reach the Kid. Charles, Paul's longtime housekeeper, answered. "Hello, Miss Natalie. It's so nice to hear from you! Unfortunately, the Kid is in Vegas with Paul and the rest of the guys," he said.

I sighed, a hint of disappointment creeping in. "Oh," I said.

Charles must have sensed my mood. "Is it important?" he asked.

"It is, somewhat. I really need to talk to the Kid, if possible," I replied.

"Just sit by the phone; I'll see what I can do," he assured me. I thanked him and hung up.

At this point, Bryan was back in his room, still upset. I went to my own room to relax with my wine and wait to see if Charles could reach the Kid.

At 10:20 p.m., my phone rang. It was the Kid. "Natalie, what's going on? Are you okay?"

"I don't want to bother you, but I have a problem," I said.

"You're never a bother. Just tell me what it is," he replied, his tone making it easier for me to talk.

I shared everything about Fang's son and how I felt helpless. "I thought if you could talk to Bryan, he might feel better," I suggested.

"Put Bryan on the phone," the Kid said. I set the phone down on my nightstand and walked over to Bryan's room to tell him the call was for him.

He initially protested, "I don't want to talk to anyone."

"Oh, I'll just tell the Kid you don't want to talk to him," I said, trying to sound casual.

Immediately, excitement shifted across his face. "Wait, it's the Kid?"

"Yep!" I confirmed.

He rushed to the living room to answer the call. I returned to my room, picking up the receiver to hang up, but then decided not to hang up. Instead, I clicked it to make it sound like I did, and then I cupped the receiver to listen in. After all, it was my son.

I heard the Kid ask, "How's my boy doing?"

"Not too good. You're going to laugh at me. This big kid beat me up today, and I'm scared," Bryan confessed.

"There's nothing wrong with being scared, Bryan. I'm afraid a lot too," the Kid replied.

"But you're never afraid! Everyone is scared of you!" Bryan retorted.

"Yes, I am. Just because I don't show it doesn't mean I don't feel it," the Kid assured him.

Their conversation continued, with the Kid promising to teach Bryan how to defend himself when he returned. "Don't worry about Monday; I'll be there with you," he said.

"But William has that huge bodyguard."

"Don't sweat the bodyguard. I'll handle him," the Kid said confidently.

I could hear the change in Bryan's tone as delight lit him up. "You're really going to come with me on Monday?" Bryan asked, incredulous.

"Absolutely. Have I ever lied to you?"

"No."

"But I want you to promise me you won't worry and that you'll have a great weekend with your mom," the Kid said. "Don't make her worry."

"Okay," Bryan agreed.

"Let me talk to your mom now, and I'll see you Monday morning," the Kid concluded.

"Thanks, Kid! You're the best!" Bryan exclaimed. Then he yelled for me to pick up. "Mom, the Kid wants to talk to you!"

"Okay," I replied, grabbing the receiver in my room. I made it seem like I was just picking up. "All right, Bryan, you can hang up now."

I heard him hang up, and I turned back to the Kid on the phone. "So how did it go? What did he say?"

The Kid laughed. "You really want me to repeat everything you just heard?"

I stumbled for words. "Damn you, Kid!" We both chuckled.

Just then, a female voice chimed in from the background. "Kid, let's go! I'm starving!"

"Hey, do you see this thing in my ear? I'll be down when I'm finished. If you want to go now, go," the Kid said, slightly annoyed.

A part of me felt jealous of whoever was there with him, but a bigger part was grateful he was putting me first.

"Sorry for the interruption. What time does Bryan leave for school in the mornings?" he asked me.

"If he takes the bus, it's 6:20 a.m. If I drive him, it's 7:00 a.m.," I replied.

"You drive him on Monday. We're all going together. I'll be at your house at 6:45 a.m. Have the coffee ready," he instructed.

"How can I thank you?"

"You can't. That's what friends are for. I'll see you Monday morning."

We ended the call, and I felt a sense of relief wash over me.

I jumped back into Natalie's story.

Oh, I remember! The Kid came down for dinner that night around 11:00 p.m., with whoever that girl was, and he said to me, "Philly, we have to go back Sunday night."

"Sunday night? I thought we were staying until Tuesday?" I asked, a bit confused.

"Sorry, we have to go. Bryan has a problem, and we need to help fix it," he replied.

"Bryan? Natalie's Bryan?"

"Yes," he confirmed.

"But he's just a kid! What kind of problem could he have?" I asked.

"I'll explain later," he said cryptically.

Later that night, the Kid spoke with Paul and arranged for us to fly back to LA instead of driving.

Paul shrugged and said, "You kill me! Go ahead and take the plane."

So that Sunday night, the Kid and I found ourselves flying back to LA on Paul's private jet. He filled me in on all the details during the flight about what had happened and how we were going to resolve it.

Natalie picked up her story.

All I know is that on Monday morning at 6:45 a.m., my doorbell rang, and in walked the Kid, Philly"—she pointed to me—"and a twelve-year-old boy I'd never met before. Everyone said hi, and the Kid introduced the boy, whose name was Barry, to my son."

"Bryan, say hello to your new cousin, Barry. Barry, say hi to your cousin Bryan," the Kid instructed.

Both my son and I exchanged bewildered glances.

"If anyone asks, Barry is your cousin," the Kid added.

We played along and quickly discovered why. After grabbing a cup of coffee, we headed out to school. The Kid said to me, "You drive. Bryan, Barry, and I will ride with you. Philly and Johnny, a made guy from Rocco's crew, will drive together and follow us."

Johnny was sitting in his car when we walked out of my house.

During the drive to school, I asked, "What's the plan? What are you going to do?"

"I'm going to deal with the problem," he said confidently.

"How?" I pressed.

"You'll see—just trust me," he replied.

We arrived at the school and came to a halt.

"Which entrance does William get dropped off at?" the Kid asked.

"Over there." Bryan pointed.

"Park at that entrance," the Kid instructed.

I quickly noticed that Philly and Johnny had disappeared. Just then, William's limo pulled up.

"That's his car," Bryan said nervously.

"Okay, let's go, boys," the Kid said, turning to me. "Stay here and don't say a word."

My nerves flared as uncertainty crept in, but deep down, I trusted him completely.

The Kid walked over to the limo with Bryan and Barry. The back door swung open, and William stepped out, his bodyguard following right behind—a towering figure at six foot three, built like a brick wall. William paused, seeing Bryan and Barry with the Kid. The bodyguard stepped closer, looming over the Kid. I edged closer, straining to hear.

Barry confronted William. "I heard you roughed up my cousin?"

William stayed silent, so the bodyguard threatened Barry. "If you're not careful, I'll make sure he kicks your ass too."

Barry glanced at the Kid, who nodded. In a flash, Barry launched a kick, connecting with William's head. William stumbled back against the car.

"Come on, tough guy! I'm right here!" Barry taunted.

The bodyguard interjected. "You think you're funny?"

"Why are you getting involved? Let the kids sort this out," the Kid chimed in.

"This ends now. If that Kid touches William again, I'll break his arm. And if you say anything, I'll shut you up for good!" the bodyguard threatened.

Those were the last words from him; the Kid swiftly punched him square in the throat. The bodyguard instinctively grabbed his throat, choking. The Kid followed up with a swift kick to his leg, sending him buckling, before launching a series of punches that left the bodyguard bloodied and on the ground.

Just as the bodyguard fell, I noticed the limo driver starting to get out, brandishing a gun. Suddenly, Philly and Johnny reappeared. Johnny smashed the passenger window with a shotgun, causing the driver to freeze in panic. As the driver swung his arm out, Philly slammed the door onto his arm, likely breaking it. The gun dropped from his grasp as he recoiled in pain, realizing he'd met serious trouble.

The Kid leaned over the downed bodyguard and grabbed his hair, lifting his head.

"You want to continue this? I'm not hard to find. But next time, I won't be so nice."

He let the bodyguard's head drop. The Kid turned to Philly. "Throw this piece of garbage in the back seat."

Johnny and Philly lifted the bodyguard and tossed him in the car before shutting the door.

"Take him to a hospital," the Kid ordered the driver.

The driver groaned. "I can't drive; I think my shoulder is broken."

"If you can't drive, you're of no use to me," the Kid stated, prompting Johnny to pump the shotgun ominously.

The driver flinched. "I can drive! I can drive!" he stammered.

"I thought so," the Kid replied. "Now, William, get in the front passenger seat of the limo; you're not going to school today."

Barry seized William by the collar. "If I hear you touched my cousin again, I'll be back, and next time, you won't walk away."

William nodded, fear evident on his face as he climbed into the car.

The Kid turned to the driver. "When you get back, tell Fang what happened, and let him know the Kid said he knows how to find me if he wants to continue this discussion."

"Okay," the driver said, and he sped off.

After everything settled, I noticed two police officers who had been watching from the school steps walking over. Johnny quietly slipped into a side street, still holding his shotgun. I half expected the Kid to be arrested.

The police officers approached, one of them asking, "Hey, Kid, is everything okay? Do you need anything?"

"No, but I appreciate it," the Kid replied; then he told Bryan to head to class.

"Thanks, Kid! And thanks, Cousin Barry," Bryan shouted as he walked into school, joined by other kids who had witnessed the scene. It felt incredible to see his smile again.

Once we got into the car, I turned to the Kid and said, "You're amazing."

He smiled modestly.

"It's lucky you knew those cops," I joked.

"I didn't, but I guess they knew me," he replied with a chuckle.

We both laughed, and in that moment, I knew everything was going to be all right for Bryan. Bryan never had another problem with William at school. In fact, he used to tell me that William went out of his way to avoid him—and whenever they did cross paths, he was always unusually polite. Fang and the bodyguard never mentioned the incident again. I figure they looked into the Kid and realized it was best to steer clear.

CHAPTER FOURTEEN
JOANNE

*N*atalie locked eyes with Joanne and gave a subtle nod. "Your turn," she said, her voice steady but inviting.
All heads turned in unison, a silent ripple of anticipation passing around the table. Conversation hushed.

Joanne took a breath, fingers curling around the edge of her glass as she gathered her thoughts. "I can't top that last story," she began, "but I've definitely seen the Kid instill fear without ever throwing a punch. And I've also witnessed him in action, trust me."

"Tell us!" Claire urged, leaning forward in anticipation.

"All right," she said, leaning in with a knowing smile. "Here's my first story."

It was a Friday night, around 11:00 p.m., and I was out with two girlfriends. We'd decided to hit the Loft—this was after the incident Philly mentioned—you know, when the Kid made quite the impression, shall we say. By now, the entire LA nightlife scene knew who the Kid was. His name carried weight, not just with the nightlife crowd but with every wannabe and made guy in LA.

We were posted up at the main bar, sipping cocktails and soaking in the hum of the DJ's set. The place was packed—models, wise guys, wannabes—and we were just looking to enjoy the vibe, nothing more. Then they showed up. Three of them. Mid-twenties, puffed up with overconfidence and overpriced cologne. You could spot their type a mile away—wannabes who wanted everyone to think they were somebody.

The ringleader leaned in with a fake grin and said, "Ladies, can we buy you a drink?"

I smiled politely. "We're good, thanks." That should've been the end of it. But he didn't take the hint.

"What do you mean you're good?" he asked, stepping in closer, his eyes scanning like he was doing us a favor. "You're turning me down? Do you know who I am?"

I raised an eyebrow. "I'm sure you're all very important guys. But we're fine. Really."

His expression shifted, cocky amusement replaced by irritation. "You don't walk into a club like this, dressed like that, and turn down a drink from a guy like me."

My patience was starting to wear thin. "What exactly do you mean by 'dressed like that'?"

He smirked. "I mean, you girls look hot. Like you're out here hunting for some classy guys."

I held his gaze. "Well, if you spot any, feel free to send them our way."

That did it. His eyes narrowed, and without warning, he grabbed my arm—tight. "You don't talk to me like that, bitch."

Instantly, my friends were up. "Let her go!" one shouted, while the other shoved at his shoulder.

He laughed and let go, but not without a lingering stare and a smug grin. "Okay, okay, let's start over," he said, his voice dripping with insincerity. "We just wanted to be nice. Buy you a drink."

I'd had enough, but I wasn't going to make a scene. Not yet. "Honestly," I said, "I'm waiting for my boyfriend."

He raised an eyebrow. "Oh, so that's the problem. Forget about him. He's not here. I am."

"I can't," I said, letting a small smile curl. "He's got a temper."

That got a laugh out of all three. "Oh, really? I'm so scared of your angry little boyfriend." He leaned in again. "When he gets here, I'll handle him. Then we'll have that drink."

I tilted my head, amused. "I don't think you know how tough he is."

He was getting louder now, cockier. "I don't give a fuck how tough you think he is! I'll put two behind his ear, just like that."

My smile vanished. "Please don't," I said quietly. "I really don't want anything to happen to Dominic."

The name didn't register, not right away. I could see it in his face. No alarm, no recognition.

"Dominic, huh?" he scoffed. "What's his last name?"

I shrugged, feigning innocence. "You might know him better by his nickname."

His tone turned mocking. "Oh, this'll be good. What is it?"

I leaned in close, voice low, deliberate. "They call him the Kid."

Everything stopped. His smirk dropped.

For a good three seconds, silence enveloped the group. The trio stood there, jaws slack, eyes wide, processing what I'd just casually mentioned. It was like I had flipped a switch, and their bravado had evaporated into thin air. At that moment, I knew I had them right where I wanted them.

"The Kid? What kid?" the leader stammered, suddenly at a loss.

At that moment, I glanced up at the platform and saw the Kid walking in with my cousin Philly. The energy in the room was electric, filled with lively music and chatter, but I raised my voice over the noise. "Dominic! Dominic!" I called, waving my hands to get his attention.

The Kid was engaged in conversation, glancing down at the bar area, completely unaware of my deliberate use of his first name. But then, finally, he caught sight of me and pointed in acknowledgment. Immediately, I saw the wannabes look up and realize who it was, as they recognized the Kid's distinctive presence.

The leader nearly fell to his knees, literally begging me not to say anything. "I didn't know! Didn't realize! I don't want any trouble!" he said, panic written all over his face. "I'll do anything! Just please don't say anything!"

At that moment, part of me felt a pang of sympathy for them; I had never seen three tough guys look so petrified. The Kid and Philly walked down from the platform and approached me, wrapping me in a warm hug and greeting my friends, completely oblivious to the underlying tension, or so I thought. Philly did the same, shooting a wary glance at the wannabes standing nearby.

The Kid—always perceptive—knew I didn't associate with wannabes. He turned to the leader standing next to me, his eyes narrowing slightly. "Are these guys bothering you, Joanne?" he asked, looking directly at the leader.

I saw Philly subtly shift behind the leader, getting close to the other two wannabes, bracing for anything. Faced with the Kid, I briefly considered telling the Kid what had transpired, but I decided against it.

"No, Kid, they're fine," I replied. I wanted to make my point without escalating the situation too violently.

The Kid, with a steely gaze, placed a hand on the wannabe's shoulder and said, "I'm glad. Because if anyone bothers her"—he gestured to me—"they'll be dealing with me. Do you understand?"

The wannabe's expression morphed from arrogance to sheer terror, his body trembling as he stuttered, "Yes, Kid! Absolutely! Of course!"

"Good. Now go away," the Kid ordered firmly.

"Thank you, Kid!" the wannabe gasped, and the three of them turned on their heels and disappeared.

It was an incredible display of power, and while I had enjoyed the moment, I also felt a twinge of discomfort. After that night, I couldn't get attention from any guy in the club. It was hard to get one to talk to me. It was as if the Kid's reputation had cast a shadow over my own dating prospects.

Everyone at the table laughed, and Graham said, "What about the story of him in action?"
Joanne said, "Oh right," and began her second story.

In my family, we always prided ourselves on staying on the straight and narrow—well, almost everyone. My cousin Philly was the black sheep.

Philly glanced at Joanne, and they both laughed.

My cousin Leslie, on the other hand, was a talented pop singer from the '60s, and she was close friends with Jimmy. She's sitting right over there at Table 7.

The year my grandmother turned eighty-five, my mother wanted to do something special. She chose a catering hall called Leone's in Malibu for the celebration. It was August of that year when she made all the arrangements, booking for the Saturday of Thanksgiving weekend to keep costs down. It was also just one day before Grandma's actual birthday.

My mother confirmed the details with the owner and gave him a deposit to book the room and the date. Excitement bubbled as she sent out invitations, planning a surprise for Grandma. The Kid was invited, too, but he called to say he'd be in New York for Thanksgiving and couldn't make it.

But then, two weeks before the party, my mother answered a phone call that shattered our plans. I overheard her say, "You can't do that. All the arrangements are made! What am I supposed to do now?"

When she hung up, tears streamed down her face. I rushed to her side, asking what was wrong.

After what felt like an eternity, she managed to tell me, "The catering hall called. They said there was a mix-up, and we can't have that date anymore. They'll return the deposit, but the next available date isn't until after Christmas. What am I going to do?"

I felt fury boiling inside me. "They can't do this!" I protested.

But my mother shook her head, resigned. "Joanne, you know those people that run that place. What can we do?"

My mother would never think of asking her nephew Philly for help; though she loved him, she hated his path in life. So, I didn't mention it.

Leslie happened to drop by that evening, and after hearing the news, she attempted to console my mother, but to no avail. We talked until the early hours, trying to figure something out.

As my mother finally went to bed, Leslie turned to me and said, "We need to talk to the Kid."

I hesitated. "I don't want to get him involved. Then Philly will get involved, and it'll only upset my mother more."

Leslie countered, "If we don't go talk to the Kid, I'll just call Jimmy, and Jimmy is just going to call the Kid anyway. Let's just go talk to the Kid ourselves, see if there is something he can do."

Eventually, I agreed, despite feeling apprehensive.

After a few hours of restless sleep, we left for Paul's house at around 7:00 a.m. The sun had just begun to rise as we pulled up.

When Charles answered the door, he looked surprised to see us. "Miss Joanne, Miss Leslie, is everything okay?" His shocked expression was understandable; who paid a visit at that hour?

"Is the Kid home? It's really important," I asked.

Charles must have sensed the urgency in my voice because he replied, "Please, make yourselves comfortable in the living room. I'll go wake him."

As he climbed the spiral staircase, I whispered to Leslie, "We shouldn't have come."

"Stop," she said firmly.

Charles returned shortly and told us, "He'll be right down. Would you like some coffee or breakfast?"

We declined, hearts pounding with anxiety. The Kid finally came down, wearing only cut-off shorts. Damn, he looked good. He flashed a charming smile as he approached us.

"This better be good," he said, and after greeting us with hugs, he noticed my distress. "What's going on, Joanne? You look upset."

So, I told him everything—the last-minute cancellation, our worry over Grandma's birthday, the lack of alternatives. I made him promise not to involve Philly, and he agreed.

"I'll be right back. Get some breakfast," he said before heading upstairs to shower.

When he returned, looking fresh in jeans and a T-shirt, he asked, "Ready to take a ride?"

It was around 8:30 a.m. by then. Leslie drove her two-seater Mercedes convertible with the top down. I sat on the Kid's lap as we headed to the catering hall.

Upon arriving at Leone's around 9:30 a.m., it was already bustling with preparations. We made our way upstairs to the office, where a sweet young receptionist sat at the desk. Standing nearby was a large, intimidating man who looked like he meant business.

The Kid instructed me to ask for the owner, Alex. When I did, the receptionist immediately rang him but returned with bad news: "I'm sorry, he's busy, and you don't have an appointment. He'll be returning your mother's deposit this week." I could see sympathy in her eyes.

At that moment, the Kid stepped in. "Excuse me, sweetheart, can you do me a favor? Ring him back and tell him the Kid is here to see him. And tell him I don't wait in lines."

She looked stunned but picked up the phone and called him back. His response was immediate. He opened his office door and said, "Kid, so good to see you; please come in." We all walked in, including the large man stationed outside the door.

The Kid declared, "We don't need Frankenstein here, Alex."

At that moment, the burly man lunged forward, and suddenly, kicks and punches filled the air. Before we even had time to understand what was unfolding, the Kid had knocked the guard unconscious. In one swift motion, he reached under the man's left pants leg at his ankle and pulled out a gun—I couldn't help but gasp in disbelief. Somehow, he knew exactly where it was hidden; I still don't know how.

Alex stood frozen, unable to move. With the gun now in hand, the Kid strode over and settled onto the couch. "Sit down, Alex," he commanded in a tone that brooked no argument. One by one, we sat down, even as the massive man lay still on the floor.

Alex complied, and the Kid began, "I have a story for you. You should listen closely. I was invited to a significant birthday party here in two weeks for a very special lady. Now, imagine my disappointment when I find out that party is suddenly canceled. They had already paid you a deposit, booked the room, and now they're distraught."

"I had no idea they were your friends," Alex said. "You just don't understand—I had no choice."

The Kid said, "I'm listening."

Alex continued, and you could hear the fear in his voice. "Henry came in on Thursday and said he wanted to have a party for one of his kids here on that Saturday. I told him I was booked, and he told me to unbook it or there would be problems. I didn't want any trouble with him."

"You must want trouble with me then?" The Kid's icy gaze made Alex shake his head immediately.

"No, no, Kid, never."

The Kid continued. "Here's what's going to happen, Alex: you're going to call Joanne's mother as soon as we leave and tell her how deeply sorry you are. You'll reassure her that her party is back on, and as a gesture of goodwill for the mix-up, you will give her a 15 percent discount.

"And you're going to promise her that it will be the best birthday party anyone has ever had. And Alex, it better be.

"Next, call that asshole Henry and tell him to find another venue for his party—because under no circumstances is he having it here that day. You tell him I said so. And if he's got a problem with that, he knows where to find me. Got all that, or do I need to tattoo it across your forehead?"

The expression on Alex's face was priceless. He simply said, "I got it all, Kid. It will be the best birthday party anyone has had." Alex nodded vigorously.

As we were leaving, the Kid turned to Alex and said, "Don't fuck this up, Alex, you understand?"

"Absolutely."

"One more thing, Alex. I'll be here for this party. It better be spectacular."

"Absolutely," he said once again.

The Kid turned to the half-conscious guard sitting on the floor now. "If you want to continue our discussion, Alex knows where to find me." The man remained seated, giving the Kid the space he needed. The Kid took the clip out of the gun and emptied one in the chamber, then tossed the gun on the couch.

Once we were outside, the Kid smiled and said, "Can I go get some sleep now?"

Leslie and I erupted into laughter. "Kid, I love you," I said. "You're the best. Are you coming to the party?"

"Unfortunately, no. I've got to be in New York, like I said, but I want Alex to believe I'm coming so he'll go above and beyond to ensure everything's perfect. Don't worry; Philly will be there. Alex doesn't want any part of him either."

After dropping the Kid off, Leslie and I returned home. My mother was beaming, barely able to contain her excitement.

"You'll never believe what just happened! The catering hall called, and they worked everything out. The party is back on, and they're giving me a 15 percent discount for the mix-up! They're even upgrading the liquor to premium and adding a lobster course at no extra charge!"

I exchanged glances with Leslie, both of us keeping quiet about what had really happened. A few weeks later, at the party, my mother discovered the truth. When she learned what the Kid had done, no one could ever say anything negative about him again. He became a saint in her eyes.

The party itself was extraordinary—the food, drinks, and service were exceptional. As the night wound down, I walked over to Alex, who was diligently ensuring everything was perfect.

At that moment, Philly approached us and asked, "Is everything okay, Joanne?"

I thought Alex might faint.

"Everything is perfect," I replied enthusiastically. "Alex did a fantastic job."

Philly turned to Alex and said pointedly, "The Kid sends his regards."

Alex, still looking a bit shaken, responded, "Thank you. I hope the Kid will be satisfied."

"Yeah," Philly replied simply, a knowing smile on his face.

CHAPTER FIFTEEN
NASHVILLE

I jumped back in. "That reminds me of the Nashville romance. I remember when the Kid started seeing Cindy Wagner—the country singer who hadn't yet become a household name."

One day, the Kid suggested we take a ride over to Capitol Records; Paul was having a recording session. We used to hang out there often, soaking in what felt like private concerts. The place had this laid-back, behind-the-curtain vibe—like you were getting a glimpse of something pure before it hit the world."

As we walked into Capitol, the Kid greeted security at the entrance—they nodded in recognition, and we continued on. Paul was always in Studio 1, and we knew our way around. While strolling through the building, we noticed a group heading toward another studio.

In that group was a gorgeous blonde, around five foot two, with an arresting figure and a face that could launch a thousand dreams. The Kid's eyes locked onto hers, and a silent recognition passed between them.

He nudged me, saying, "Come on, I have to know who she is." We trailed them until they entered Studio 12.

There was a security guard at the entrance to each studio, so the Kid casually asked, "Who is that?"

The guard, familiar with him, replied, "That's Cindy Wagner; she's a country artist here to record a crossover song."

The Kid thanked him, and we slipped inside. The room wasn't crowded, so we claimed seats in the first row. Soon enough, the band started rehearsing, and Cindy began to sing a few bars. When she looked our way and smiled, it was clear something had just begun.

The Kid smiled back and murmured, "Sounds great so far."

Almost as if drawn by fate, she stepped down a few steps and came over. With a lighthearted spirit, she addressed the band. "Give me five." Then she turned to the Kid, asking playfully, "Am I supposed to know you?"

He replied with equal playfulness, "I don't think so, but this is a great place to start," and they both laughed.

In the midst of the banter, one of the stage bosses hollered, "Hey, Cindy, are these guys bothering you? Time is money, so let's go!"

His tone carried an edge, but the Kid stood and turned to him with a look that silenced him immediately—a look that said everything without a single word.

The man's bravado faltered, and he muttered, "Whenever you're ready, Cindy," in a subdued manner.

"Do you have that effect on everyone?" Cindy asked the Kid.

With a touch of humor, he replied, "Nah, just on guys who disrespect my friends."

She smiled, and before heading back behind the glass, she asked if he would stay and listen while she performed.

"No one's getting me out of this seat," he retorted. "Give it your best, gorgeous."

And then she sang—a soulful rendition of "Tears on My Pillow" that captivated everyone in the room. When the song ended, the Kid stood up and clapped vigorously, and the entire room joined in the applause. Afterward, she came over again, and the two of them chatted for a while.

Soon, she mentioned she had to go back behind the glass to record again.

Almost impulsively, the Kid asked, "How about dinner tonight?"

At first, she explained she had plans, then paused and said, "I'll break them—I would love to."

"I'll pick you up at seven," the Kid said.

"Great, I'm at the Beverly Wilshire."

As we said our goodbyes and readied to leave, the Kid couldn't resist one final stare in the direction of the guy who'd disrupted the moment on stage—a silent gesture that made his point without words.

I chuckled. "You had to do that," I said, and we both shared a laugh.

That evening marked the beginning of the long-distance relationship between the Kid and Cindy. They would take turns flying back and forth each month. Although Cindy was about five years older than the Kid, and desired more than just a transient romance, their fling lasted almost six months before they called it quits. Yet, despite the end of the romantic chapter, a genuine friendship endured between them.

About three months after it ended, the Kid came to me and said, "We're going to Nashville—me, you, and Rocco."

I hesitated. "I know it's not to start things up with Cindy again if we're bringing Rocco along."

The Kid said, "No, it's not. Cindy called me last night. There's a big-shot producer at RCA Nashville who told her flat out: either she entertains him privately, or she'll never sing in Nashville again. Her career is on the line."

I couldn't help but mutter, "This asshole has no idea what a mistake he's made."

The Kid just grinned and replied, "No, he doesn't—but he will soon."

Before our trip, Rocco made a call to Louisiana to Fabrizio, the boss of the Venti family who controlled Louisiana and its surroundings. I remembered that Fabrizio had once told the Kid that if he ever needed anything, just to give him a call—after we'd helped his grandchildren on the beach in LA.

We flew into Nashville to find two of Fabrizio's guys waiting for us. As we introduced ourselves, one of them, Vincenzo, said, "Fabrizio said that whatever you need done will be done."

The Kid called Cindy to check when she was scheduled in the studio again.

"Not until I agree to his conditions," Cindy said.

"Hang tight," the Kid said. "I'll let you know when things change."

Soon after, she met us for dinner.

As we dined, Cindy asked the Kid, "So what are you going to do about him?"

With a playful smirk, he replied, "Nothing, except stare at him."

The comment reminded us all of that memorable moment when the Kid's glance had spoken volumes—prompting a light, shared laugh.

The next day, Vincenzo picked us up, and we drove to the office of this producer, whose name was Austin. Vincenzo's reputation in Nashville preceded him. As soon as we walked in, it was clear that fear was in the air. Austin wasn't expecting a visit. As usual, Austin had two goons flanking him.

Vincenzo approached him. "We have a problem," he said. "Let's go to your office to discuss it."

As we stepped into Austin's sprawling office, I couldn't help but think that Austin looked as if he wished he'd never opened that door. It was about to get real, and I sensed that the producer was in for a lesson he wouldn't soon forget.

The Kid fixed his gaze on Austin. "Do you know who I am?"

The look on Austin's face was priceless.

At that moment, I delivered a punishing blow to one of Austin's goons, hitting him in the gut with such force that I lifted him right off the ground. He collapsed immediately.

The second goon didn't dare move; Rocco stood beside him, a .45 trained against his head. We needed to make a statement.

The Kid continued. "They call me the Kid. Fabrizio asked me if I wanted him to handle this for me, but I said no. I want to look this jerk-off in the face when I tell him how close he is to not breathing anymore."

Just then, the guy I had hit started to get up, so I delivered another punch, sending him right back down.

The Kid glanced at me. "Philly, I think they get the message. Rocco, put it down." Then he turned his full attention to Austin. "Now, Austin, I'm going to say this only once. I'm assuming you didn't know, so let me be clear: Cindy is my girl. In other words, she's with me. When she says 'jump,' the next words out of your mouth better be 'how high?' If I hear that you so much as looked at her cross-eyed, you'll wish I had put you six feet under right here and now. Am I clear?"

Austin stammered, "I'm so sorry! I had no idea. Vincenzo knows I would never disrespect the family."

"I better hear that she is your number one recording artist, because anything less will likely make me very unhappy," the Kid said. "If I'm unhappy, we will be back. And the next time we talk, it will end differently. Clear?"

"Absolutely," Austin replied, visibly shaken.

"Okay, I think we're done here."

As we turned to leave, Vincenzo said to Austin, "Fabrizio wanted me to tell you that if he has to send me back here, it will be very unfortunate."

Austin nodded. "No, Vincenzo, tell Fabrizio this will never happen again."

Vincenzo acknowledged him with a nod, and we all exited.

Cindy never had any more problems in Nashville after that. Vincenzo drove us back to the airport, and the Kid said, "Tell Fabrizio I owe him. Anything he needs, all he has to do is ask."

We all shook hands and returned to LA.

When we landed, Cindy called the Kid to inform him that Austin had reached out to ask her to come in and record, apologizing profusely. "What did you say to him?" she asked.

The Kid chuckled. "I just stared at him." They both laughed.

That would be the last time I saw Cindy until she performed in LA a decade later. I brought my wife to the show, and we hung out with her backstage for a while. She truly was a remarkable woman and entertainer.

CHAPTER SIXTEEN
THE KID LEAVES LA

Shortly before the Kid and I turned twenty-three, Pop passed away from natural causes, and his son, Carl Jr., who was named after his grandfather, Carl Sr., assumed control of the family. Although we lost a bit of clout with his passing, things stayed relatively steady—until Paul came under FBI scrutiny.

Suddenly, our world was upended. Agents questioned us incessantly, trailed our every move, and obtained warrants for our business records. It was a trying period, and only when Paul was eventually exonerated due to a lack of evidence did the heat finally subside.

I thought things had finally settled down—until one day, the Kid pulled me aside and said, "We need to talk."

Over lunch, he opened up and told me he needed a change. When I asked what kind of change, he said that although we were doing well in the private sanitation business, he felt stuck. His mother had been urging him to come back to New York, and after thinking it over, he'd decided it was time to go back to school and deepen his understanding of business. He was drawn to the idea of building something real—something legitimate.

I tried to convince him to remain in LA—keeping the business intact while attending college in Southern California—but for a week we debated the matter until he made it clear he had to leave.

The following week, the Kid informed Marino of his plans. Marino, ever pragmatic, told him he was making the right decision and wished him well. We cashed him out of the business, and in 1983, at the age of twenty-three, the Kid left Southern California with $250,000 in cash. With his departure, I found myself drawn once again to the lifestyle I had always secretly craved—the life of a wise guy.

After much pondering, I called the Kid and asked him to put in a good word with Carl Jr. for me. You couldn't just walk up to someone in the family and say, "Hey, I want to join." It didn't work like that. You had to be recommended by someone who was already made. Now, the Kid wasn't made himself, but he had the juice—the influence—with the family to make it happen.

The Kid did everything he could to talk me out of it, but I was stubborn. He looked at me and said, "Philly, we ran with a lot of those people. We were in deep—connected in a hundred ways—but we were never one of them. We never had to take orders to hurt people or do things we didn't want to do. Sure, we hurt guys, but only the ones who came after us, interfered in our business, or the ones who tried to hurt people we cared about."

Then he paused before laying it out plainly.

"You know what it takes to get made. It means doing work. Real work. That means killing someone. It doesn't matter if you actually pull the trigger or not—you're in on it. Maybe it's a stranger, maybe someone you've had dinner with—someone who's never done a thing to you or anyone you love. That's something I couldn't do. And I know you, Philly . . . I'm not sure you could either. So, ask yourself: Are you really ready to cross that line?"

I looked him in the eye. "Kid, you know this is what I've always wanted. You've been the one holding me back all these years, always shielding me from that final step. But things are different now. You're not here anymore. You chose a different path. And didn't you always tell me: we deal with the reality in front of us, not the one we wish we had? This is my reality now. I need to do this. I'm asking you to make the call. And if I'm being honest, I'm hoping I'll have your blessing too."

Eventually, he gave in. "Philly, I will always have your back no matter what."

A few weeks later, I got the word: Carl Jr. wanted to see me. We sat down at DanTana's, his favorite spot in LA. Over a plate of pasta, he got right to it. "I hear you want to choose our life," he said.

"I do," I answered simply.

He leaned back, studying me. "Why now, Philly? You've had plenty of chances before."

I told him the truth. "It's always been in me. The dream, the pull. But when I was with the Kid, it felt like we were wise guys without wearing the stripes. We lived it—but we never signed our names to it."

Carl smiled, nodded. "That makes sense. I understand," he said. "And I believe you've got what it takes. I'm putting you with Arnoldo—my nephew—one of our captains. He'll see what you're made of. And when the day comes that we think you've earned it, we will ask you to join us. In the meantime, you do everything Arnoldo tells you."

The next day, I received a message from Arnoldo asking me to meet him at a local coffeehouse at 7:00 a.m. I arrived early, within minutes of the scheduled time.

Arnoldo didn't waste any time. "You're now with me. Lesson number one: when I tell you to meet me at a certain time and place, you better be there at least thirty minutes early in case I'm early. I don't wait for you—you wait for me. Understand?"

I responded immediately. "Yes, sir."

From that day forward, I made it a point to be thirty to forty-five minutes early for every meeting with him. I spent countless hours by his side—driving him around, acting as his chauffeur and bodyguard, and learning the ropes of the street business. Ten years my senior and a lifelong mobster, I quickly came to respect his streetwise teachings and the lessons he imparted about conducting and earning money in our way of life.

Just under two years later, on July 16, 1985, I was proposed and officially inducted into the family. Once I was "made," Marino and Joe took over the operations of the garbage business completely. They were well-connected and respectable men, but now I was their key connection. I rarely went to the office because I was occupied with the Poporri family business. The private sanitation business would now serve as my front—a place I could wash money and show a legitimate income.

I built my own crew and diversified our ventures—from loan sharking, bookmaking, and hijacking to anything we could get our hands on. I did my best to follow the principles I'd learned from the Kid, such as not harming anyone who wasn't involved or deserving—but not every member of my crew shared that restraint. Some were full-blown outlaws, caring only about the profits, regardless of the cost or injury to others. I had to accept this as part of the life, but did my best to keep it contained.

As my crew continued to grow and generate more money, I was promoted to captain in 1990. I had now become part of the Capo regime of the Poporri family, answering solely to Carl. Although we spoke occasionally, I hadn't seen the Kid in three years—until the day Paul died of natural causes.

Paul's funeral was a major event, attended by everyone who was anyone. Naturally, the Kid flew in and spent a week with Paul's family.

During his stay, we spent some quality time together. One day, he came by my social club and met a good number of my crew, some of whom he already knew from back in the day. The Kid settled in, and we started catching up.

At one point, someone needed to talk to me, so I asked the Kid to hang on for a minute, promising I'd be right back. While I was in the back talking, I heard a commotion and rushed out. What I found shocked me: one of my guys was lying on the floor, and the Kid was standing over him with a gun in his hand.

"What happened?" I asked, alarmed.

The Kid looked down and said, "Is this the scum you associate with now?"

Again, I pressed. "What happened?"

The Kid gestured toward a cleaning girl who had witnessed the incident. "This degenerate grabbed her ass and told her to get on her knees. I told him, 'Grow up, lowlife,' and he jumped up and pulled a gun on me. He's lucky this isn't ten years ago; otherwise, you'd be scraping him off the floor right now."

"He pulled a gun on you?" I exclaimed, noticing all my guys standing around, frozen. None of them dared move, knowing who the Kid was and what our relationship entailed.

I walked over to the guy on the floor who had drawn the gun. I extended my hand to help him up, and as soon as he was on his feet, I landed a punch that sent him crashing back down. I think I broke his jaw.

"You two, get him out of here," I ordered two of my guys.

I turned back to the Kid and apologized.

"Hey, it's not my jaw that's broken," he replied with a grin.

We both chuckled, deciding to go out for dinner at a popular local Italian restaurant.

Two of my guys drove us there, and we were seated right away, bypassing the line outside—one of the perks of my status.

The Kid leaned over and said, "Looks like La Cosa Nostra suits you well."

We both laughed heartily. It was great to catch up with him. A few days later, he left for New Jersey, and I didn't see him again until that fateful phone call that would change my life.

The gentle clink of silverware faded into a background hum as Graham's wife, Thessaly, poised and curious, turned toward me. Her voice was warm, the kind that invited confessions without pressure.

"So," she said, tucking a wisp of light brown hair behind her ear, her eyes sharp with the glint of genuine interest, "what's the Kid been up to all these years?"

I leaned back in my chair, took a slow sip of wine, and said with a grin, "I can tell you—but it's not a short story."

The table broke into laughter, and Graham replied, "We've got nowhere to be."

Natalie, Joanne, and my wife already knew pieces of what I was about to share, but the rest leaned in, clearly hungry for every detail. I told them that some of what I'd learned about the Kid after he left LA had come to me secondhand—sometimes even third—but every story had eventually been confirmed to me by the Kid himself. And with that, I began.

After the Kid left LA in 1983, our lives split in very different directions. For me, things were going along just fine for a while—until, in 1990, everything changed. My former captain, Arnoldo, was arrested on a laundry list of charges that could have easily put him away for life.

Overnight, although I was already a captain, I found myself given more responsibility, with Carl asking me to be acting captain of Arnoldo's crew as well. Before long, my crew, now closely associated with Arnoldo's crew, became known as the most feared in all of LA.

Of course, the FBI soon started zeroing in on me. While New York was in turmoil—with the five families under heavy investigation and everyone scrambling just to avoid jail—the West Coast wasn't entirely off the hook. The pressure built up until, one day, as I was walking to my office, I was arrested.

In an instant, everything shifted. I spent the next six months shelling out hundreds of thousands of dollars to attorneys, investigators, and anyone I thought could help. Every avenue I tried seemed hopeless. I knew that a conviction would mean a very long stretch behind bars, probably for the rest of my life, given the harsh sentences the Feds were doling out to made guys.

Then, in an almost miraculous twist of fate, the Feds brought me to trial—only for their key witness against me to die of a heart attack three days before the proceedings were set to begin. I had nothing to do with it, but the outcome was clear: the charges were dropped, and I walked free.

That, however, didn't keep the Feds off my trail. I learned to be extremely cautious, and for the next ten years, I managed to stay out of further trouble.

I was slated to eventually become underboss—acting in that capacity for some time—but things changed again when Carl's nephew, Arnoldo, was made underboss after being released from custody. That same key witness was going to testify against him as well, and I found that I preferred not to draw any more unwanted attention from the Feds, so I was fine with that decision. Somehow, the constant pressure eased, and life continued on.

All the while, the Kid was back in New York. We would talk from time to time, although our conversations grew more infrequent as the years passed. Still, I knew deep down that the bond we had built would never truly die.

CHAPTER SEVENTEEN
TERESA

When the Kid returned to New York—he made a sharp break from our turbulent life in LA. Focused entirely on school, he steered clear of fights and trouble, always knowing when to walk away and avoid chaos. I like to think he made his mother proud, although I doubt she ever fully grasped the reality of what we lived on the West Coast.

He settled into his mother's timeworn Brooklyn home, sharing space with his spirited younger sister, Gloria, three years his junior. Almost immediately, every familiar creak of the old floor and the lingering scent of family dinners unleashed a tidal wave of childhood memories crashing back at him, stirring long-forgotten laughter and bittersweet echoes of the past from his father and grandfather.

By 1986, he had earned a four-year degree in just three years, majoring in finance, economics, and marketing—a true testament to his drive and intellect. Shortly afterward, he opened an office on 3rd Avenue in Brooklyn in the Bay Ridge section and took an audacious leap by launching a magazine devoted to technology—a venture that proved wildly successful. By 1992, he had amassed a few million dollars—a fortune, at least by our standards.

In the early days of launching the magazine, he sifted through countless résumés, each boasting impressive scholastic credentials. The interviews followed—one after another, a parade of qualified candidates. But then, amidst the routine exchanges and polished responses, one applicant stood apart from the rest—a stunning young woman named Teresa Garcia.

Two years his junior, Teresa stood at five foot four with long, flowing brown hair that shimmered naturally and captivating brown eyes that held your attention. Her flawless, porcelain skin and every delicately sculpted feature hinted at a beauty that was both refined and arresting. What made Teresa even more unforgettable was her unique blend of Italian and Spanish heritage. Having emigrated from Spain to the US with her family at age five, her subtle accent told the story of her roots, adding an intriguing layer to her charm. When she spoke, her sexy, engaging voice commanded the room.

After her interview with the Kid was finished, he was convinced he had to hire her. It wasn't long before it became clear that a special chemistry was developing between them.

From the moment Teresa joined the Kid's team, their relationship remained strictly professional. She excelled in her role, attending meetings, managing marketing and sales calls, and working long hours alongside him.

Over time, their shared dedication and countless conversations forged an unspoken connection. The Kid found himself looking forward to each day, not just for the work but for the moments spent with Teresa. Her elegance was effortless, a quiet confidence woven into every graceful movement. The way her heels framed the curve of her legs only deepened her undeniable presence, commanding attention without a single word. And she certainly had his.

Their business trips to Manhattan evolved into something more. Meetings turned into opportunities to explore the city's finest restaurants, where the Kid discovered a newfound appreciation for wine.

Teresa joined him in this journey, and together they cultivated their palates, transforming each meal into a shared experience of discovery. Over glasses of rich reds and crisp whites, their conversations deepened, spanning everything from business strategies to the most personal corners of their lives. These moments became a foundation for their growing bond.

Nine months into her tenure, the Kid invited Teresa to accompany him on a business trip to Las Vegas, assuring her she'd have her own room. Excited by the prospect of visiting Vegas for the first time, Teresa agreed. During the car ride to the airport, their conversation shifted from business to music as the driver played nostalgic tunes. As they listened to the first chorus of the song "Turn Around, Look at Me" by the Vogues, Teresa reached over and took the Kid's hand and held it.

Surprised but moved, he turned to her and said, "I feel the same." They held hands all the way to the airport.

On the flight, the connection between them grew stronger. Seated in first class, the Kid turned and kissed her gently, saying, "You are a very special lady."

"And you are an incredible man. Watching you work and how you handle people and business makes me smile."

Their conversation flowed effortlessly, touching on everything from their dreams to their shared values.

At the hotel, as they waited in line to check in, Teresa leaned in and whispered, "We only need one room."

The Kid smiled and arranged for a suite. That weekend marked the true beginning of their relationship. From that point on, Teresa became an integral part of the Kid's life, sharing in every aspect of his world.

They discovered they were perfectly aligned in their tastes for music, movies, fine wines, and food, as well as their shared faith, family values, children, dreams of the future, and passionate lovemaking.

Their first day in Vegas was spent entirely in their suite, emerging only at 9:30 p.m. for dinner. Teresa asked the Kid if she had satisfied him, to which he replied, "No one has ever satisfied me like you do."

She confessed, "I know you have had far more experience than me, but no one has ever touched me the way you have. I've never felt this kind of passion with anyone."

The Kid smiled. "This is just the beginning. Let's take a shower, get dressed, and go have some dinner. You wore me out—I need energy."

They laughed together, their connection deepening with every moment.

After the business meeting the following day, they decided to extend their stay by three days, spending their time relaxing, enjoying each other's company, and solidifying the bond that had begun to flourish.

Then, in a move that shocked all of us back in LA, within a year of their Vegas trip, the Kid decided to propose to Teresa. After they returned to Brooklyn, he spent every day with her at work and every weekend together until it was clear that he wanted more.

One day, he called his trusted friend Blue Eyes—Vincent Palozzi—a powerful captain in the Battista family and asked for a recommendation: a reputable diamond merchant he could rely on. Blue Eyes connected him with a diamond wholesaler on 47th Street in Manhattan. The Kid met with the merchant, and after a deliberate exchange of hushed words and subtle glances, he purchased a perfect two-and-a-half-carat round blue diamond. This exquisite gem, its deep blue facets catching every stray beam of light, was meticulously set into a sleek white gold band—a symbol of refined taste and an unwavering resolve to make a statement.

Armed with the perfect ring, the Kid invited Teresa out to celebrate in style. He told her about a newly opened fine dining

French restaurant in New York called La Rose d'Or—a name that carried its own air of exclusivity—and mentioned that there was normally a three-month wait for a Saturday night reservation. However, he had managed to secure one for them that Saturday at 7:30. Always eager to spend time with the Kid over fine wines and exquisite cuisine, Teresa readily accepted.

Though Blue Eyes belonged to a different family than the Kid's grandfather, and though he was twenty years his junior, their bond was unmistakable. The Kid's grandfather had once been a mentor to Blue Eyes, and that respect carried through to his support of the Kid—even though the Kid never introduced him to Teresa. In his quest to forge a new life, the Kid deliberately kept his mob family connections out of his personal world.

That memorable evening, a limo whisked them from Brooklyn into Manhattan and to La Rose d'Or. By 7:30 p.m., they were seated at a corner table with a stunning view overlooking 5th Avenue. They uncorked a spectacular bottle of Corton Bressandes, a French Grand Cru Burgundy, and savored an unforgettable dinner.

After dinner, Teresa excused herself to the restroom. When she returned, she noticed a blue velvet ring box resting on the table in front of her seat. Her eyes widened as she looked at the Kid. With a big smile, she picked up the box and opened it.

Overwhelmed, she turned to him, embraced him tightly, and the Kid softly asked, "Will you marry me?"

With watery eyes and heartfelt joy, she replied, "Yes, yes, yes. I love you so much."

In the days that followed, they discussed the details of their future together—from whether she wanted a lavish wedding, to which family members should be invited, to where they would live. Teresa made it clear that the only thing she truly desired was to be his wife; a grand wedding was not necessary. The Kid, however, countered that instead of delaying for tradition's sake, why not seize the moment and get married soon? They decided, then and there, to tie the knot eight weeks from that night.

Teresa didn't come from an affluent family—her family lived modestly, and finances were always tight. Early on, the Kid sat down with her parents and made it clear: he would be covering the cost of the wedding, and he didn't want them to feel the slightest obligation. "Having your daughter as my wife—and all of you as my extended family—that's more than enough," he told them sincerely.

After some thoughtful family conversations, they chose Micali Terrace in Brooklyn for the reception—a venue arranged through Blue Eyes, who quietly held an ownership stake in the catering hall. The ceremony took place at the Basilica of Regina Pacis, or Regina Pacis Church as the locals called it. The church was grand yet warm, and the moment Teresa walked down the aisle in her sweeping white gown, she looked nothing short of radiant. The reception that followed was intimate—just around fifty guests—but full of love, laughter, and a quiet sense of new beginnings.

None of us received an invitation. Later, the Kid explained that starting fresh in New York meant cutting ties with everything from his past on both coasts—even with some of his New York connections, like Blue Eyes, who were left off the guest list. At first, I was upset—jealous even of his decisive break—a choice I soon secretly wished I could have made for myself.

After getting married, he and Teresa decided to start a new chapter in New Jersey. They left Brooklyn and built a modest home in Morristown, New Jersey, and within a year, Teresa was pregnant with their first child. In just six years, their family blossomed into a household of four children—two boys and two girls, with one boy and one girl arriving as twins. Life had a slow, peaceful rhythm that felt entirely their own.

It was during these years that Teresa gently guided the Kid back to God. In our years together in LA, I never once saw him set foot in a church—even though we both grew up Catholic. It wasn't that our faith had disappeared; rather, we never felt the need to prove our beliefs from a pew. But when Teresa entered his life, everything changed. Whether it was gratitude for her love or the precious blessing of their children, the Kid found a renewed purpose in faith. Now, without fail, every week became sacred: he and Teresa, surrounded by their children, attended church religiously, drawing solace and strength from their shared devotion.

The Kid had rekindled a deep closeness with his mother, as well as his sister, Gloria. They were an important presence in every family gathering, involved in all their activities, and always ready to lend a loving hand.

Babysitting his children was his mother's joy, a role that also paved the way for a special bond with Teresa. In her eyes, Teresa was the center of their universe—she believed the sun rose and set around her. Teresa wasn't just an incredible mother to the children; she was the perfect wife the Kid needed to complete his world. Teresa spent countless hours with his mother, sharing more than just the daily routines. They would embark on leisurely shopping trips, always on the lookout for something special in every store.

The Kid's sister, Gloria, thought of Teresa as a sister. Back at home, the three joined forces in the kitchen—sharing recipes, chopping vegetables, simmering sauces, and preparing meals that carried the warmth of family traditions. Amid the bustle of raising the children, every moment together deepened their bond, weaving a tapestry of shared care and resilience that enriched the entire household.

Teresa's family remained in Brooklyn, but even after she and the Kid settled in New Jersey, the bond never wavered. They often made the trip across the bridge for big family gatherings, blending seamlessly with the Kid's family.

From the very first introduction, her parents embraced him without hesitation, treating him not just as Teresa's future husband but as one of their own. The two families got along effortlessly, their get-togethers filled with laughter, stories, and the kind of warmth that made it feel as if they'd known each other forever.

When the Kid first met Teresa's family, her brother Manuel was still in school and studying to be a writer. At a Sunday dinner, soon after Manny had graduated, he asked the Kid if there might be an opening for him at the magazine.

"Let me think about it," the Kid said, "and I'll get back to you."

Later that evening, as they drove home to New Jersey, Teresa asked, "What do you think about my brother working for you?"

"I didn't want to commit without first talking to you," the Kid said. Noticing Teresa's surprise, he continued. "I want to know your thoughts first because—as you know—if I hire him, I'll treat him like everyone else. I like Manny, but if he doesn't measure up, he'll need to look for another job. I need to be sure you're okay with that."

Teresa smiled. "Thank you for checking with me. I'm well aware, and I'm completely fine with it."

The following week, the Kid hired Manny to start at the magazine.

A few years later, in 1995, the Kid pulled off another bold move. He invested a million dollars in a tech startup called Looking Glass, a company with ambitions to revolutionize the way the Internet functioned. I'm not exactly sure what he saw in it at the time, but looking back, it turned out to be one of the best investments anyone could've made. While most were hesitant to take the risk, this enabled him to negotiate extremely favorable terms. By 1997, he owned 13 percent of the company, had a seat on the board, and held unique privileges: veto power over mergers and acquisitions and a no-dilution clause on his shares. He clearly took everything he'd learned from Marino, the streets, and business school and used it to write another successful chapter in his life.

By the late '90s, the board had agreed to let Goldman Sachs take Looking Glass public within two years, marking a major transition. During that time, one board member—Walter McNeill, a hothead who fancied himself a tough guy—began going to other investors, offering to buy out their shares at a steep premium. Some jumped at the chance for a guaranteed profit and cashed out early.

But when it came to the Kid, things weren't so simple. His shares carried the same weight as anyone's in volume, but with the added power of those special privileges—privileges that made his stake exponentially more valuable to anyone looking to consolidate control. Walter, in particular, had his sights set on them. He knew that if he could get his hands on the Kid's shares, he'd have the leverage to cut a sweetheart deal—even with a company like Goldman Sachs.

One day, during a board meeting, Walter once again put his money where his mouth was. He offered to buy the Kid's shares at nearly triple the price the other investors had been paid. The Kid, however, maintained his calm and politely refused.

That's when Walter's temper flared. He stood up abruptly and thundered, "Do you know who I represent?" His outburst echoed through the boardroom; a startling moment given the usual corporate decorum.

Unfazed, the Kid replied in his characteristically cool manner, "No, I guess I don't, but it doesn't really matter—I'm not interested in selling my shares."

Walter, still seething, shot back, "We will see about that," and then stormed out of the meeting.

One of the other board members suggested that the Kid file a police complaint over the incident. The Kid dismissed the idea with a simple remark: "There's no need for that—Walter probably just had a bad day." In that moment, it was clear the Kid wasn't just making business decisions—he was setting boundaries and ensuring that no one could use their connections or bluster to dictate terms over him. It was yet another example of how he controlled the situation with quiet confidence, never compromising his hard-earned advantages.

The following weekend, the Kid attended a charity function with his wife, Teresa. I can't recall exactly where the event was held, but for some reason, the Kid insisted on driving his own car that night. He had just taken delivery, in May of 1999, of a brand-new 2000 Mercedes CL500—a car so rare that only three black-on-black versions existed in the United States.

In fact, the dealer had offered him $20,000 not to take delivery after hearing that Scottie Pippen of the Chicago Bulls was willing to pay $50,000 over sticker price for the car. True to his character, the Kid said no and kept the car.

After the charity event wound down, the Kid and Teresa were among the last to leave. Outside, the parking lot was almost deserted. The Kid told Teresa, "You stay here, and I'll go get the car."

But Teresa, relishing the clear, beautiful night, insisted, "No, I'll walk with you." So after saying goodnight to the few people lingering outside, they strolled together arm in arm into the parking lot.

Since the Kid left LA, his commitment to training never wavered. Even after escaping those dark memories, he maintained a rigorous routine, hitting the gym with a disciplined intensity that kept his sculpted, lean, powerful frame. His passion for martial arts wasn't just about physical fitness—it was a statement of control, a way to master his own destiny. In those early days, he even took time to share his expertise with Teresa.

Together in the gym, he patiently taught her basic self-defense techniques, guiding her through every punch, kick, and controlled movement. As she watched him work the heavy bag—with each powerful strike and precise kick—her eyes lit up with admiration. She was captivated not only by his skill but by the fluid grace with which he moved, a testament to years of dedication to martial arts and proper conditioning.

He showed her how to stretch, stay limber, and remain alert, instilling in her both confidence and resilience. Yet, despite all the intensity of his training, she never saw him in a real confrontation. His combat skills remained a practiced art, honed in the safe space of the gym rather than tested in the chaos of the outside world.

Just as they reached their car, another vehicle screeched up beside them. Two large men jumped out, and in an instant, the Kid reacted on instinct—he scooped Teresa up behind him, as if expecting the worst. For a split second, it looked as though these men might be armed.

Instead, one of them stepped forward, his tone chilling as he said, "We have a message for you. Maybe after we break both your legs and mess up your pretty wife, you'll rethink selling your shares." As the threat hung in the air, one of the men brandished an aluminum baseball bat.

That night marked the first time Teresa witnessed the Kid engaged in a conflict like this. She later described the next sixty seconds as something utterly indescribable—moments of raw intensity that left her petrified. The kind of confrontation that etches itself into your memory forever.

Both big men lay on the floor, blood everywhere, their bodies marked with multiple contusions. When it was all over, the Kid turned to his wife and said, "Get in the car."

Without a word, they climbed into the vehicle, and he started the engine, pulling away from the chaos behind them.

Teresa, still in shock, asked, "Aren't you going to call the police or an ambulance?"

"No," he replied firmly. "This is something I need to handle myself."

She pressed him with a few more questions, but it was clear he didn't want to discuss it further. Sensing the weight of the situation, she let it drop.

Later that night, my phone rang. I answered, and it was the Kid's voice on the other end. "I may need you and a few of your guys," he said.

I didn't ask for details. I simply replied, "Let me know when, and we'll be there."

He said, "Thanks," and hung up, then swiftly called Carl Jr.

Explaining the situation to Carl, the Kid asked for a favor. He wasn't entirely sure which New York family was behind Walter's attempts to seize control of his shares in Looking Glass, but he knew someone needed to make it clear that this needed to stop—immediately. Carl, who had always held the Kid in high regard, understood the urgency. After all, the granddaughter of Pop, whom the Kid had stood up for at that club years ago, was his daughter.

Carl agreed to look into it and make the necessary calls. A few days later, Carl called the Kid and said he found out it was someone in the Battista family. He spoke with Joey Doves, and Joey assured him it would stop. It was evident that word was passed along, because a month later, during the next board meeting, Walter walked in, his head bowed—a stark contrast to his previously brash demeanor. The Kid sensed immediately that someone had spoken to Walter and that the message had landed.

At some point during the meeting, Walter stood up and, facing everyone, apologized for his outburst against the Kid at the last meeting. He assured them it would never happen again and, crucially, he never mentioned the sale of the Kid's shares again.

Everyone present quickly realized that the Kid wielded considerable influence. From that day forward, he noticed a distinct change in how they treated him. It was reminiscent of the respect he had always garnered in LA after that unforgettable night in the Loft. The Kid had made his mark once more, and everyone knew it.

Teresa chose to let the night's unsettling incident in the parking lot slip into silence. She sensed that the Kid wasn't yet ready to explain everything in detail—and deep down, her trust in him ran beyond words.

Later that evening, after the board meeting, the Kid called her with a soft apology. He explained that he had kept her in the dark over the past few weeks because he wanted to protect her and the kids. He suggested they open a special bottle of wine that night and talk, promising, "It's time for me to share a story with you."

In response, with gentle affection, Teresa simply said, "No matter what it is, Dom, I love you too." At that time, she still knew him only as Dominic, unaware of the full weight of his past and his nickname, the Kid.

That night, after the kids were settled, as the soft glow of candlelight danced across the quiet living room and the gentle clink of wine glasses punctuated the silence, the Kid leaned back and began to unravel the tangled tapestry of his past for Teresa—a life steeped in both pain and peril long before he'd met her. His voice, low and reflective, carried her back to a time when he was just a boy struggling in a world fractured by loss and hardened by the mob influences that swirled around his family.

"Listen," he began, "as you know, I lost my father when I was ten. That loss—when I was so young—shattered our little world. My mother, my sister, and I were left devastated. But then my grandfather, who I was always very close to, and the rest of our extended family stepped in.

"See, on my mother's side of the family, things were never simple. The mob was woven into our very existence. My aunts helped my mother and guided Gloria, and my grandfather, a captain in the Barbieri family, took me under his wing. I used to ride with him everywhere, watching in silent awe as he handled people, commanded respect, and exuded a mixture of strength and menace that made everyone think twice. In my young eyes, he was my hero—a man everyone feared who could do no wrong, even if his world was far from ordinary."

He paused, his gaze far away as memories flooded him.

He looked over at Teresa, who sat silently, her chin resting on her knuckles, waiting for the next words.

"I remember my mother's stories when she was growing up—her house was often raided by the police. Once, when the authorities came pounding at the door, she grabbed all the betting slips scattered on the dining room table and hid them under her mattress, desperate to shield her family. My father, the gentlest soul you could ever meet—always ready to give the shirt off his back—had nothing to do with that life or that world. Though 100 percent Italian, he was the antithesis of what my grandfather represented. And yet, I was caught between them. I admired my father's decency, even as I couldn't help but be drawn to the raw power of my grandfather's world."

Teresa, listening intently, her eyes fixed on him, finally spoke.

"In all the conversations I had with your mother, she never once mentioned anything about her father being involved in the mob."

"I'm sure she didn't," the Kid replied. "It's something she's embarrassed about and wants to forget.

"When I was about eight years old, I spent most Friday nights in the basement of my house, where card games were a regular tradition. The kitchen, smaller and brightly lit, was where the women played cards and cooked. In the larger adjoining room, the men gathered around a table for a higher-stakes game, though nothing crazy. I had always wanted to play, especially since my grandfather had taught me the basics years earlier. But the answer was always the same—I was too young.

"On one particular Friday night, I tried once again to join the kitchen game, only for the women to shoo me away.

" 'Go bother the men,' one of them said with a smirk.

"Taking her advice, I wandered into the main room and asked for a seat at the men's table. My father, who rarely ever played cards, wasn't feeling well and had stayed upstairs in bed. He had given me five dollars to play. Still, the men at the table flatly refused.

" 'No way you're playing here,' one of them told me.

"Disappointed but determined, I sat just a few feet away, quietly watching the game unfold. Then the sound of footsteps echoed down the basement stairs. Every head turned as my grandfather descended. The moment he appeared, I ran to him and threw my arms around him.

" 'Grandpa, I want to play,' I pleaded.

"The mood shifted instantly. A seat was immediately made available for my grandfather—no one questioned it. My grandfather looked at me and asked, 'You want to play?' When I nodded, he smiled and said, 'Come sit on my lap. You can play my cards.'

"I climbed onto his lap and looked around the table, especially to the man who said I couldn't play at this table. No one objected. No one said a word. With quiet focus, I played—and even won a few dollars.

"It was in that moment that I realized, with the clarity only an eight-year-old could have, that my grandfather wielded enormous power. In that basement, among those men, his word was final. And to me, it meant everything."

Teresa leaned in closer, drawn to every word as if piecing together a mystery that had always been hidden in plain sight. The Kid poured her another glass of wine, then settled back into the couch.

"When I was nine, I was riding in a car with my grandfather. We were in the back seat, while two of his guys were in the front. We were headed into the city for lunch when, as we passed Broom Street in lower Manhattan, one of the men in the front remarked, 'There's Roberto.' "

"Almost immediately, my grandfather said, 'Pull over—I want to talk to him.' The guy sitting in the front passenger seat got out to approach Roberto.

"After a tense three minutes, it was clear that Roberto wasn't agreeing to what was being demanded of him. I could see the anger in my grandfather's eyes as he told me to 'stay here' and stepped out of the car. I watched in quiet horror as he walked over, grabbed Roberto by the neck, and slammed him against the wall. I don't know the exact words exchanged, but I saw the fear and panic spread across Roberto's face. I guess he didn't know my grandfather was in the car. Finally, my grandfather released him after uttering something.

"All I saw was Roberto, panic-stricken, nodding, 'Yes, okay, okay.' "

"Without missing a beat, my grandfather got back into the car and said, 'Let's go to lunch,' as if nothing had happened. Later, when I asked what had happened with Roberto, my grandfather looked at me seriously and said, 'Don't worry about it. One day, you will understand.' I knew from that moment my grandfather was feared and respected."

Teresa shifted in her seat.

The Kid's voice softened further as he shared a memory that still haunted him.

"When I was eleven, I walked into the basement of one of the car washes my grandfather owned—only to find him in a rage, beating a man against the wall, while two of my grandfather's men stood behind him. I remember the blood trailing down that man's face, and the moment my grandfather saw me, he hushed his own fury. He told his guys to deal with it, and he took me by the hand and walked me upstairs. 'Just forget what you saw, Dominic,' he said, his tone as cold as the concrete surrounding us. 'Learn that this world is tough—sometimes you have to stand up for yourself.' I never managed to forget it."

Teresa, her eyes brimming with tears, whispered, "I thought stories like that only happened in the movies."

The Kid gave a small smirk, nodded, and said, "I can attest—many of them are true.

"When I was fourteen, I started playing cards in a storefront with a group of older guys—a bunch of local regulars who weren't connected to the mob but simply enjoyed a good card game. I soon found myself there, enjoying the camaraderie and honing my skills, playing at least twice a week. By the time I was fifteen, before leaving for LA, I was at the store one day when two older girls—maybe around seventeen—walked in.

"They were talking with the store owner, Louie, and I joined their conversation. I knew I had the attention of one of the girls, which was flattering being only fifteen, when suddenly Richie, one of the older guys I'd never been particularly fond of—and who clearly saw me as nothing more than a kid—swaggered in and inserted himself into our conversation.

"After about ten minutes, with none of the girls paying attention to Richie, he abruptly stood up, tossed a ten-dollar bill onto the table, and barked, 'Hey kid, go get us some coffee.' I was mortified. I almost lunged for a chair to smash him with, but knowing he was twice my size, I swallowed my anger. I took the ten dollars and shuffled up the block to buy the coffee. When I came back, I placed the coffee on the table along with the remaining change and announced that I had somewhere to be.

"That afternoon, feeling both humiliated and determined, I went home and made a call. With my grandfather in the hospital for some tests, I reached out to Sonny—one of my grandfather's trusted men—and told him everything. I swore that if Richie ever insulted or bothered me again, I'd pick up a chair and smash it across his face.

"Sonny assured me, 'Don't you worry; I'll handle it.'

"But I pleaded, 'No, please don't—I want to handle this myself.' Sonny agreed, telling me to keep him updated.

"The next day, I returned to that store and sat with Louie, confessing every detail of what I just said. Louie, who knew who my grandfather was, muttered, 'Oh no, they're going to kill him,' though I didn't yet grasp the full weight of those words.

"What I hadn't known was that Richie had already gotten in deep trouble with the family—he'd been caught fooling around with someone's wife. A big no-no in that life. It turned out that Richie's mother was the sister of a made guy who had stepped in and pleaded with the boss for his life. They agreed to let Richie keep breathing but warned that if he ever crossed any line again, his time would be up.

"I simply said, 'Oh, well, I hope he wears a watch.' Louie, who had been very friendly with Richie, gave me a look and shook his head.

"The following Friday, during a big card game at the store, Richie walked in and immediately smiled as he came over to me to say hello. I only nodded, fully aware that the tide had turned. Later that night, sitting at the main table with seven other guys, I ended up winning a big pot with a full house. Seizing the moment, I stood up, picked up twenty dollars from the winnings, and glanced to my left at Richie. I tossed the money his way and said, 'Richie, go buy coffee for everyone.'

"The room fell silent. Richie understood that this was his defining moment—a choice between facing his past transgressions or accepting the consequences. He picked up the twenty dollars, left to get the coffee, and upon returning, set the coffee down before simply walking out. I never saw him again.

"That night was my first true taste of the power my grandfather's world wielded—a lesson in respect and consequence that I would carry with me forever."

Teresa leaned in and took a big sip of wine, eyes wide with wonder. "It's like you're telling me scenes straight out of a movie."

The Kid smiled, a flicker of memory dancing behind his eyes. "That was my life," he said softly. "Growing up, that was all real.

"Following the card game story, I found myself hanging out in the schoolyard near the house one day. There were about ten of us, cracking jokes and messing around. I made a joke about Sebby, and suddenly, the whole group froze, waiting for him to pounce. But instead of popping me, Sebby just laughed. It was a surprising moment, considering our history.

"Sebby was this big kid, a few years older than us, standing about six feet tall and weighing over 200 pounds. I, on the other hand, was a skinny 150 pounds at best. For months, whenever I hung out in that schoolyard, Sebby would rough me up—throwing me to the ground, standing on me, and generally making my life miserable.

"One day, I was driving down the block with Sonny in his black Cadillac; as I mentioned, he was one of the made guys in my grandfather's crew. As we passed the schoolyard, Sonny slowed down, watching the group of guys hanging out. I spotted Sebby and said, 'There's that fucking Sebby.'

"Sonny immediately stopped the car and turned to me. 'What about him?' he asked.

"I told him, 'He's always punching the shit out of me.'

"Without hesitation, Sonny pulled over and honked the horn. The sound cut through the chatter, and everyone in the schoolyard turned to look. Sonny pointed at Sebby and motioned for him to come over with his finger. Sebby jogged up to the car, bending down to greet Sonny. 'Hey, Sonny, how are you? What do you need?' he asked, all smiles.

"Sonny didn't waste any time. 'Do you know my boy Dominic here?' he said, gesturing toward me.

"Sebby's demeanor shifted instantly. 'Sure, I know him. Hey, Dom, how are you doing?" he said, trying to play it cool.

"I stayed silent, letting Sonny handle it. Sonny leaned in slightly and said, 'He's with me. Do you understand?'

" 'Absolutely,' Sebby replied without hesitation.

"Sonny nodded. 'Okay, you can go,' he said, dismissing him. As Sebby jogged back to the group, Sonny turned to me and said, 'He won't bother you anymore.'

"I looked at him and simply said, 'Thank you.'

"That day, I learned a powerful lesson about intimidation and the weight of influence. Sonny didn't need to raise his voice or his hands—his presence alone was enough to change the dynamic entirely."

The Kid took a long sip of wine before continuing, his eyes glistening with both regret and resolve. "I grew up in this world. Those business trips to Los Angeles with my grandfather only enhanced it. That world was both exhilarating and brutal. After my father passed, those trips became more frequent, almost like a way to fill the void he left behind. But by the time I was fifteen, I decided to leave for LA—to run away from the pain, the loss of my father, from all that heavy history, hoping to forge a new identity.

"My grandfather agreed to let me go, and he made arrangements with Paul to watch over me. He convinced my mother it would be better for me. Once there, I wound up getting involved with a lot of connected people in LA."

◆◆◆

The Kid even told Teresa stories about Mikey and the two-year stint at a CIA training school—the kind of stories that, even as a kid, taught him to hide his vulnerabilities behind a hardened exterior.

"I've told you some of the stories about how I grew up under the influence of my grandfather," the Kid said. "But what I don't talk about enough is how wonderful my father was. Even though I lost him so young, he left me with lessons that shaped the core of who I am.

"My father always spoke to me about church and Jesus. Every Sunday, the four of us went to Mass together—him, my mother, my sister, and me. Since before I was in first grade, he'd read me stories about Jesus, and I remember how deeply those stories stuck with me. In fact, in first grade at Our Lady of Guadalupe School in Brooklyn, I won a religion medal for telling my class the story about the Good Samaritan—something my father had taught me. That was the kind of man he was: kind, honest, and deeply rooted in faith. To him, God, family, and country were everything.

"One moment in particular will stay with me for the rest of my life. I was about seven years old. My father had just sold an old car—a 1949 Studebaker—for two hundred dollars. I was outside with him when the buyer came by. The man handed over the money, shook my father's hand, and started to leave. But before he could go, my father reached into his pocket, pulled out twenty dollars, and handed it back to him.

" 'Use this to buy a new front tire,' he said. 'It's bald. I'd feel better knowing you replaced it.'

"The man looked surprised but took the money, nodded, and thanked him. I stayed quiet, like I was always taught. But once the man was gone, I asked, 'Dad, why did you give him the twenty dollars? He didn't ask for it.'

"My father looked at me and said, 'Because I don't want it on my conscience that I sold someone a car with a bad tire. What if he's driving with his family and gets into an accident because of that tire? I'd feel awful. That's not something I could live with.'

"I didn't fully understand it then, but I never forgot it. As I got older, I realized what that moment said about my father. He was a truly good man.

"So yes, I was always conflicted—torn between the values of my father and mother and the powerful, often darker world of my grandfather. As you can probably tell by now, that struggle was always there—between what I was born into, what I lived in LA, and what I knew was right."

Teresa chimed in, her voice tinged with longing. "I really wish I could've met him."

The Kid's smile softened. "Me too," he said quietly.

His voice softened, deliberate and vulnerable, as he spoke directly to her. "I didn't leave things out to deceive you, Teresa. I kept them from you because I wanted to shield you—from a world I'd already turned my back on. A world that once defined me but no longer held any place in the man I wanted to become."

He took a breath, the words carrying weight. "When I left LA, I didn't know exactly what I was looking for—only that I needed something different. I couldn't become my grandfather, no matter how much I loved and respected him. And I didn't want the life my father had either—honest work, constant struggle, and dying too soon without ever getting ahead. I needed a new path. I think my father would have wanted that for me too."

He looked at her with quiet intensity. "Then I met you. And it all became clear. You and the kids . . . You're everything. That night in the parking lot—what you saw—it wasn't who I am anymore. Just a flash of the past. A reminder of how far I've come."

She reached over, gently resting her hand on his. "That must've been hard . . . walking away from everything you knew."

"It was," he said softly. "But I knew if I stayed, I'd either end up behind bars or buried. You can only straddle two worlds for so long before one of them pulls you under. I chose freedom. I chose us."

He leaned forward, his gaze intense and sincere. "I needed to share those memories, so you'd understand why I do what I do, and why I promised to always protect you. Even now, I have to occasionally draw on old connections—like the incident triggered by someone from the Battista family in New York, who wanted a piece of my shares in Looking Glass. Back then, if I were still that impulsive kid from LA, those men who attacked us in the parking lot would be dead today. But I made the calls that needed to be made, and now it's settled."

He wove in more details as the conversation meandered into recollections of his early nicknames. "You know," he said with a wry smile, "back in LA, rarely did anyone call me Dom or Dominic. Everyone knew me simply as the Kid. It was a name I earned long ago—a part of who I was, even if I've changed since." His eyes shone with a mixture of nostalgia and determination. "But truly, my life began when I met you. All of these chapters—the losses, the lessons—led me here, to a future where I could be both strong and gentle, where I could let go of my past and build something beautiful with you."

After a long, meaningful pause, he admitted, "After telling you everything, I feel closer to you than ever."

Their shared silence was punctuated by a deep, unspoken understanding. Later that night, their passion ignited—as if the truth had cleansed him of remnants of guilt and regret. And in the days that followed, Teresa told him that she was so grateful for that confession. She said it allowed her to see all the missing pieces of who he truly was, and she loved him all the more for it.

In that vulnerable moment—wine, memory, and raw emotion mingling together—the Kid had shown his scars and his strength. He had laid bare the origins of his tumultuous past to build a future defined not by that legacy but by the promise of love and safety for her and the children.

CHAPTER EIGHTEEN
TROUBLE

"**A**ll right, guys—I don't know about the rest of you, but I need a quick bathroom break," I said, standing up. On the way, I bumped into the Kid, who was lingering near the hallway on the phone. As the Kid hung up, I grinned and said, "You're missing some legendary stories about us growing up."

The Kid chuckled. "I'm sure you remember every single one . . . in cinematic detail."

I laughed. "I'm dying to tell them the story about the Pill."

"The Pill?" the Kid said, raising an eyebrow. "That never happened."

We both burst out laughing.

Still grinning, I headed into the bathroom, but my mind drifted. The Kid might deny it—but I remembered every single detail.

◆◆◆

That following year, when Goldman Sachs took Looking Glass public, the Kid made nearly three hundred million dollars in a single day—a windfall that changed everything for him and those around him.

About a year before that deal closed, he had already taken a bold new step by launching a private security firm called Seal Team Six Security. Drawing on the expertise of former military special forces and paramilitary police units, he started small, mainly offering personal bodyguard services to high-net-worth individuals. But as his political connections grew, so did the scope of his business. He began securing state and government contracts, which marked a major turning point and helped establish the firm as a serious player in the industry.

After the Looking Glass IPO, he used a portion of the proceeds to expand Seal Team Six Security—hiring more personnel, scaling operations, and aggressively bidding on large-scale contracts. The company was officially on its way.

Then, roughly six months after selling half his shares—and about a year and a half after starting up Seal Team Six Security—news reached the Kid that things weren't going well for me. The authorities had arrested me, this time on a RICO case, with fresh recordings and a new corroborating witness coming forward. The witness turned out to be none other than Sammy the Pill, a crew member whose ambitions had once led him to push the group toward dealing drugs. Years earlier, the Kid had warned me to cut ties with Sammy and keep him out of our circle. Following that advice, Sammy had stayed away for quite a while. However, after the Kid left Los Angeles, Sammy eventually resurfaced in my new crew. Though his past behavior was well known, his knack for earning money meant that he was tolerated despite lingering concerns. Now I wanted to kill him.

I remember it like it happened yesterday. The Kid called me out of the blue and said, "We need to talk." He told me to hop on the next plane and meet him in Vegas. It was September 7, 2001. I'll never forget that date because, of course, it was just four days before 9/11. When I landed at McCarran, the Kid had arranged for a limo to pick me up. Once I got to the Bellagio, I made a beeline for his suite. We embraced like old friends, reunited, and he immediately opened a bottle of exquisite white Grand Cru Burgundy.

Now, we had always been more of vodka men, but by that time the Kid had turned into a real wine snob. He joked, "Do you want vodka?" and I just grinned and said, "I'll have what you're having." That bottle turned out to be incredible, and I'll admit, it was the beginning of my own transition to fine wines.

After we settled in, the Kid said, "Tell me what's going on."

I glanced around the room at our company: there was Peter, a sharply dressed guy on the opposite couch with a notepad on his lap, and a well-built younger man stationed by the fireplace. The Kid introduced them: "This is Peter Flynn—hands down one of the best criminal defense attorneys in the country. And that guy, John Jr.—but I call him JJ—he is my Rocco."

I immediately understood the gravity of that statement. By this point, the Kid's security business was growing, and I knew that if he brought Peter and JJ along, they were as trustworthy as they come. I'd later learn that JJ was an ex-SEAL with extensive counter-terrorism training—the kind of guy you want by your side when trouble's brewing.

Then, we got down to business. I explained that the Feds had me on RICO charges, and they were coming down hard with some very damaging recordings. Those recordings even implicated Carl Jr. I knew the Kid felt he owed a debt of gratitude to Carl for making some phone calls regarding the Looking Glass shares, so this all hit close to home. Peter chimed in, saying that he was already somewhat familiar with the case. Apparently, as soon as the Kid told him about it, he started calling in favors to see just how deep the Feds' evidence went. Peter added that once I formally hired him as my attorney, he'd have free rein to request all the evidence.

Without missing a beat, I said, "You're hired." I admitted a bit of embarrassment, confessing that I was a little strapped with legal bills at the moment—but I was good for it.

The Kid quickly interjected. "Philly, why are you talking stupid? I already told you Peter's with us. There's no need for any legal bills."

I managed a smile, with an expression of thank you.

"Don't say a word," the Kid said. "Just let Peter continue."

As we dove deeper into the discussion, I mentioned that the Feds had a key witness lined up to corroborate the recordings. The Kid leaned forward and asked, "Who's the witness?"

"Sammy Blancho—his nickname is 'Sammy the Pill,' " Peter said.

The Kid's face grew heated. "Where is Sammy now, that drug-dealing piece of shit?"

I looked at Peter, admitting I hadn't the faintest idea. Neither of us knew.

The Kid shook his head. "You never listen to me, Philly. I told you he was a piece of shit and that one day he'd bite us in the ass."

I just nodded in agreement. I figured the Feds were keeping him locked up somewhere, probably on the off chance that someone from Carl Jr.'s family might come after him.

The Kid then turned to JJ. "Find out," he said, and JJ nodded.

Peter pressed for more details about the recordings. I explained that I'd only heard two of the recordings the Feds used to try and push me into flipping on Carl. Of course, I'd never consider doing that.

One tape captured a conversation between Carl and me about a gas tax scheme, where the family was siphoning off five cents per gallon from every gallon of gas sold in California and Nevada. I wasn't directly involved in that operation, so I couldn't say exactly how much money was at stake, but it was a lot. I remembered a gas distributor threatening to blow the whistle, and Carl had told me to "go straighten him out." I went in with two of my guys and Sammy, and after a week in the hospital, that distributor decided to keep his mouth shut.

The other recording was of me making it very clear to a bookie that he needed to come up with my money that week—otherwise, he'd have a hard time walking on two stumps. The bookie did pay up, and now, apparently, they were trying to flip him as well, though I suspected he was too scared to testify. The Feds claimed they had more recordings, though I really couldn't say.

Peter assured me he'd request to see all the recordings once they started the formal indictment process.

At one point, the Kid asked Peter if he needed anything else; Peter said, "No."

Soon after, our meeting broke up—Peter got up, handed me a client agreement and asked me to sign it, which I immediately did. Then he shook my hand and told me not to worry. He also shook hands with the Kid before leaving.

After Peter exited, the Kid turned to JJ once more and said, "Find him," and JJ nodded before heading out.

Left alone with the Kid, I couldn't help but ask, "How can I ever thank you?"

Without missing a beat, he replied, "Stop talking stupid. Would you be there for me if I needed you? Were you there when I called you out of the blue and said I might need you and your guys?"

"Of course."

"Then why are you thanking me for being here for you?"

I just chuckled. I knew that despite everything, the bond we built over twenty-plus years was as strong as ever.

The conversation then took a more personal turn. The Kid looked me straight in the eye and asked, "After we get through this, are you ready to walk away from the life for good?"

"For sure," I said. "I'm done. But you know how tough it is finding something that pays enough to cover everything."

The Kid smiled and reassured me. "No, it won't be that hard. My business is growing so fast, I have the perfect spot for you. I need someone I can fully rely on and trust, and that someone is you. We'll talk more about that later. For now, let's get you past these legal hurdles."

Changing the subject as if to lighten the mood, he said, "I'm starving—come on, let's go grab something to eat."

We headed down to Prime Steakhouse, located in the Bellagio, where we enjoyed an incredible meal paired with a spectacular bottle of Chateau Lynch Bages. That night, I savored a great red Bordeaux—a moment that solidified the beginning of my own journey into becoming a wine snob, all thanks to the Kid. I started trading in my vodka for really fine wines.

We spent the rest of dinner reminiscing about old times, and I felt a deep sense of relaxation and renewed optimism—a feeling I hadn't experienced in a long time. Then I realized it was getting late, so I said, "If you want to head back up, I understand. I'm sure you're not alone on this trip? Remember, I know you."

The Kid laughed. "I'm not that guy anymore, Philly. Teresa is all I need. She fills my cup like I never thought any girl could, in ways I never knew existed."

"I think that's great," I said. "I'm really happy for you. I truly am. I can't wait to meet her."

"You will when this is over," he said.

The next day, I flew back to LA while the Kid returned to NJ. Before I left, he handed me a rather bulky cell phone—by today's standards, it was nothing like my current flip phone—and said, "Only use this phone when you need to talk to me or Peter. Keep it with you at all times, because this is the only number I'll call you on. It's a top-security, encrypted sat phone—untraceable and untappable."

I said, "Okay," and from that day on, that phone never left my side.

Looking back, that trip to Vegas was more than just a high-stakes meeting—it was a turning point in my life. Despite all the legal troubles and old ghosts coming back to haunt me, the Kid's support reminded me why our bond endures. And in that moment, sharing a fine meal and great bottles of wine, I felt ready to face whatever came next.

I went back to LA and resumed my regular routine, keeping a very low profile. I didn't reach out to Carl or anyone from my crew—especially not the other captains—since no one knew who was being monitored or recorded. About a week later, the secure phone the Kid had given me rang. I answered, and a voice—not the Kid's—stated, "We located him. We will be in touch."

I knew that meant JJ had found where Sammy was being held, and by whom. That was all I had to go on at the time.

Soon after, the phone rang again, and this time it was Peter. He explained the details of the Feds' case against me. Their evidence was mostly circumstantial, but the recordings gave them extra leverage. The critical point in their case was the eyewitness testimony of Sammy the Pill; he was expected to corroborate everything on those tapes. Peter warned me that the Feds intended to serve an arrest warrant in the morning, and he advised me to make myself available. He even said he'd fly out that night to be there in the morning when it happened.

Sure enough, the next morning, Peter arrived at my house around 8:00 a.m. I had sent my wife Amy to stay with her folks—I didn't want to subject her to what was about to unfold. Then, at 9:00 a.m., the doorbell rang. Peter answered the door, and FBI agents announced they had a warrant for my arrest. Peter led them into the kitchen where I was seated. They instructed me to stand and then read me my rights. As they turned me around and applied the handcuffs, I distinctly recall Peter asking, "Is that really necessary?"

The agent replied curtly, "I'm sorry, I have no choice. Those are my orders."

Before I knew it, I was being led out of my house and placed in their car, with a few neighbors watching. I must admit, the whole ordeal was incredibly embarrassing. Despite having seen many guys go through similar situations, even a tough guy like me felt a sting of shame.

I was taken to the local FBI office and soon after brought before a judge. The judge—a no-nonsense kind of man—set my bail at a staggering five million dollars. For someone like me, with no prior convictions, that figure was exceptionally high, but the prosecutor claimed I was a flight risk.

Peter protested to the judge to no avail. Fortunately, Peter had a bail bondsman in the courtroom waiting, and soon, I was posted. I knew the Kid had put up five hundred thousand dollars to secure my release and had even guaranteed the remaining $4.5 million if I ever tried to flee. The judge, visibly irritated that I was able to make bail so easily, grumbled something about how it should have been set higher, before fixing my trial date for August 1st. That gave us three months to prepare for what lay ahead.

I went back to my daily life and tried to continue a low profile—no calls to anyone in the life. About a week later, my secure cell phone rang. The Kid's voice came through: "I'll be in LA tonight. We'll meet tomorrow. I'll send a car for you," and then he hung up.

The next morning, the secure phone rang again. This time, a message said, "A limo will pick you up in one hour at the Burger King on Stratmore." I knew that location, so I quickly grabbed my things, told Amy I had to go, and left the house. I drove to the Burger King, parked, and waited by my ride. Soon enough, I saw a limo pull up.

The back door opened, and out stepped a gorgeous blonde I'd never seen before. She called out, "Philly, baby, you look great!" I couldn't help but smile. As I headed to get in the limo, she threw her arms around me in a big hug and declared loudly, "We're going to have a great time today!" Then she hopped in, and I followed.

Once the door closed, the limo drove off. A moment later, I heard the soft click of a button as she activated the divider so the driver couldn't overhear us.

"Hi, Philly, I'm Cecelia," she said. "The Kid thought it would be best if whoever is following you thinks we're spending the day in a room at the Ritz." I just nodded. We didn't exchange much more until we pulled up to the Marina del Rey Ritz-Carlton.

As the driver pulled in front, Cecelia grinned and said, "Let's get out, arm in arm, and act all lovey." We did just that. But as we began walking in, I noticed a black Ford with two men in suits parked about a hundred feet behind us. That's when I knew—we were being followed.

Inside, Cecelia led me straight to the elevators. She used her key card to call the PH floor, and when the elevator doors opened, she said, "It's to the right," pointing down a corridor. We turned right and walked down the hall until she suddenly stopped.

"This is my door," she announced, handing me a key card and pointing to another door at the end of the hall that would be mine. I walked down the hall and inserted my card and stepped inside, where I found the Kid sitting on a couch and JJ standing near a window. The Kid got up, and we shook hands and hugged. I greeted JJ, who merely nodded—just like Rocco used to do back in the day.

The Kid then got down to business. "The Feds have Sammy at a safe house in New Mexico. He's always got two armed marshals with him," he explained. "Peter tells me that if Sammy testifies, there's a good chance you'll be convicted. That leaves us just one option: he can't be allowed to testify, or at least not the way the government expects." He paused and asked, "What are your thoughts?"

I looked him in the eye and said, "Get me in that house, and I'll put two in his head."

He shook his head and replied, "That's one option, but is it the best one?"

I pressed, "What do you mean?"

He explained, "If we go down that path, the Feds might trace it back to either you or Carl—and that would only make them more relentless. They might never stop coming after you."

"Do you have another idea to keep him from testifying?" I asked.

The Kid leaned in. "We're not trying to silence him; we just want him to testify in a way that works for us. What if we uncover something he cares about more than himself?"

I scoffed. "That doesn't exist."

He laughed. "Normally, I'd agree with you—but I think we might have found something no one else knows about."

"I'm listening," I told him.

Then, almost casually, the Kid revealed, "He has a sister."

I almost laughed out loud. "No, he doesn't," I said. "In all the years we've known him, I've never heard him mention one, nor have I ever seen one."

The Kid smiled knowingly. "That's what makes her so perfect. Apparently, Sammy has a sister who married a congressman when he was fourteen. She's about ten years older than him, and she raised him—she was like a mother. I know his own mother died when he was born."

"I always thought he was raised by his father," I said.

"His father was around, but it was his sister who did all the nurturing," the Kid said. "That's why he's so close with her. And the reason we never heard about her is that after she married that congressman, she wanted nothing to do with her family— her father was a drunk and a half gangster. So, she moved away when Sammy was fifteen. By the time Sammy started coming around us, his sister was long gone. Sammy kept in touch with her in secret, though, and now she's got a daughter as well."

"How did you find all that out?" I asked.

The Kid laughed. "JJ's very good at what he does."

I turned to JJ, raised my glass in a silent salute, and thanked him. That was the first time I saw JJ smile—a quiet nod that said it all.

The Kid laid it out: "Here's my idea. We have his sister and her daughter picked up a few days before Sammy is supposed to testify. We stage it so it looks like we're going to kill both his sister and his niece if Sammy doesn't do exactly what we tell him. My guess is he'll comply. It's a gamble, so I want you to make the call. We can handle it however you see fit—either your way or this way. Remember, Philly, if we guess wrong and he testifies the way he did on the interrogatories, you could end up with thirty years. But if we get him to recant, you might finally get the Feds off your back."

I sat, thinking it over for a long minute. "What if we grab the two of them and Sammy still refuses to say what we want him to say?" I asked.

The Kid sighed. "That's part of the gamble. If we grab them and he doesn't cooperate, you're stuck, because by then, he's already testified, and you're in deep trouble. But you know there is no way we will hurt either one of those girls, no matter what."

I nodded. "Of course I know that, Kid. I know you."

"Okay, let's try it," I said. At least I know that if I go down on these RICO charges because of Sammy's testimony, Sammy won't get to see me behind bars."

The Kid leaned back. "You can count on that. If we pull this off right, and luck is on our side, there's a good chance everything will just vanish, and the Feds will leave you alone for good."

"No one outside this room will ever know what we're doing. Peter will only be asked, in an ideal scenario, what he'd like Sammy to say on the stand—the details, the how and why, are unimportant." I agreed, feeling the weight of the plan.

We ordered some in-room lunch for the three of us, paired with fine wines, and spent the next few hours reminiscing about the old days—stories for JJ and to keep my nerves steady.

Around 5:00 p.m., I hugged the Kid goodbye and shook hands with JJ. I told the Kid I'd wait to hear from him.

"I probably won't be in touch for a while," he said. "I'll handle everything. Just sit tight and know it's being taken care of."

I felt strangely confident that it would all work out.

Then, as I was about to leave, the Kid picked up his phone and called Cecelia. By the time I got to the door and opened it, there she was, waiting to walk me out, arm in arm. We climbed back into the limo, and she drove me back to the Burger King.

"Thank you," I said. "I'm sure we'll see each other again."

She smiled warmly, gave me a big hug and a kiss on the cheek, and replied, "I'm sure."

Even now, thinking back, that day in Vegas is still etched in my memory—full of high-stakes plans, old alliances, and the ever-present risk that comes with everything we do. But I knew one thing for certain: with the Kid's support and our decades-long bond, I truly believed we'd find a way through it all.

Peter kept in touch with me through those tense weeks leading up to the trial. We'd meet in a conference room at one of Los Angeles's most prestigious criminal law firms. Although Peter's own office was in New York, his connections stretched everywhere. As the trial drew nearer, I began to feel a little apprehensive, but Peter always reassured me things were going well. Still, I couldn't help but ask if he was confident about Sammy's testimony.

He looked me in the eye. "If Sammy testifies the same way he did during his interrogatories, we're in trouble. But I'm hearing his testimony might be different this time."

He didn't say who was feeding him that info, but both of us already knew the answer.

The trial began with jury selection, and Peter Flynn's team was working hard behind the scenes. Once the jury was finally seated, the first few days passed with the prosecutor playing recordings for the jury to hear. Aside from the two recordings I'd already heard, nothing new seemed to come up—though I suspected the Feds had played their best material for me in an attempt to get me to flip.

Then, on Wednesday, Peter informed me that Sammy was scheduled to testify the following Tuesday. That gave us almost a week of breathing room—but then the Kid learned some inside information that neither Peter nor I had. Apparently, someone in the federal prosecutor's office was feeding the Kid details, and it turned out to be a godsend.

The very next morning, as the pale desert sun crept over Nevada's barren landscape, Sammy's sister and her daughter were "picked up"—quietly removed from their separate residences and transported to a nondescript house in the middle of nowhere. Discreet video cameras were fixed at strategic angles, capturing every grim detail as both women, with emotional fear across their faces, held up the front pages of the *New York Times* and the *Wall Street Journal*—a silent, potent message broadcast for anyone to see.

Meanwhile, JJ, ever the strategist, quietly orchestrated a critical meeting. He reached out to Sammy's longtime attorney—a cautious, loyal man known for keeping things clean—and explained the situation. JJ needed him to arrange a meeting between Sammy and another lawyer, someone JJ trusted completely, to deliver a message that, while unconventional, would be in Sammy's best interest.

That messenger was Robert D'Angelo, a seasoned attorney and loyal ally who had earned JJ's trust over years of quiet service.

The plan was simple—but bold. At a private safe house, Robert would accompany Sammy's attorney under the pretense of joining the defense team. Once seated with Sammy, the attorney would excuse himself—claiming he needed the restroom—leaving Robert alone to speak freely.

Initially, Sammy's attorney balked. The idea clearly unsettled him. But JJ leaned in, eyes cold and steady. "Do you want to test me?"

That single line, calm and firm, dissolved any resistance.

Later that day, both attorneys arrived at the safe house. Sammy, eyeing the unfamiliar man warily, turned to his attorney. The man introduced Robert as a new legal advisor brought on to assist with the case. Then, as planned, he excused himself, needing the restroom.

It was then that Robert made his move. With deliberate precision, he opened his laptop and played a DVD—a recording captured earlier that morning. On the screen, Sammy's sister appeared, firmly clutching the *New York Times*, while his niece held aloft the *Wall Street Journal*. Robert's tone was icy as he laid out the ultimatum: if Sammy didn't follow his instructions exactly, he would never set eyes on his sister or niece again.

Faced with the grim choice between potential jail time for perjury and the absolute loss of the family he loved, Sammy swallowed his fear. He silently acknowledged that cooperation was, in that moment, the only viable option—even if it meant sacrificing years in prison.

I hadn't known any of this yet. Up to that point, I assumed Sammy's sister and niece might be taken on Sunday, since his testimony wasn't due until Tuesday.

After lunch, the courtroom buzzed as the prosecutor stood and declared, "Your Honor, the prosecution would like to call Sammy Blancho to the stand."

Immediately, Peter jumped up. "I object—this witness wasn't scheduled until Tuesday, and I haven't finished preparing my cross-examination." I'm not sure Peter knew what was really happening behind the scenes, but he wasn't willing to let the schedule be disrupted if he could help it—especially if it might hinge on the timing of Sammy's testimony.

The prosecution countered that a scheduling change forced them to switch the order of witnesses. Peter insisted this was deception, but the judge overruled him. "Counselor, you may call your witness," he said to the prosecution.

In walked Sammy. I remember staring at him with eyes that could kill. He didn't even look in my direction as he took the stand, got sworn in, and faced the barrage of questions from the prosecution.

"Please state your name for the record," the assistant US attorney said, standing before the witness box.

"Sammy Blancho," the witness replied. "Though most people know me as Sammy the Pill."

The courtroom murmured briefly at the nickname, prompting the judge to raise a cautionary eyebrow.

"And your occupation?" the prosecutor asked.

"I was a drug dealer," Sammy replied flatly.

The prosecutor narrowed his eyes. "You say 'was.' Are you no longer involved in that line of work?"

"Not since the FBI picked me up," Sammy said. "They've had me in protective custody ever since."

The line of questioning shifted. "Mr. Blancho, were any promises made to you by the government in exchange for your testimony here today?"

Sammy nodded. "They said they'd talk to the AUSA—assistant US attorney—about reducing my charges if my testimony helped convict the defendant and Carl Jr. Poporri, whose trial is next month."

The prosecutor steered the questioning toward the night of February 23rd. "Were you present when Carl Jr. had a conversation with Philip Fiore—also known as Philly—regarding how to 'handle' a gas station owner in Los Angeles?"

"No," Sammy said, shaking his head. "I wasn't there."

A brief silence fell over the courtroom. The prosecutor raised an eyebrow and turned toward the jury box, then retrieved a folder from the prosecution's table.

"Mr. Blancho, that's not what you testified to during your deposition," he said, flipping to a marked page. "Allow me to refresh your recollection."

He read aloud: " 'I was present, listening to the conversation between Philly Fiore and Carl Jr. regarding the handling of that gas station owner.' "

Sammy shrugged. "I said what I thought I needed to say at the time."

The prosecutor leaned forward. "Are you admitting you lied under oath during your sworn deposition?"

Sammy smirked slightly. "Let's just say ... I said what I thought I should say."

The prosecutor's tone turned sharp. "Mr. Blancho, you do realize that you are under oath right now—and that what you're describing constitutes perjury? That's a felony offense. You will face jail time."

Peter, seated at the defense table, rose instantly. "Objection, Your Honor—counsel is badgering his own witness."

"Sustained," the judge said firmly. "Watch your tone, counselor."

The prosecutor glanced at the bench, then exhaled sharply. "No further questions at this time. We reserve the right to recall this witness."

"Granted," the judge replied.

Peter rose and approached the witness box, buttoning his jacket. "Mr. Blancho, let's clarify a few things for the jury."

He spoke calmly but deliberately. "To be clear: you were not present during any conversation between Philip Fiore and Carl Jr. Poporri about a gas station owner in Los Angeles?"

"That's correct," Sammy answered.

"Have you ever personally heard such a conversation?"

"No. Only on recordings the FBI played for me during questioning."

Peter nodded. "And prior to those recordings, did you even know there was an alleged illegal gas scheme involving Carl Jr.?"

"No. I wasn't aware."

Peter paused for effect, then asked, "Has anyone—law enforcement, the prosecution, or otherwise—threatened you or offered any inducement to alter your testimony here today?"

"No," Sammy said. "I wasn't threatened or promised anything."

Then, he leaned slightly forward, voice steady. "But I do know Philly. And when I saw him here, sitting in this courtroom . . . I knew I couldn't let an innocent man go down for something he didn't do."

Peter held his gaze a moment longer, then turned toward the judge. "No further questions."

"Thank you, Mr. Blancho," the judge said, nodding. "You may step down."

Sammy stood, his expression unreadable, and exited the witness stand.

As the court recessed for the day, the tension slowly lifted. I watched the jurors file out, and for the first time in weeks, I could breathe again. The damage to the prosecution's case was undeniable.

Back in the hallway, Peter clapped a hand on my shoulder and gave a rare smile. "We're in a good place," he said. "The jury's going to struggle to reconcile recorded conversations with a live witness who just denied them under oath."

He glanced at his watch. "Take the weekend. Get some rest. I'll see you Monday."

That evening, I went home and relaxed with my wife, Amy, over a fine bottle of wine. Out of the blue, my secure cell phone rang, and I heard the Kid's voice saying, "Peter tells me things are looking up."

I was almost speechless.

He continued. "Hopefully, soon this will all be over, Philly, and we can begin again. Hang in there, and we'll talk soon." Then he hung up.

Monday morning arrived, and by 9:00 a.m., we were back in the courtroom, the tension thick in the air. Everyone sat in anticipation as the judge took the bench and called the session to order.

"The prosecution may call its next witness," the judge announced.

But instead, the assistant US attorney stood and addressed the court with an unexpected declaration: "Your Honor, in light of the material inconsistencies in the testimony of our key witness, the government moves to dismiss all charges against the defendant, Philip Fiore."

Gasps echoed across the courtroom.

I froze, hardly able to process the words.

The judge gave a quick nod, then turned to me. "Mr. Fiore, all charges against you are hereby dismissed with prejudice. You are free to go. Bail is exonerated, and the record shall reflect your full release."

It was over—just like that.

After everything, I walked out of that courtroom not as a defendant but a free man

I immediately stood up, smiling broadly, shook hands with Peter, and then turned to find Amy sitting in the first row. We embraced tightly, and in that moment, I felt the beginning of a new life unfolding before me.

As soon as they processed my release, we left the courthouse. I immediately grabbed the secure cell phone Amy was holding and dialed the Kid—this was the first time I'd used that phone to call him. He picked up on the first ring, and I said, "I'm ready for whatever you have for me."

Without hesitation, he told me to get my things in order, put my house on the market, and head to New Jersey as soon as possible. He mentioned that business was going well and that he was looking forward to having my help.

"I'll be there as soon as I can," I said. "There's just one problem—I'm not sure Carl Jr. will let me just walk away. You know our world, Kid."

The Kid replied calmly, "I already anticipated that, so I spoke to Carl. He is grateful for what we did, and he understands the situation and has agreed to let you go, as long as everything you've built stays with the family."

I couldn't help but marvel at his foresight.

"You're amazing," I said. "I'll see you as soon as I can."

And with that, we ended the call.

Unbeknownst to me, early Saturday morning—after the government case had collapsed on Friday afternoon—the Kid quietly flew to LA on a private plane to meet with Carl Jr. During their meeting, the Kid asked Carl to release me, to allow me to walk away from the life. The Kid wanted me with him now. Carl understood, and grateful for the Kid's role in his own case unraveling, he agreed—but only with two strict stipulations.

First, he demanded that I leave everything he'd built in LA to the family, with no compensation. Second, I was not to return to LA for a few years, allowing my release from the life to settle. The Kid agreed, and after they shook hands, he returned to the airport. By Saturday night, he was back in New Jersey, sitting down to dinner with Teresa and the kids.

It took about two weeks for my wife and I to wrap up everything before leaving. We eventually landed at Newark Airport on Friday, September 23, 2002, ready to start a new life. Meanwhile, the case against Carl Jr. had been dropped by the prosecution after Sammy's sudden change in testimony—and Carl was once again in the Kid's debt, as we both knew who was really behind Sammy the Pill's change of heart.

CHAPTER NINETEEN
NJ OFFICE

The Kid arranged a stunning apartment in the Morristown area for Amy and me, a temporary haven while we adjusted to the area and looked for the perfect house to call our own. He even secured a brand-new Mercedes for me and a Range Rover for Amy, little luxuries to ease us into our new lives. The very next day, I drove to the Morristown office—a striking, modern building nestled in downtown Morristown, New Jersey. I took the elevator up to the top floor—the tenth floor—and when the doors slid open, I stepped into a spacious, light-filled area defined by gleaming glass walls and a reception desk nestled behind two large glass doors.

I approached the reception area and announced, "Hi, I'm here to see the Kid." The two receptionists exchanged puzzled glances. One said, "There is no kid here. Are you sure you have the right office?" Chuckling, I corrected myself. "I'm sorry—I'm here to see Dominic Argianno."

Her eyes lit up as she inquired, "What is your name?"

"Philly Fiore," I replied.

"Please hold on," she said, picking up the phone.

A couple of minutes later, I noticed a tough-looking blonde emerging from the back. She strode over and introduced herself, "Hi, I'm Alice Bower. Please, follow me." Alice led me through a magnificent office space that boasted panoramic views of downtown Morristown. We strolled past a sprawling glass conference room and approached a pair of mirrored glass doors that concealed another office. After a soft knock, she opened the door to reveal the Kid seated behind a sleek, modern desk. At the sight of me, he rose quickly, and we embraced warmly.

Smiling, he quipped, "I see you met Alice. Come, sit down, and let's talk."

As the door closed behind Alice, I couldn't help but remark, "Two-way glass, impressive."

He laughed, and we spent about an hour talking before he guided me around the office, introducing me one by one to most of the team.

The real turning point came the following day when the Kid welcomed me into his inner circle. During a staff meeting in the expansive conference room, he invited me to sit among his closest advisors. I quickly realized that he was managing his operation much like he did back in LA—albeit with key differences, now operating largely within the bounds of legality. His trusted inner circle was a tight-knit team:

- **Alice Bower:** The smart, sassy, and capable office manager—a former captain in the military whose toughness was legendary.
- **John Rodgers:** The young and aggressive sales director, an ex-Delta Force operator who negotiates most of our government contracts along with Frank Rotundo.
- **Jim Rodriguez:** An IT genius and former Air Force computer whiz, fluent in five languages and capable of hacking into any system with the ease of those savvy TV experts.
- **Peter Flynn:** The brilliant lawyer who managed my case. Though he wasn't ex-military, his advice was rock-solid, and the

Kid always consulted with him before skating too close to the edge on legal matters. Peter had an office there on the tenth floor, but was rarely there, except when the Kid needed him. His main law office was in NYC.

• **Frank Rotundo:** A very sharp business lawyer, who was involved in many parts of the business, especially government contracts and proposals.

• **Howard Cohen:** Our in-house CPA. He was a master at reading financial documents.

• **Shelia Murphy:** Head of Human Resources. She worked very closely with Alice.

• **Sophia Rossi:** Head of Advertising, Marketing, and Public Relations for the entire company. Former TV anchor who works closely with John and the Kid.

• **John Jr. Sorrentino (JJ):** The Kid's indispensable right-hand fixer, a man who could handle any problem that sprang up. Over the years, JJ and I forged a strong friendship as we worked very closely.

Anyone wishing to reach the Kid outside of this circle had to go through Alice, a task made challenging by her fierce protectiveness and unwavering loyalty. For the first few weeks, the Kid had me sit in on meetings, gradually acclimating me to the way things ran. I spent time with each member of the inner circle, absorbing every detail of their roles and the dynamics of the operation.

After about five weeks, I finally felt ready and said, "Hey Kid, I'm ready. What do you want me to handle?"

He locked eyes with me and replied, "I want you to start working with JJ. Let him show you the ropes. Most of it should come naturally, given how we grew up. Our business is growing too fast for one person to do everything JJ handles, and I need someone I trust with my life."

I looked him in the eye and said, "Thank you," and we both shared a sincere smile.

With that, I left his office and crossed the hall to JJ's office, ready to embrace my new challenge.

That day marked not just a pivotal shift in my career but the true beginning of a new chapter—a turning away from the past and an eager step into a future built on trust, loyalty, and shared ambition.

A few weeks had gone by, and during that time, I spent a lot of time with JJ, asking him all sorts of questions. JJ was very open and didn't seem to hold anything back. I knew the Kid must have spoken to him and told him to trust me completely; otherwise, he wouldn't have shared as much as he did.

One day, JJ walked into my office and said, "Let's take a ride."

As we drove, I asked, "What's going on? Where are we headed?"

He said, "The Kid's had me watching a guy named Jason. Real piece of work. Known for abusing girls, but he's never been convicted. Teresa mentioned a friend of hers suspects Jason's been abusing her daughter, Carol. The girl's too scared to leave him—he's threatened her. Teresa asked the Kid if someone could talk to him."

JJ went on. "This morning, I heard from a detective buddy I reached out to. Turns out, Jason was being investigated for something similar last year. The detective was sure he was guilty but couldn't gather enough to charge him. Everyone's afraid of the guy. That raised a red flag for me. I called the Kid to update him, and he told me to have a conversation with Jason. His words were, 'Make sure Jason understands it's in his best interest to stay away from Carol.' I figured you and I should handle it together."

The Kid agreed.

I grinned. "Now you're speaking my language." We both laughed.

Jason was working construction in Seaside Heights. We parked a block away and dressed the part—hard hats, clipboards, casual business wear. JJ had everything in his trunk. We looked like site inspectors, which helped us blend in.

Ten minutes in, we spotted Jason crossing between two buildings. "There he is," JJ said. He was working with two other guys. We followed them into a small on-site office.

JJ called out, "Jason, you got a minute?"

The workers froze. Jason looked up. "Who the hell are you two?"

JJ replied calmly, "I apologize if that sounded like a suggestion."

Now we had their attention. One guy gripped a hammer. The other held a saw. JJ focused on Jason, trusting me to watch his back. One of them adjusted his grip on the hammer, getting twitchy.

"It's your choice," I said, opening my jacket to flash the .45 on my hip. "But I can promise you, it won't end well."

They exchanged glances. One muttered, "Let's go grab coffee." They dropped their tools and walked out.

"Private conversation," I warned as they left. "Keep it that way." They nodded.

Jason stared at us. "What do you want?"

JJ said, "Just to talk."

"So talk."

JJ stepped forward. "Let me be clear so there's no misunderstanding. You've been seeing Carol. That relationship? It's over. Done. If you even think about her, let alone speak her name, we'll be back. And next time, there won't be words. Got it?"

Jason sneered. "Fuck you both."

Standing behind JJ, I said calmly, "Thank you."

He went for a 2x4. Too slow.

I caught him mid-reach and drove punches into his gut until blood spilled from his mouth. Then I broke his leg.

JJ warned, "We need to be careful. Too many people saw us walk in."

I nodded.

As Jason writhed on the ground, I drew my .45 and pressed it into his mouth.

"Please, Jason," I said. "Give us a reason to come back."

He nodded. Message received.

We walked out. The two workers we'd passed earlier were loitering near the site entrance. JJ looked at them.

"If you remember anything about today," he said, "someone else will come help you forget."

They just nodded, terrified.

Back in the car, I said, "Damn, that felt good."

JJ laughed. "Hell yeah, it did."

Jason never contacted Carol again. He disappeared like smoke. Turns out, sometimes the best way to send a message is to make sure it's heard loud and clear.

I finally met Teresa, and, of course, the Kid had known my wife Amy from his early days in LA. Though, I hadn't started dating Amy seriously until after the Kid had already returned to New York. It wasn't just another meeting—it felt as if fate had decided that the time had come for all our worlds to converge.

Our first weekend in New Jersey, the Kid and Teresa took Amy and me to their favorite restaurant—daBenito Ristorante in Union. The moment we stepped inside, the air was rich with elegance, the scent of fresh basil, and slow-simmered sauces. Crystal glasses gleamed under soft, golden light, and the quiet hum of conversation was punctuated by the gentle clink of silverware on porcelain. It was exactly the kind of place I'd expect the Kid to frequent—refined yet welcoming, with an unspoken sense of privilege for those who belonged there.

Over a glass of an DRC La Tache Grand Cru Burgundy—one of the Kid's favorite wines—he told me he'd held countless meetings in this restaurant. The owner treated him and his guests like family, always ready with a private dining room when business required hushed voices and discretion.

That night, we dined in the private wine room—a space steeped in old-world Italian charm. Cool, patterned tile spread across the floor, while mahogany-redwood wine cabinets lined the walls. Around us stood empty large-format bottles, relics of the most expensive wines in the world, each one a silent witness to nights of indulgence and deal-making. I would soon sit in this very room for my own meetings, where the food was flawless, the service unshakably precise, and the wine list could rival any in Manhattan.

At dinner, I couldn't help noticing how seamlessly Teresa fit at his side. She laughed easily, her hand finding his without thought, her eyes locking on his as if no one else in the room existed. She pulled everyone into the conversation with a warmth that felt effortless. Something had shifted in him. For years, the Kid had drifted from one woman to another, relationships fading as quickly as they began, but here he was—settled, anchored, transformed. Their bond was so natural, so deep, I could have sworn they'd known each other forever.

As I watched them talk, I thought back to a night in Vegas, when I had expected to see some glamorous woman waiting for him after our meeting. Instead, he had simply told me, "I have no need for other girls, Philly—Teresa is all I need."

By then, the Kid had already shared much of his past with her. He'd spoken of his triumphs and trials, giving her enough to understand the man sitting before her, without pulling her into the shadows of his old life. Some truths, he left unspoken, not out of deception but protection. Still, he made sure she was woven into every joy of his present—and the way she looked at him, it was clear she felt the same.

Amy and I began spending more time together with the Kid, Teresa, and his children. We'd plan weekend outings that reminded me of the old days—just the Kid and I, always side by side—but now with an added warmth and familial vibe. Amy and I had been together for years, sharing our quiet life, and despite never having our own children, we soon after began to feel a parental instinct toward the Kid's children.

I recall one summer afternoon, all of us strolling through a local park, the laughter of his children blending with our conversations. I couldn't help but think, "If anyone ever hurt these kids—especially the girls—they'd never recover." The protective instinct was overwhelming, and it was that feeling that solidified our bond as a family.

At dinner that night, I heard Teresa call him "Kid" for the very first time. Amy and I just smiled knowingly. With her characteristic charm, Teresa laughed and quipped, "I think I'm spending too much time with you two—you're starting to rub off on me."

The Kid just laughed in reply, and it felt like a quietly significant moment between us all.

Meanwhile, our professional lives were undergoing a transformation of their own. Over the next year, as the business expanded and our earnings soared, the Kid's influence grew even further. I'd see him in tailored suits, negotiating government contracts with the same confident charm of a man who's overcome so much—yet still holding onto the remnants of that gritty past we all knew so well. To me, watching him thrive wasn't just about the money or the business; it was seeing him embrace a new kind of life balanced on both sides of the old world and the new possibilities.

I also began to notice subtle shifts in the way the Kid interacted with those around him. In the inner circle, trust was the currency. Names like Alice, John, Sophia, Frank, Howard, Jim, Peter, and JJ weren't just colleagues—they were now like brothers and sisters, each indispensable to the operation. Every meeting, every off-the-record conversation, was a reminder that while the past was never entirely gone, it could be transformed into something positive, something sustainable.

Over the following weeks, as I worked long hours absorbing every bit of wisdom that JJ had to share about the new way of running things, I felt more at home than I ever had before. The Kid's presence wasn't just a reminder of our wild past—it was a constant beacon for the future. I could see that he had truly found his soulmate in Teresa. Their connection was magnetic.

There was a real joy in his transformation; the Kid was no longer a lone wolf flitting through a sea of transient relationships but a man committed to his wife, his family, his business, and to the possibility of redemption.

Looking back now, I see how everything fell into place. The old days of reckless camaraderie had evolved into something deeply rooted in trust, loyalty, and the hope for a better tomorrow. Together—with Amy, the Kid, Teresa, the children, and our inner circle—we were building a future that honored our past but wasn't bound by it. In those moments, whether we were laughing over a simple dinner or closing a business deal, it was clear that life had truly gotten better. And as I stood there surrounded by family and friends, I couldn't help but feel that our journey was only just beginning.

I remember one wedding like it was yesterday. Rebecca—a talented girl from our office—had invited a lot of people from work to her big day. At our table, I sat with Amy, the Kid and Teresa, JJ with his girlfriend Susan, Alice and her husband, John and his wife, along with Jim and his girlfriend. Not too far away, a guy nicknamed "Slippery" was seated at the next table. He was an associate with the Romano family. He knew who the Kid was and wasn't likely to challenge him.

It was around 11:00 p.m. and the drinks were flowing. Suddenly, Slippery started yelling and verbally abusing his wife. The atmosphere shifted instantly; everyone at their table grew uncomfortably quiet. Before long, the bride herself—clearly disturbed by what was unfolding—came over to our table and asked the Kid quietly if he could calm him down.

Unflappable as ever, the Kid replied, "Go enjoy your wedding; he's leaving." Then he turned to me and JJ and said, "Please deliver a message for me. Tell Slippery I said goodnight—he is leaving."

JJ and I exchanged a knowing nod before we got up and made our way over to Slippery's table.

I approached him and said, "The Kid has a message for you." I could see him smirking, probably expecting some kind of pleasant note. I continued. "The Kid said goodnight."

With a smile, Slippery replied, "I didn't know the Kid was leaving—let me go say goodnight to him."

I put my hand on his shoulder as I took a deep breath and said, "The Kid isn't leaving—you are, and it's happening right now."

That change in tone silenced the entire table. Slippery looked at me, defiant at first, and said, "I'm not leaving."

I leaned in and clarified. "Maybe what I just said sounded like a suggestion. Let me make it crystal clear: You have one minute to stand up and walk out. After that, you'll be carried out. Am I clear?"

He paused, weighing his options, and finally muttered, "Yeah, maybe it's time I leave." He got up along with his wife and another couple, and they left the wedding. I never saw him again.

A couple of weeks later, after Rebecca returned from her honeymoon and came back to work, she pulled me aside. "Thanks for what you and JJ did at the wedding," she said warmly.

I couldn't help but ask, "It was my pleasure—but how on earth did Slippery get invited?"

Rebecca chuckled and explained, "He's a cousin of my husband. They hardly ever speak."

I shook my head. "Well, I'm sure now they won't be talking anytime soon."

We both laughed, and I added, "If he ever gives you any more trouble, just let me know."

She smiled gratefully and said, "Thank you."

That night echoed with the realization that even in our old world—where loyalty, unspoken rules, and respect ruled every interaction—you could still make a stand for what was right.

And for me, that memory is a reminder that sometimes, a few well-chosen words can change the course of an evening and set things straight for good.

A few weeks later, the Kid called me and JJ into his office one morning, his expression serious. He looked straight at JJ and said, "Gerard Swanson is a kid at my daughter Teresa's school. Find out where his father is."

Without missing a beat, JJ got up and walked out.

I looked at the Kid and said, "What's up?"

The Kid explained, "This kid, Gerard, smacked Teresa at school yesterday. The school said they handled it, and Gerard was suspended for two days. Teresa went up to the school afterwards and met with Gerard's parents and the principal. Teresa told me they weren't very apologetic; in fact, the father even said, 'It was only a smack—be glad it wasn't a punch.' Then, when Teresa fired back, 'You should be thankful I'm sitting here and not my husband,' he just shrugged and replied, 'Yeah, yeah, I'm sure he's really tough.' "

He continued. "Last night, when I went in to talk to little Teresa before she went to sleep, she told me, 'It's okay, Dad, don't worry—it doesn't hurt anymore.' I said, 'I'm glad it doesn't hurt anymore,' even though I could see a small bruise forming on her cheek. I asked her if she was afraid of this boy, and she simply said, 'No, I'll just stay away from him. If he bothers me again, I'll tell you, and then he'll be afraid.'

"I asked her, 'Really? Why do you think he'll be afraid of me?' She said, 'Everyone is afraid of you, Dad. I can see how people act around you.' That kid's wisdom amazed me. I told her, 'For an eleven-year-old, you're one perceptive little girl, Teresa. Go to sleep, and we'll talk tomorrow.'

"I went downstairs and relayed the conversation to Teresa. She shook her head and said, 'Imagine if she saw what I witnessed in that parking lot.' I simply smiled.

"Then, Teresa turned to me and asked, 'Dom, you're not going to do anything, are you?' I put my hands on her shoulders and said, 'Teresa, everything will be fine. Remember this: no one—and I mean no one—will ever touch you or any of the kids and walk away smiling. Just leave it alone, and I'll handle it.' "

The Kid then laid it out: "I'm going to have a conversation with Gerard's father. I'm going to explain to him just how big a fucking deal this really was and send him a message he won't misunderstand."

Without hesitation, I said, "I'm coming with you, and this isn't a request."

The Kid smiled, nodded, and said, "Okay."

By that time, JJ had returned—he'd gathered the information he was tasked with.

The Kid stood. "Let's go."

"You guys are not going without me," JJ said.

So, the three of us left the office together and headed over to track down Gerard's father, ready to set things right.

We arrived around 11:30 a.m. Gerard's father, also named Gerard, was a wannabe trying to carve out a place with the Battista family. He was hanging around a local restaurant in Lynchburg, New Jersey, which was just opening for lunch. As we stepped inside, the air was filled with the rich aroma of brewing coffee.

We took a table in the front, noticing only one occupied table was at the back, where four knock-around guys lingered, casting wary glances in our direction. They had the unmistakable vibe of wannabes too, none of us recognizing their faces. We thought they could be packing heat, but so were we. We were licensed to carry because of security work with Seal Team Six Security, which made us ready for whatever this lunch might throw our way.

When the waitress approached with menus, we ordered coffee first. The Kid, with his sweet manner, asked her, "Is Gerard around?"

She looked momentarily taken aback but then nodded and

pointed toward the back. "He's at the table in the back," she said.

The Kid grinned wide and replied, "Oh, I didn't even see him back there! Thanks. Let me go over to say hello."

As soon as she walked away, the Kid's excitement was palpable. He said, "Let's go introduce ourselves." He led the way, and we trailed behind.

As the Kid approached the men at the table, he confidently called out, "Excuse me, gentlemen, is one of you Gerard?"

We formed a semicircle behind him—me to his left, JJ to his right—and I felt the air grow thick with tension. The four men looked at one another, uncertainty etched on their faces.

The Kid broke the silence. "I just wanted to thank Gerard for handling the situation at my daughter's school yesterday." At this, one of the guys looked up, as if a light bulb had gone off.

The Kid turned to Gerard, extending his hand. "Gerard." When Gerard reached out, the Kid firmly gripped his hand and, with a swift motion, pulled him to his feet. Instantly, the atmosphere crackled with anxiety. More patrons were trickling in for lunch, and the tension in the room was palpable.

"Do you boys know who I am?" the Kid asked. They exchanged furtive glances, confusion flickering in their eyes. "Let me clarify something," he said, lowering his voice ominously. "If any one of you so much as twitches, you'll die right here in your chairs." At that moment, both JJ and I had our guns in our hands, subtly positioned at our sides—not that we really needed them, but the threat hung heavily in the air.

The Kid continued. "When we're finished here, I want you to pick up the phone and call Blue Eyes. Tell him the Kid stopped by. He'll explain who I am."

That name hit like a thunderclap. Blue Eyes.

The two men exchanged a look—tense, alert. They were tied to the Battista family, and Blue Eyes wasn't just anyone—he was a captain, and a feared one. Now, they were fully locked in. The mood shifted. Respect. Fear. Suddenly, they were listening.

"Now, Gerard, do you really think it was okay for your son to smack my daughter?" The silence hung thick. Gerard just stared at him, seemingly lost for words. "Don't make me ask you again," the Kid warned.

Reluctantly, Gerard replied, "No, but she's okay now, and it's over."

The Kid countered, "It may be over for her, but it's not over for you. You were pretty tough when you spoke to my wife at school yesterday. No one talks to her like that."

With a precise motion, the Kid spotted a back room separated by a sheer curtain, which was thankfully vacant at the moment. He dragged Gerard through the curtain, while JJ and I stood by the table, keeping watch on the other men. Not a soul moved. I turned to them and said, "Relax, boys. If we wanted you dead, you'd be dead already." They seemed to take my words to heart, visibly easing up.

The Kid's voice rang out as he leaned close to Gerard. "Listen closely, Gerard. You need to grasp how this can never happen again. If it does, there won't be room for discussion next time." In a flash, the Kid hit Gerard squarely in the gut, before delivering a powerful blow to his jaw that sent him crumpling down. He hoisted Gerard back up against the wall and said, "If your son ever looks at my daughter with anything less than a friendly smile, I'll split you in two, and if you ever disrespect my wife again, you will wish I killed you right here. Do you understand?"

Gerard met his gaze, fear evident, and simply said, "Yes."

"Good," the Kid replied, stepping back as he released Gerard. He emerged from the curtain, turning to us and saying, "I think we're done here," and we all began to walk away.

From that moment on, there wasn't a single issue at the school concerning little Teresa. Word must have spread quickly.

Just days later, we heard that Gerard had wound up in the hospital—an accident at the restaurant, they said. But those who knew the inner workings suspected Blue Eyes had played a hand in it, his frustration over Gerard's failure at the school boiling over. Maybe it wasn't just loyalty to the Kid's grandfather; maybe it was personal. Blue Eyes had a daughter and a granddaughter, and he had never been one to tolerate disrespect toward the women closest to him.

Life settled back into its usual rhythm, smooth and predictable. That was, until the ominous Friday of Labor Day weekend in 2004—when everything would begin to unravel.

CHAPTER TWENTY
SAD TIMES

I remember that day as if it were painted in slow motion—a day heavy with unspoken dread and vivid shades of heartache. A couple of weeks earlier, Teresa had mentioned to Amy that she wasn't feeling well and needed to see a doctor. None of us gave it much thought at first, assuming it was one of those fleeting bouts of discomfort. But after the doctor ordered a battery of tests, the results came back on Friday of a three-day holiday weekend, and everything changed.

I walked into the Kid's office that afternoon, and the atmosphere hit me like a cold wave. The usually confident and unflappable expression on his face was replaced with a grim seriousness I'd never seen in him before—a face etched with worry and sorrow. He was on the phone, and I motioned silently, wondering if he needed me to leave, but he lifted his hand, a silent command that I stay. When he finally ended his phone call, I stepped closer and asked in a quiet, tentative tone, "What's up, Kid?"

He leaned forward slightly and, with a gravely lowered voice, instructed me to "Close the door." As the latch clicked shut, the space seemed to contract around us. His eyes, normally steely and composed, shimmered with an emotion that betrayed the weight of his pain. "I'm leaving for the day," he began, pausing as if bracing himself against the words. "Teresa just got off the phone with the doctor—and the news ... it isn't good." I could see the tremor in his hand as he spoke—an emotion so rare from him that it struck me like a punch in the gut.

He explained that Teresa had been diagnosed with advanced ovarian cancer—an unwelcome specter that cast long, dark shadows over everything we'd built. The Kid was determined to be by her side and exhaust every possibility to cure her. They would seek answers from multiple top oncologists, even on a holiday weekend—something that only his influence could secure. His voice softened almost to a whisper as he added, "I just need you and Amy to help out with the children."

I didn't hesitate. "Of course," I said, the words feeling both like a promise and a prayer. "We'll do whatever you and Teresa need."

He nodded, his eyes flickering with a semblance of resolve amid the despair, and simply muttered, "Just pitch in with them and pray."

Even though I knew the stakes were impossibly high, and that the medical world rarely bent its schedule—especially on a holiday weekend—I also knew that when the Kid made the calls, even the best in the business would step in.

Those next three months dissolved into a blur of teary farewells, hushed conversations in dimly lit hospital corridors, and a constant undercurrent of sorrow that seeped into every corner of our lives. Amy and I became steady pillars for the Kid and Teresa, our home always open whenever Teresa needed a few hours away—a temporary refuge where her quiet strength could breathe and her children could manage awkward smiles in the face of uncertainty. Amy's compassion deepened as she spent nearly every waking moment by Teresa's side, whether at our house or, more often, at the Kid's, alongside his mother and sister, Gloria. I couldn't help but admire how the women forged an unspoken sisterhood—one born of shared hardship. In time, it drew all of us even closer together.

The Kid, once the indomitable force who had led our wild escapades and high-stakes deals, now seemingly wandered through his empire in a daze. He was consumed, every thought and breath focused solely on Teresa and their children. With his business acumen dulled by pain, I found myself stepping into the breach, ensuring that the company ran like a ship with a steadfast helmsman even as its captain struggled to stay afloat.

Then came the day that crystallized our collective resolve. The Kid had been out the previous day, taking Teresa to see two different specialists.

It was Tuesday morning when he walked into the office around eleven, the same heavy look in his eyes weighing him down. Without a word, he went straight to his office.

I followed, closing the door behind us with deliberate care. "I need to know what's going on," I said, my voice low, earnest, and edged with desperation. "Don't shut me out—we're family."

In that hushed room, the Kid did something I had never witnessed: he sat on the couch in his office and began to cry. Not the controlled, grudging tears we'd seen in passing, but full, unabashed tears that revealed raw vulnerability. For five long minutes, he just sobbed quietly—the kind of moment that rewrites all the memories of his near-invincibility from our younger days, back when even Mikey's fists couldn't make him break down like this.

I sat beside him, gently patting his shoulder, whispering, "It's okay, Kid, let it all out. I'm here for you."

After what felt like an eternity, he managed to catch his breath and confided, "I can't believe that with all the money, influence, and power I have, there's not a single thing I can do to fix this for her." His voice cracked as he added, "Philly, all our lives we fixed things for people—no matter what it took. But this . . . I feel helpless."

I asked him, cautiously, "What exactly did the doctors say?"

He explained that the prognosis was grim: Teresa's ovarian cancer was very advanced. The head oncologist at both hospitals—the top two oncologists in the country—concurred. They both implied: don't get your hopes up.

"Unfortunately, Philly," he said with a bitter shake of his head, "I believe them."

The days that followed blurred into long hours and sleepless nights. While I busied myself holding down the company—a patchwork of voices and opinions in our cramped boardroom that had once been our playground for daring decisions—I often caught myself daydreaming of a time when things were simpler. That memory of the Kid, once so vibrant and unstoppable, now seemed permanently stained by the gravity of Teresa's illness.

I recall one particularly charged afternoon when tensions hit their peak in our conference room. The Kid's inner circle—JJ, Alice, John, Jim, Peter, Frank, Shelia, Sophia, and a few other executives—had gathered in a tense meeting, passionately debating over key decisions, each person convinced of their own plan to steer the company forward. Then, as if commanded by fate, the Kid walked into the office, saw everyone in the conference room, and decided to walk in.

The chatter instantly died, replaced by a silent, electric stillness. He stood at the head of the table, surveying the room with eyes that reflected both sorrow and steely determination.

"I'm not sure what's going on in here," he said, his voice resonating with quiet authority, "but I'm only going to say this once: until I am ready to refocus on business—and I don't know when that will be—Philly speaks for me. Is that clear?"

JJ was the first to respond, "Yes, boss," and one by one, every single person nodded in agreement.

In that moment, my pulse surged with a mix of pride and an intense, personal responsibility. The Kid might not have declared me the only one smart enough to hold down the fort, but he trusted me implicitly. I knew he believed, without a shadow of a doubt, that if things got rough, I'd be the one to take one for the team—just like old times. The Kid then turned and exited the room, leaving behind an unspoken promise of loyalty and kinship.

Standing there, surrounded by my colleagues—my new family—I addressed them softly, "I hope I can count on everyone's cooperation to keep things running smoothly until the Kid returns to us whole again."

JJ was the first to rise, declaring, "I'm with you, Philly."

One by one, the others followed, their nods and murmurs of agreement echoing like a solemn vow.

That day, the colors of our lives seemed both muted and strangely vibrant, muffled by grief yet glowing with a fierce, unyielding bond. Together, as a family forged in fire and hardened by life, we would face whatever came next.

I remember those three months after Teresa's diagnosis as a drawn-out haze—a bittersweet lull where everything seemed to go on without a hitch, yet behind every laughter and every meeting in the office, there was an ever-present cloud of sorrow. The Kid was hardly ever around, and when he was, he drifted through the days as if somewhere else entirely. He would drop by the office maybe once a week for a few hours, sometimes with the children, and I'd do my best to fill him in on what was happening in the world outside his grief. Every time, he'd just nod and mumble, "Whatever you think, Philly, is fine with me," as if my words barely reached him.

One evening, Amy and I stepped into the quiet, dimly lit hospital suite, its sterile white walls softened by the gentle glow of a bedside lamp. Teresa lay on the bed, her eyes heavy and distant under the haze of morphine, a serene, almost otherworldly look upon her face. Beside her, the Kid was there, cradling her with a tenderness that seemed to hold back the storm of grief. The scene was heart-wrenching in its vulnerability.

Amy, overwhelmed by the sight, trailed slowly to one of the couches, where tears streamed down her cheeks like a silent testimony to our shared sorrow. I moved closer to the Kid and, in a quiet voice laden with concern, asked, "Do you want us to leave?"

With a gentle shake of his head, he murmured, "No, just give me a moment."

He got up, and we all sat on the couches. We tried to fill the heavy silence with words of comfort, but every syllable fell flat against the weight of our collective grief. In that room, filled with the soft beeps of monitors and the quiet murmur of distant voices, our words became little more than fragile whispers in a sea of sorrow.

Then came that fatal phone call.

It was a quiet Sunday night, around 12:30 a.m., and Amy and I were lying in bed, distracted by the muted glow of the TV. Out of the blue, my cell phone rang. Amy and I exchanged a weighted glance; we both knew this wasn't just any call.

I answered, and on the other end, I heard the familiar, steady voice of Roger—the director of Memorial Sloan Kettering Hospital and a trusted friend of the Kid's.

"Philly, it's Roger," he said gently. "I'm sorry... Teresa's gone."

I could barely breathe for a moment. I paused, then added, "Is the Kid there?"

"He was."

"I'll be right over," I said.

Amy and I began to dress in a daze. I asked her, "Where are you going?"

She looked at me with those tear-filled eyes and replied, "With you."

I tried to be firm. "I think I should go alone. There's nothing you can do now, and I think the Kid would prefer to have just me there."

Even as tears welled in her eyes, she nodded okay, with a resigned, heartbroken smile.

Within thirty minutes, I was pulling up to the hospital. Outside the presidential suite, I saw JJ sitting on a couch, looking into space.

He perked up when he saw me and said, "The Kid is inside."

Stepping into the presidential suite where Teresa lay, time slowed to a crawl. There she was—still and silent on the bed, her delicate face almost too serene to be real, with an eerie resemblance to those countless lifeless bodies I'd seen over the years. But this was different.

The Kid was sitting on the bed, holding her lifeless hand, tears running down his cheeks. With his head bowed, the raw grief in his eyes shone through a new vulnerability I'd never seen before.

"I can't believe it," he whispered hoarsely. "After everything we've been through, I've never felt pain like this."

I nodded solemnly; words felt futile. No woman could ever hurt him like losing Teresa did; she was his anchor, the one who made him whole.

I sank into one of the leather couches closest to Teresa's bed, in her large hospital suite, now eerily quiet without the hum of machines that had once kept her alive. The wires and tubes were gone, a final farewell to the devices that had fought to sustain her.

The Kid walked over and sat beside me in silence, his gaze fixed on her still form. He wasn't ready to let go; he wanted to hold onto every fleeting moment, every trace of her presence. He admitted, his voice barely audible, that he had spent hours lying by her side, each second stretching endlessly in the shadow of loss.

He said that, at one point during the night, Teresa managed to whisper through the haze of morphine, "Don't die with me, Dom—the kids need you." Her words, fragile yet profound, hung in the air—a testament to her love and selflessness.

Overwhelmed, he responded, his voice trembling, "I love you so much." It was a raw confession, filled with sorrow and gratitude for the life they had shared.

Those were her final words.

As he sat there, the weight of memories and unspoken grief pressing down on him, he realized that life without her felt unimaginable. The void she left behind was vast and unrelenting, and the ache of her absence lingered with every breath.

After a long, pained silence, I suggested gently, "Kid, let's go get a cup of coffee."

He agreed, and as we slowly left the room, I watched him approach her bedside. He bent down, pressed a soft kiss to her forehead, and murmured, "I love you," as if trying to imprint that love into the still air—a final goodbye that broke my heart anew.

Later, in the hospital's presidential suite coffee break room, in the dim light of a long, sleepless night, we talked quietly about the next steps. The Kid's voice was low and resolute despite the sorrow: "I want the wake at Catalino Funeral Home."

I immediately picked up the phone—it was 3:00 a.m. by then—and called the man himself. Catalino Funeral Home, one of the largest in New Jersey, was practically a kingdom of mourning.

Mario, the owner, was a familiar face from way back. I recalled a time I'd gone with JJ to talk to a guy named Jason regarding a young girl, Carol—Mario's daughter—and how he had come by the Kid's office to thank him personally. In that memory, the Kid's generosity and protectiveness shone through. Now, I explained the urgent news to Mario on his cell phone. He was deep in sleep, but he promised to be at the hospital within the hour.

When Mario arrived, his presence brought a quiet dignity to the room. He offered his condolences to the Kid, who listened with haunted eyes.

"I want the viewing on Wednesday and the funeral on Thursday," the Kid said firmly. Then, lowering his voice, he continued, "And Mario, I need you to do something else. I want the entire funeral parlor—no matter what it costs. No one else is to be viewed on Wednesday."

Mario's expression was one of determined understanding as he said, "That might be difficult, but I will do whatever needs to be done to make that happen. I'll make the arrangements; you'll have the whole place."

I couldn't immediately grasp why the Kid wanted such absolute privacy, but as the wake unfolded, the answer crystallized.

That Wednesday, from 2:00 p.m. until 10:00 p.m., more than five hundred people flooded the wake at Catalino Funeral Home. There were faces I'd only seen in the pages of high-powered magazines: governors, senators, congressmen, cabinet secretaries. Senior FBI agents, CIA and Secret Service operatives—almost every major federal agency was represented, even the elusive head of the NSA. And then, as I wandered amongst the throngs, I recognized figures from the Kid's shadowy past—old made guys I had known from both New York and California.

I saw Blue Eyes, and I nearly fell off my chair when I saw Carl Jr. walking in, looking as nonchalant as if he'd just stepped out for a coffee. For those few hours, every corporate coup, every whispered alliance between the criminal element and law enforcement, felt suspended in a fragile moment of unity. Despite our differences, everyone had come to pay their last respects. It was as if the Kid—once a wild force of nature—had woven together a tapestry of loyalty so complete that every enemy and ally alike stood aside in honor.

After the funeral on Thursday, as the last of the mourners drifted away, the Kid turned to me, his eyes still laden with sorrow. "I'm not sure I'm coming back, Philly," he said softly.

I clapped him on the shoulder and replied, "Take all the time you need. Stay with the kids. I'll keep things running. Teresa would want you to go on—she'd want you to be strong for them."

He simply murmured, "Yeah, I know," a barely audible concession to the weight of his grief.

That night, I lay awake replaying every moment, every tear, every whispered goodbye. In the midst of unbearable loss, I vowed to honor Teresa's memory by protecting the Kid and the children—by running his business with the kind of fierce loyalty that had defined us since we were young. And even though the color of our lives had darkened into deep blues and grays, there were still glimmers of light—memories of love, respect, and unbreakable bonds that promised, somehow, we would find our way through even the darkest of nights.

The Kid didn't step foot in the office for the next two months. It was like an endless stretch of waiting, each day marked by the same routine: I'd call him, hoping to hear even a flicker of the old Kid in his voice.

But every time, his response was distant, almost mechanical: "Whatever you think, Philly, is fine with me."

It was as if he was trapped in a fog, and no matter how hard I tried, I couldn't pull him out. I kept telling myself he just needed time, but deep down, I worried he might never snap out of it. I would invite him over for dinner with the children all the time, but rarely did he come, and when he did, it was only to talk about Teresa and how much he missed her. Eventually, he stopped coming.

Then, one Monday morning, without warning, he walked into the office. It was like seeing a ghost—familiar yet changed. Everyone stood up to greet him, their faces lighting up with cautious hope. He nodded politely, but you could tell he wasn't ready for small talk. He called the inner circle into his office, and as we gathered around the table in his office, he spoke with quiet determination. "I'm going to start coming back to work," he said. "I need to try to focus again. But if you see me slipping—if I'm not thinking clearly—I want you to say something."

One by one, we nodded, a silent promise passing between us. And just like that, the next chapter began.

For the next six months, he buried himself in work like a man trying to outrun his own thoughts. Slowly but surely, the pieces started to fall back into place. The team gelled, the business thrived, and the Kid began to find his rhythm again. But outside of work, he was a different man. He went home almost every night to be with the children, rarely stepping out except for the occasional business dinner. It was like he'd built a wall around himself, and no one—not even me—could break through.

One day, I decided to try. I walked into his office, and we started talking about nothing in particular—just the usual banter to pass the time. Then, out of the blue, I said, "Kid, why don't you go out more? I think it might be time."

He looked at me, his eyes heavy with a sadness that hadn't faded. "Philly," he said, "you've known me all my life. Never did a girl dig so deep into me that I couldn't move on. But Teresa did. I just can't seem to get past losing her."

I tried to lighten the mood. "Well, maybe if you gave it a chance, you'd meet someone who could help take your mind off her," I suggested.

He gave a half smile and said, "Maybe. But I just don't want to right now." Then, with a hint of his old humor, he added, "Philly, you know, no one loved sex or being with girls more than I did."

I couldn't resist. "That's for damn sure—you've slept with half the female population in LA!"

He laughed—a real, genuine laugh—the first I'd heard from him in eight months. For a moment, it felt like the old Kid was back.

But then his face grew serious again. "I just feel so guilty," he admitted. "I wish there was something I could've done. Sometimes I almost wish someone gave her the cancer, so I could spend all my time tracking them down and making them pay over and over again." His words hung in the air, heavy with the weight of his grief. In that moment, I knew he wasn't ready to move on—not yet. We talked for a while longer, and then I left him to his thoughts.

Another day, while chatting in his office, I mentioned that Amy was going out that night to a play with some girlfriends and asked if he'd like to grab dinner.

He paused, then said, "Let me call my mother and see if she's okay with the kids." After a quick call, he nodded and said, "Sure, let's go grab a bite—I could use that."

That evening, we drove into the city and headed to Sparks Steakhouse. The place was bustling, packed with people waiting for tables, but Andre, the head maître d', spotted us immediately and came over to greet us warmly. Without hesitation, he led us to a table near the bar, bypassing the crowd. The atmosphere was lively, yet intimate, and we settled in, talking about everything—our childhoods, Teresa, his kids, and even a bit of business. Over dinner and a magnificent bottle of wine, the conversation flowed effortlessly.

As we were finishing up, Blue Eyes walked in with two of his guys. He spotted us and came over, exchanging pleasantries. "Come to the bar and have a drink with me," he said.

The Kid nodded, "Sure."

We joined him at the bar, which was just as crowded as the rest of the restaurant. The Kid ordered a grappa, and I followed suit. As we talked, a loudmouth in a group of three couples to our left started raising his voice at the woman he was with—a strikingly pretty girl who had been laughing at something moments before.

His words sliced through the lively hum of the bar: "How about I slap you in your mouth? Would that be funny too?" He punctuated his threat by shoving her—not hard enough to knock her down but enough to make his point.

The Kid didn't hesitate. In a flash, it was like stepping back into 1980. He smacked the guy hard, square in the mouth, splitting his lip and leaving him stunned. Blood began to drip down the man's chin as he stood there, frozen. The Kid's voice was sharp and unwavering. "Why don't you push me, tough guy? Or is it only girls you pick on?"

One of the loudmouth's friends made a move toward the Kid, but before he could get close, I stepped in front of him, my glare stopping him dead in his tracks. He froze, and no one else dared to move, as Blue Eyes's guys made their presence known.

The loudmouth, still shocked and bleeding, stammered, "I didn't mean anything by it. She's . . . my girlfriend. We just had a disagreement."

The Kid didn't miss a beat. "I feel bad for her then, because she can do a lot better than you, fatso," he shot back, his words cutting deeper than the smack.

Andre, ever the professional, quickly stepped in to defuse the situation before it spiraled further. He offered the group a table, and they wasted no time accepting. The tension in the air began to dissipate as they shuffled away.

That was the first time I'd seen the Kid use his hands since we visited Gerard at the diner in New Jersey. It was a reminder of the fire that still burned within him, even after all these years.

On the drive back to New Jersey, the Kid leaned back in his seat and said, "That felt good—though I would've liked to pulverize him."

It was the first time I'd seen him like his old self in a long while. But deep down, I knew the anger and grief over Teresa was part of what triggered him. I wasn't sure what—or who—could ever help him move past her.

The next three months passed quietly, uneventfully. The Kid kept his head down, focusing on work and his children, but the shadow of Teresa's loss never left him. It was like a part of him had been buried with her, and no amount of work or laughter could bring it back. Still, I held onto hope. If anyone could find a way to heal, it was the Kid. He just needed more time.

CHAPTER TWENTY-ONE
PHILADELPHIA

One day, I was sitting in the Kid's office, shooting the breeze with him, when his cell phone rang. He glanced at it, answering in that unmistakable warm tone, "Beth, how are you, sweetheart? What's going on?"

I watched his face change in real time—as if dark clouds had suddenly gathered behind his eyes—while he listened intently. After a moment, I heard him say, "I understand. I don't want you to worry. What's his name?" When Beth replied, his tone shifted to reassuring firmness: "Stop worrying, I won't say a word. Just relax. I promise you there's nothing to worry about. Jimmy will be fine. You go back to doing what you were doing; I will handle it. I love you too."

He hung up, then shot me a look as he picked up his desk phone and dialed quickly. "JJ, come in here, please," he ordered. When JJ arrived, the Kid gestured to close the door behind him, which made it clear: nothing from this conversation was to leave the room.

Fixing his eyes on both of us, he launched into the details. "Jimmy's flying back to Philly this weekend to visit his sister, who's in the hospital for minor surgery," he said. "He called me yesterday to tell me he would come by the house and see the kids when he was done visiting with his sister, probably Monday or Tuesday. But here's what I wasn't told until now—apparently, there was an incident involving Jimmy at a restaurant in LA two weeks ago when he was out to dinner with Beth." He paused, his voice thick with disbelief. "I can't believe I hadn't heard about this until now.

"It seems Jimmy got into an altercation with some loser named Adam Civino, who'd had too much to drink. Jimmy had stepped away from his table with Beth to talk privately with someone at the bar. While there, he accidentally bumped into Adam, who took offense and—without hesitation—smacked Jimmy hard enough to knock him into the bar. Fortunately, a few of Carl Jr.'s guys happened to be dining there that night. They stepped in quickly, intervening on Jimmy's behalf, and defused the situation before it escalated further. But as Adam was being escorted out, he made a threat: 'If you ever come back to Philadelphia, you'll have a real problem.' "

"Beth urged Jimmy to call me, but he brushed it off, saying no need to bother the Kid; Adam was just drunk and mouthing off. Now, with Jimmy returning to Philadelphia this weekend, Beth's scared out of her mind. She thinks Adam's a loose cannon—and this time, he might actually follow through."

The Kid's jaw clenched as he continued. "We're not taking any chances. JJ, I want you to find out everything you can about this Adam Civino. I need you to do it now—we don't have much time. Get the intel, and then we'll decide how to handle it." Without a word, JJ nodded and left the office, the urgency of his task hanging in the air.

The Kid's eyes softened just a fraction as he said, "When we get the info, I suspect we'll find he's some wannabe—a minor associate of the Locatelli family in Philadelphia." We waited for JJ to return. After an hour, he did.

He said, "About three months ago, Adam had an incident with a girlfriend of Alphonse—Joey Doves's son, who was temporarily running the Battista family in New York while his father was in prison. Alphonse was furious.

"He reached out to Carmine Locatelli—head of the Locatelli family in Philadelphia—wanting him dead. Carmine refused, saying Adam was a good earner and maybe Alphonse's girlfriend shouldn't have been hanging around in Philadelphia. And to top it off, after all that, Adam refused to apologize. If Joey hadn't been in jail, things might have gone differently—but with the Locatelli family backed by the Barbieri family, Alphonse let it slide, though he was livid."

The Kid's expression hardened into resolve. "Philly, reach out to Alphonse on my behalf and tell him I want to meet tonight. Normally I would call Blue Eyes, but I want to leave him out of this for now. Let Alphonse know I've got something for him he'll appreciate—but we have to meet tonight." The Kid hadn't seen or spoken to Alphonse directly since that night in LA—when I stopped the Kid from making a fatal mistake—but I quickly reached out through one of his captains, a guy I'd become somewhat friendly with. Quickly, the message was passed along, and Alphonse agreed to the meeting.

That very night, JJ, the Kid, and I drove through the lively, rain-slicked streets to Marco Polo Restaurant on Court Street in Brooklyn—a dimly lit, atmospheric joint known for its hushed conversations, excellent food, and underworld clientele. JJ and I sat at a table with three of Alphonse's guys, our eyes darting nervously around the room as anticipation built. In a secluded corner, the Kid sat face-to-face with Alphonse, their conversation private and heavy with unspoken history.

Later, when the meeting wrapped up, we all headed out. On the ride back, the Kid recounted the conversation. "I told Alphonse, 'It's been too long. A lot has changed between us. I know we got off on the wrong foot, but as far as I'm concerned, the past is the past. I'm over it—and I hope you are too. We've both got a problem, and I might have a way to help us both.' "

The Kid paused for a beat, then added, "Alphonse just looked at me and said, 'I'm listening.' "

The Kid then detailed the situation with Adam—the scumbag who had dared to threaten Jimmy, and by extension, our world. "I want to send a message," he declared, his voice low and measured. "I would like your backing, so that there's no repercussions. When I handle this, it'll be my way—no official permission. Adam isn't made, and although I can take some heat, it'll be easier if the Battista family in New York stands behind me. After all, Adam's nothing more than a scumbag."

Alphonse's eyes darkened, and in a gravelly tone he said, "I want him dead."

The Kid paused, weighing his words, then replied, "So do I— though that might be pushing it too far. The message I send will be long-lasting, and I'll keep your name out of it. When he's in the hospital, you can send flowers. He'll know exactly what that means."

There was a moment of charged silence before Alphonse's face broke into a wry smile. "I got your back, Kid. And by the way, you're a hell of a fighter."

The Kid responded, "And you have a hell of a punch; no one ever hit me that hard." They both laughed—a brief, knowing laugh that seemed to make the weight of the conversation a little lighter. They stood, shook hands, and embraced warmly. In that moment, I knew the Kid had forged a new alliance—one that might just tip the scales back in our favor.

That night, as the neon lights of Brooklyn blurred past in our rear-view mirror, I couldn't help but feel that amid all the strife and heartache, our little family—this tangled web of loyalty, loss, and hard-won alliances—was holding strong. And despite everything, there was a glimmer of hope that soon, justice would be dealt with, and once again, our world could find a semblance of balance.

Then the Kid said, his voice cutting through the hum of the car's engine with a firmness that brooked no argument, "JJ, you and Philly—take whoever else you need—and get down to Philly.

I want you both to scout things out and, by Friday, I want this handled." His eyes were steely as he continued. "Philly, I want you to be the one who sends the message. That way, if the Locatelli family raises any issues, they'll know it came straight from me. I want him to spend a good week or two in the hospital. Make sure he's awake so he can hear every damn word: 'If you so much as think about touching Jimmy, you'll wish I put two in your head right here and now. Got it?' " JJ and I both nodded in unison.

The Kid paused for a beat, a wry smile playing on his lips, then added, "Philly, aren't you going to ask why I want you handling this instead of me?"

I shook my head, a firm grin breaking through as I replied, "When have I ever doubted you? You want me to handle it, the message will be sent without question."

The Kid's smile broadened as he concluded, "All right. I'll handle any fallout with the Locatelli family—though I doubt there'll be any—but you never know."

Later, I told JJ, "We need some backup that we can trust— people who really know the Philadelphia area."

He grinned and said, "I know just the guys." With that, he made a couple of calls on his cell as we dropped the Kid back at the office. The next morning, we left the office together—JJ behind the wheel. We made two more stops to pick up two trusted ex-Seals who JJ vouched for. We had hundreds of ex-military on our payroll, but for a job like this, we needed real specialists—ones who wouldn't hesitate if things went sideways.

As we drove down to Philadelphia, I laid it out for the new guys: no one was to lay a finger on Adam except me. They exchanged nods, clear as day what our priorities were. We checked into the Prince Edward Hotel in downtown Philadelphia around noon. The lobby's low lighting and the steady murmur of guests couldn't mask the tension in our veins as we dropped off our bags and immediately hit the street.

We scouted the nightclub we'd heard Adam frequented. Thanks to JJ's prior work—he'd secured mug shots of Adam, making him easy to spot—our mission was already half won.

That night, we headed to the club. As luck would have it, we immediately spotted Adam at the far end of the bar. He was with two other guys and a girl—a picture of relaxed menace. We stayed low, nursing beers and admiring a few good-looking women to blend in. By around 12:30 a.m., Adam looked visibly intoxicated; his swagger slackened as he draped his arm around the girl and made his way to the exit. We knew better than to strike while he was with company, so JJ and I texted our two ex-Seals to tail them discreetly.

We lingered in the club until about 1:00 a.m., then headed out. Not long after, our phones buzzed with a text: Adam had been spotted at a house just outside Philadelphia. We didn't know if it was his place or the girl's, nor how long he'd be staying. We quickly drove to the address. JJ checked with a detective contact he had in Philly—it turned out the property was rented to a young woman. We assumed this was the same girl he'd been seen with.

After a brief scan of the neighborhood—no cameras in sight—we parked and waited as dawn approached. At around 7:30 a.m., as first light glinted on dew-soaked streets, we finally saw him: Adam emerged from the house and made his way toward his car, which we had already identified.

Every detail of that night was etched into my mind: the Kid's unwavering command, the careful planning, and the cold, calculated resolve we shared to send the message. And as I watched Adam walk out into the early morning light, I knew that justice—and a stern reminder of who controlled the game—was about to be served.

I told JJ, "Let's take him right now." The urgency in my voice sent a shiver down my spine as we began to approach our target, our footsteps muffled by the biting cold of the morning air. It was early, the streets eerily empty in the cold morning temperature, and I could sense his apprehension. It didn't take long for him to realize we were coming for him; I watched his eyes widen as he bolted toward his car, panic propelling him forward.

I couldn't let him get away. He likely had a gun in the car, but he wouldn't make it that far. Just as he reached for the car door, I lunged, grabbing him just before he could slip inside. He swung wildly at me, a desperate attempt to fend me off, but I ducked low, feeling the rush of adrenaline as I dodged his punch. That was the moment I unleashed a storm of my own, delivering blow after blow to his lower body. I could hear the sickening crunch of shattered ribs beneath my fists, each strike fueled by a mix of anger and determination.

When he finally crumpled to the ground, I focused my attention on his face. Blood sprayed like a vibrant red flag as I struck his jaw, fragments of teeth littering the pavement around us. With a final, decisive smash of my knee to his nose, more blood gushed forth, painting the ground in a grotesque pattern. He lay there, dazed and disoriented, and I reached into my pocket for the smelling salts I had stashed there, knowing I would probably knock him out cold. I waved the vial under his nose, and he gasped back to consciousness, eyes fluttering open in confusion. I grabbed a fistful of his hair, lifting his head and forcing him to meet my glare.

"Can you hear me?" I asked, my voice low and steady. His faint groan was all the confirmation I needed. I pulled out my .45, pressing the cold barrel against his trembling lips. "Listen carefully," I said, my voice cutting through the chaos around us. "I have a message from the Kid. If you even think about looking at Jimmy cross-eyed, you will wish I killed you right here and now. Do you understand me?"

The weak, defeated "yes" that escaped his lips was music to my ears. I let his head drop back to the pavement, a finality in the gesture that signified his defeat.

But I wasn't quite done yet. I turned his leg and snapped it at the knee with a sickening crack, ensuring he wouldn't be walking for a while.

JJ and I walked away calmly, as if nothing had happened, heads down, blending into the early morning shadows. We didn't run; we moved with purpose, unhurried, avoiding the gaze of any curious onlookers who might question us.

The other two guys picked us up around the corner, and we piled into the car, heading back to the hotel. My heart raced as I texted the Kid: "The sun is up." He would know exactly what that meant—it was done. There were no repercussions, not a single trace left behind, as if this act of violence was merely a figment of a collective imagination, whispered in the dark.

The following week, the Kid got a call from Blue Eyes. He wanted to meet. They arranged lunch for the next day at the Kid's favorite restaurant in Union, New Jersey—daBenito Ristorante.

It was my first time meeting Blue Eyes in person. After the handshakes and small talk, he and the Kid took a private table in the back. Lunch traffic was light, and the quiet made privacy easy. I stayed at the bar, enjoying a perfect plate of pasta while chatting with the bartender I knew well.

On the ride back to the office, the Kid filled me in. Blue Eyes said Antonio Locatelli, boss of the Locatelli family in Philadelphia, had been asking questions about the Adam Civino "message" sent in his city. Antonio had spoken to Alphonse and requested a sit-down.

"Alphonse wants you to know he's got your back," Blue Eyes told him. "Antonio knows it was you who sent the message. I'll keep you informed if there's any reason to look over your shoulder. The meeting is set for next week."

The Kid didn't waste time. "Assign a team to watch me and my family until this is resolved," he said. I took care of it immediately. Any time one of them left the house or the office, eyes were on them.

Two weeks later, Blue Eyes called again. Another lunch—this time in Brooklyn, with Alphonse. JJ drove the Kid and me to Marco Polo Restaurant, while a surveillance team followed, and another team scouted the area in advance.

Inside, the Kid and Blue Eyes joined Alphonse at a table in the back. I sat with JJ and a couple of our guys alongside Alphonse's crew. Fifteen minutes later, I watched them stand, hug, and kiss on the cheek. The meeting was over.

On the ride back, the Kid explained. Alphonse had met with Antonio. It was agreed that the message to Adam was justified. Adam had threatened Jimmy, and Alphonse had his own vendetta against him.

Alphonse told Antonio, "My father sends a message from prison. If there's any retaliation over Adam, he'll take it as a personal attack on him and his family."

Antonio thought for a moment, then said, "Tell your father I understand. This is over. Adam's a hothead—he got what he deserved." Antonio even apologized for the incident involving Alphonse's girlfriend and Adam.

I kept the protective teams in place for a few more weeks, just to be sure.

About a month later, the Kid was invited back to Marco Polo Restaurant for dinner with Alphonse, a gesture of gratitude for how it all turned out.

JJ and I joined him, sitting at the same table where tension had hung heavy during their last meeting. This time, over shared plates and quiet laughter, the mood was different. A new alliance was forged—built not only on respect but on the unspoken understanding that in our world, protecting one another often meant walking in the shadows.

CHAPTER TWENTY-TWO
GERMANY

The next few months were a blur of endless work—STS Security kept growing, and we were all buried in our own tasks. Then one day, as I walked into the office, the Kid called me in. His expression was unusually serious as he began, "Philly, I received an unexpected call from a government official I trust in Germany—a man named Wilhelm Braun. He told me that Borrshose, a massive, well-connected private security firm in Germany, is in deep financial trouble. The owner, a degenerate gambler, has squandered company funds and tangled himself up with some very dangerous people. If this gets out, it could sink the firm and their lucrative government contracts. Wilhelm wants to know if I'm interested in a quick, quiet acquisition."

Intrigued, we immersed ourselves in a discussion of the pros and cons. Later that morning, the Kid convened an inner circle meeting in the conference room. With an earnest, measured tone, he laid out the details and then invited everyone's input.

Frank broke the ice with a wry remark: "Too bad the company isn't public—this news would make a great short."

The Kid's laugh was spontaneously sincere as he retorted, "Don't I know it."

One by one, colleagues voiced that if we could secure the right talent to manage Borrshose's operations in Germany, and we could get it at the right price, this move could become a major win. It would give us a global presence.

Then he posed the question that resonated in the room: "Anyone have any thoughts on who could be the right fit for us? Any of our midlevel managers ready?" A palpable silence followed until he grinned and said, "Don't everyone speak at once." Amid light laughter, he concluded by urging us to give it some thought—after all, perhaps one among us knew someone with the talent for a two-year adventure across the Atlantic. "We'll revisit this in a day or two," he said, leaving the question hanging in the air like an unspoken challenge.

That evening, over a quiet dinner at home, I brought up the dilemma with Amy. I explained that we needed someone willing to uproot their life for two years in Germany to spearhead this new venture.

To my surprise, Amy asked, "Why don't you take it, Philly?"

I chuckled, almost incredulous. "Me? You mean you'd want us to pack up, move to Germany for two years, and learn a new language?"

With a playful glint in her eye, she admitted, "It might be a new adventure for us." In that moment, the idea began to take shape.

Two days later, after many more discussions with Amy, I walked into the office with newfound determination. Finding the Kid, I said quietly, "I think I've found the person for Germany."

He looked at me, puzzled. "Who?" he asked.

I met his steely gaze and replied, "Me."

His shock was swift and genuine—he couldn't quite believe it. "Are you serious?" he demanded.

I explained that Amy and I had been talking seriously about it. "We're ready for an adventure. We want to take on this challenge," I added.

The Kid paused, then replied with a mix of regret and pride, "Philly, I'd really miss you here, but you're one of the few people I trust to expand our operations overseas. I would never ask you to do this unless I believed it was truly what you both wanted.

"If you and Amy really want to consider this, here's what you do: pack a few bags, and tomorrow night, you and Amy jump on a plane and head to Germany. Time is of the essence; if this information leaks, other bids will start coming in, and competition is not what we want. Stay in the very best hotels and enjoy the local scene—all expenses are on the company."

He leaned forward, his voice softening with encouragement. "Enjoy yourself for a week, and when you get back, if you still think this is the right move for you and Amy, we'll pursue the deal."

The next night, Amy and I flew first class out of Newark directly to Munich, Germany. The experience was surreal—a mix of plush first-class comfort, the crisp European air, and the weight of responsibility that sat on our shoulders. The Kid had left no detail to chance: Alice had our travel agent arrange flights, premium accommodations, limousines, everything we needed.

The Kid arranged with Wilhelm to set up a meeting the following day with the owner and top management of Borrshose. We arrived in Munich, where the Borrshose corporate headquarters loomed like a fortress of both tradition and modern ambition, and we fell in love with the place almost immediately.

Over the next few days, I sat through a series of meetings. I meticulously examined the company's operations and overall potential. I sent a lot of the financial information back to Howard and Frank, for their deep review. With each discussion, my conviction grew stronger—the numbers were promising, the challenges surmountable. By the fifth day, I knew that if the figures aligned, this acquisition could become one of the smartest moves we ever made.

Without hesitation, I called the Kid and said, "If the numbers work, just go ahead and close the deal. We're in." His voice, even over the phone, carried the same resolute tone I'd come to trust. In that moment, with the future of an entire empire hanging in the balance, I realized this adventure wasn't just about expanding our reach. It was about seizing a bold opportunity that could redefine our legacy.

The next day, the Kid set the wheels in motion. I remember his voice over the phone that morning—firm and decisive—when he told me not to come home yet. "We're heading to Germany in two days to get things rolling," he said, and that set a chain of events in motion that would soon redefine our operation.

Three days later, the scene shifted to the cool, brisk air of Munich. The Kid and group were whisked away by Wilhelm—the government official who had first broken the news that set this plan in motion. They made a brief stop at my hotel to drop off their bags and check in. I still recall meeting them in the spacious, softly lit lobby; Wilhelm's Range Rover waited outside like a promise of things to come.

After freshening up in our respective rooms, the Kid, JJ, Frank, and I piled into Wilhelm's Range Rover and drove through the streets of Munich toward our next destination—the new office of a company whose fate hung in the balance.

We arrived at a sleek, modern building that housed the offices of Borrshose. Guided into a sprawling conference room, the atmosphere was tense yet meticulously controlled. JJ, ever the consummate professional, immediately produced a compact eavesdropping detection kit from his briefcase and methodically scanned the room. "I think it's clean," he said with a quiet confidence that put us all at ease. The Kid nodded in agreement.

Not long after, the door swung open and in walked Hans Groubert—the owner of the company—with the restrained assurance of a man burdened by his own mistakes. Hans greeted

Wilhelm warmly; the look in his eyes confirmed their long-standing acquaintance. He was then introduced to the Kid, JJ, and Frank. I had met Hans a few days before when I arrived in Germany, and I was reassured by his impeccable English and the careful articulation with which he explained every detail of his company: the contracts secured, those pending, and the very structure of their operations.

After two hours of measured discussion, punctuated by the steady hum of urgency in the room, the Kid finally leaned forward and asked Hans, "So, what do you think the value of the company is?"

Hans hesitated, clearly unaccustomed to such direct scrutiny, and after a long pause replied, "At least one hundred million euros."

The Kid's eyes narrowed—not in disbelief but in an unspoken challenge. "Hans, you strike me as a smart, decent man," he said coolly. "But let's not play games. You're in trouble.

"If you're not bailed out quietly and quickly, there's a very good chance you'll end up in jail, and whatever money you get for this company will be confiscated to cover the funds you siphoned off illegally—on top of the fines and penalties you'll incur. You know it, and I know it."

His voice hardened as he continued, "So, let's speak frankly. Either you take my offer seriously, or I'll thank you for your time, and we'll be back on a plane to the States before the end of the day."

Hans's face drained of color. Mortification and resignation mingled in his eyes as he wondered how the Kid could possibly have known every sordid detail. In a hushed tone, Hans asked, "How much are you willing to give me?"

The Kid replied, "You're in debt for five million euros to some very dangerous people—the kind who will bleed you dry, leaving you to take the fall in the end. Here's my nonnegotiable offer: I'll pay off your five million euro debt, ensure these thugs never bother you again, and collect any evidence they have on your financial misdeeds. I'll pay you ten million euros personally, depositing the money in any account you choose, anywhere in the world, and I'll buy the company for twenty-five million euros."

I saw Hans's eyes widen in disbelief, as if a guardian angel had just appeared to save him. We were both getting an unbelievable deal. On the open market, the company was easily worth seventy-five million euros—perhaps even approaching the one hundred million Hans originally cited—but the Kid knew the value lay in a quick, discreet cash deal that would shut out external investigations and guarantee Hans's safety from his violent creditors.

After a long, breathless moment, Hans stood, extended his hand, and with trembling gratitude said, "I know you're getting a great deal, and thank you for saving me."

The Kid shook his hand firmly, sealing the agreement with a look that brooked no further argument. Hans then thanked the rest of us, and we left the conference room together.

Back at the hotel, the Kid's mood shifted abruptly as he suggested, "Let's change, and then you and Amy can show us the best restaurant in Munich."

When I went back to the room and told Amy about our dinner plans with the guys, she protested. "No, Philly—you go with them so you can talk business."

I quickly phoned the Kid's room, and his immediate retort cut through any hesitation: "Absolutely not. You tell Amy that we're not going to dinner without her. And tell her I'm starving."

I relayed his words, and Amy smiled, finally acquiescing to the plan.

That night at dinner, over a candlelit table in one of Munich's finest restaurants, the conversation wavered between serious discussion and moments of shared levity.

We sipped on a magnum of DRC La Tache—a wine so magnificent it defies description—and then, as if to crown the evening, the Kid ordered a magnum of Chateau Margaux 1990.

Both wines, extravagant and exquisite, were the finest I had ever experienced; they were a toast to new beginnings and the taste of our coming success.

The following day, while Frank and Howard were on the phone, deep in the weeds of contractual details and financing, the rest of us toured Munich—soaking in the city's vibrant mix of old-world charm and modern ambition. Frank also met with Emil Müller, a top international business lawyer the Kid had consulted before flying to Germany. Emil would prove instrumental in structuring the contractual terms with Frank to get the deal done.

Once I took control of Borrshose, I leaned heavily on Emil to help build the company. He became as valuable to me in Germany as Frank was to the Kid in New Jersey. Eventually, after conferring with the Kid, we agreed to offer Emil a sweet deal to officially bring him on board. He accepted, and soon after became a full-time member of the Borrshose team. Two days later, the paperwork was finalized, the funds were transferred, and the acquisition was complete.

But there was one more loose end to tie. The Kid phoned Yoav Ben-David, a Mossad agent stationed in Germany. Yoav had an extensive network of contacts—many of them on the wrong side of the law. The Kid explained that he'd met Yoav during an earlier operation in the States, when STS Security had worked alongside Mossad on an assignment. He liked him, trusted him.

He asked Yoav to arrange a meeting with the people leaning on Hans. An hour later, it was set. "Let's take a ride," the Kid said. "We'll talk to the ones holding Hans's five-million-euro debt."

JJ drove the Kid and me, making a few strategic stops along the way. We picked up two hard-as-nails bruisers—Rolph and Henri—former German special forces operatives JJ knew and trusted. We had plenty of ex-military on our payroll, but for a mission like this, these two were perfect: local, smart, tough, and intimidating on sight.

I would come to rely on Rolph and Henri in the years to come, with Rolph eventually becoming my JJ in Germany.

We arrived at a foreboding office complex on the outskirts of Munich that looked like a fortress. Two men armed with automatic weapons guarded the lobby as we were escorted to the top floor. Inside the upscale office of the man in charge—who introduced himself simply as Bruno—we immediately sensed we were entering a different league. Bruno was a formidable figure: tough, impeccably dressed, and exuding quiet authority. "I've heard a lot about you, Kid," he said, his tone a mix of respect and cautious curiosity.

The Kid replied coolly, "All good, I hope?" They shared a brief smile and shook hands—a gesture that set the tone for what followed.

The Kid then laid out the terms calmly but firmly: "I appreciate you agreeing to this meeting. As was discussed, we're going to pay off Hans's five-million-euro debt, and with that, your business with him is concluded. You'll never contact him again for any reason. In addition, I expect you to hand over all documents implicating Hans."

Bruno hesitated only for a moment before asking, "But how do you know I won't make a copy of those documents before handing them over?"

The Kid fixed him with a steely glare and replied, "Because we both know you enjoy breathing."

At that, I tensed, expecting a problem, but Bruno's face softened into a conspiratorial smile. "I guess the information I have on you is correct—you do have balls of stone." The Kid's unwavering silence spoke volumes, and then Bruno added, "You won't have any trouble from me; you have my word."

They shook hands one final time before the Kid said, "Have a nice day," and we all turned to leave.

Once in the car, as we drove away from the office complex, I couldn't help but ask, "Do you really believe him?"

The Kid grinned. "I do. He knows he'll have to watch his back now; he also knows we have the ear of the German government.

And more than that, he wants to keep breathing, as I said. It's the only language a man like him understands."

We all burst out laughing—a brief moment of levity after the intensity of negotiations.

Miraculously, the scandal surrounding the company's financial woes never became public. It was as if the company had been sold simply because Hans wanted out. The following day, after all the papers were signed, the Kid, JJ, and Frank flew back to the States. Amy and I followed the next day—the Kid insisting we not all travel on the same flight, just in case.

Back in the States, the Kid moved swiftly to settle Hans's debt with Bruno. He arranged, through Yoav Ben-David, to pay off the five million euros, as we had agreed. Yet, just two days later, the Kid received a call from Yoav reporting a snag: Bruno's group in Germany had another partner—Manfred—who was now causing trouble. Manfred claimed that the loan wasn't supposed to be paid off for three years, and that prepayment would cost him the rest of the "vig," so he demanded an extra one million euros to even consider it.

The Kid never quibbled about money unless someone tried to squeeze him. He calmly told Yoav to hold tight and then picked up the phone to call a man named Ziggy—a well-known figure in the Russian mafia. Although I never learned the full story of how the Kid and Ziggy had come to know each other, I remember clearly the conversation over the phone.

"Zig, do me a favor," the Kid ordered unmistakably. "Send a few guys to pay Manfred a visit and remind him exactly who he's fucking with." A terse "Thanks" followed before the call ended.

Three days later, Yoav called back with the wiring instructions for Manfred and Manfred's deep apology for the earlier confusion. The money was transferred. Soon after, the remaining documents were collected, and we never heard from Bruno or Manfred again.

That deal in Munich—fraught with high-stakes negotiation, old-school muscle, and the cold precision of international finance—was a turning point. In those months, our company had not only expanded its reach across the Atlantic but had also deftly navigated the dangerous intersections between legitimate business and the murky underworld. And as I sat back and reflected on it all, I couldn't help feeling that we had not only secured a major win but had also further established our reputation as players who got things done.

A week after the deal was sealed, Amy and I packed our bags and left the States for what would become a two-year whirlwind adventure. It was a leap into the unknown, but with the Kid's guidance and the unwavering support of the New Jersey office, I threw myself into building the European security company.

The transformation was staggering. By the time we were done, the company was three times the size it had been when we acquired it. I'd never worked so hard in my life, but the payoff was beyond anything I'd ever imagined. For the first time, I was financially set for life. And perhaps even more rewarding, I proved to myself—and to everyone else—that I was more than just muscle. I could lead, strategize, and build something extraordinary.

CHAPTER TWENTY-THREE
ANGELA

In those early days of our German adventure, my conversations with the Kid were almost exclusively about business. Every call, every meeting was consumed with strategies, deals, and plans for our venture. There was little room—or perhaps, little need—for personal chitchat, and I didn't mind; it felt like we were both pouring every ounce of our energy into making this venture a success.

But as time went on, I began to notice something peculiar. The Kid, who had once been refreshingly open with me, started growing secretive about his personal life. Whenever I tried to steer our conversation away from work—trying to catch even a glimpse of the man behind the mask—he'd deflect or abruptly change the subject. I figured it was just lingering grief from Teresa's loss or maybe embarrassment, a reluctance to reopen wounds that hadn't fully healed. As far as I knew, he wasn't dating or even going out. He seemed to be living in his own carefully constructed bubble, keeping everyone at arm's length.

Then, whispers began to filter in from our inner circle back in New Jersey. Little snippets of hushed information started to paint a picture of something stirring beneath the surface—a new pulse in the Kid's heart that I hadn't expected. It turned out he wasn't as isolated as I had assumed. Bit by bit, the stories unfolded, and I started to suspect there was far more to his silence than mere grief.

One evening, after wrapping up one of our business conversations, we settled into some lighter chitchat. The Kid said, "Philly, I gotta come clean with you, because sooner or later, you're gonna hear it anyway. You know I love you like a brother—I'm not trying to hide anything from you—but I'm embarrassed as hell to share it, and I'm not even sure why. I started going out again." His words hung in the air, tentative yet honest. He continued. "My mom, my sister, and Teresa's parents and brother have been pitching in with the kids, so I get out a couple of nights a week—sometimes on the weekends. As much as I believe Teresa would've wanted me to carry on, there's this overwhelming guilt that I can't shake."

I leaned back and said, "I'm glad you're telling me, Kid, because I was starting to worry about you. It's perfectly natural to need some companionship—to go out and feel connected. Guilt is heavy, but it tends to lighten over time, or maybe, just maybe, you'll meet someone who helps ease that burden."

He let out a wry laugh and replied, "That person doesn't exist." Still, he admitted that for the last few months, he'd been seeing a few girls. "They're great—they make me laugh, they're beautiful and sexy, they ignite a passion in me, but it's nothing more than fleeting company."

I encouraged him with a gentle smile. "Just keep at it. Maybe someday, the right one will come along."

He chuckled, dismissing the thought for the time being.

And so, the Kid started to go out again—not with any explicit aim of finding a committed relationship but simply in search of company and companionship. I always knew he was a chick magnet, a fact that never ceased to amaze me. But beneath that,

I wondered if he was in danger of reverting to his old self back in LA, that impulsive, wildly free version of him, or if time and loss had forged a new man altogether. Only time would tell what path he would choose.

There was a group of girls in the New Jersey office who would occasionally go out together after work. One Friday, they made plans to check out a new club that had been generating buzz—an upscale venue called Opal & Onyx, nestled on Broadway in downtown Manhattan. Before leaving the office, they happened to run into the Kid and casually mentioned where they were headed, half-jokingly asking if he wanted to meet them there. To their surprise, he said, "Maybe I will."

The club was rumored to be owned by Blue Eyes, whom the Kid knew well. When they arrived, the line to get in stretched down the block. They waited nearly an hour beneath the neon glow of the city, their excitement slowly giving way to impatience. Just as they were starting to consider leaving, a sleek, chauffeur driven car pulled up in front. Out stepped the Kid, dressed sharp and accompanied by a stunning blonde.

In that moment, one of our colleagues spotted the Kid and yelled his name, and with a wave, he beckoned everyone from the line to join him. The bouncers, who clearly recognized him, stepped aside with just a nod, and within minutes, the office crew had bypassed the line and entered through the club's elegant glass doors.

Inside Opal & Onyx, the ambiance was everything one would expect from an upscale NYC club—vibrant energy, elegantly dressed patrons, and a dance floor bathed in dynamic lighting. The Kid ordered a round of drinks for the group and then found his way into the VIP section with his date, watching the crowd below as they talked over music and cocktails. But then, something—or rather, someone—caught his eye. Amid the swirling lights and deep bass, his gaze locked onto a familiar figure—a gorgeous woman in a beautiful, sexy red dress moving gracefully through the crowd in four-inch heels.

Without hesitation, the Kid turned to his date and said, "Excuse me, I'll be right back," setting aside his conversation with the girl he was talking to. With quiet confidence, he walked through the crowd and approached her, lightly tapping her on the shoulder. When she turned, their eyes met, and he said softly, "Angela Esposito?"

Her eyes immediately widened and her face lit up in pleasant surprise as she replied, "I don't believe it—Dominic Argianno?"

In that instant, the years melted away into a flood of memories. They greeted each other like old friends reunited, marveling at how time had passed since their childhood days. Their conversation, filled with exclamations of, "Oh my God, I haven't seen you in forever," quickly rekindled a connection that had lain dormant for far too long.

Angela was a vision in every sense, with long, softly curled chestnut hair that framed her striking features and eyes sparkling with a familiar warmth the Kid remembered well. She exuded both class and sex appeal. At about five foot four inches, she had the poise of a Milan runway model—a face and body to die for. She radiated class, confidence, and undeniable sex appeal—a woman who turned heads the moment she entered a room.

After about only fifteen minutes of nostalgic conversation, the Kid reluctantly excused himself with a wistful look in his eyes as he asked for her number, promising he'd call soon. He made his way back to the VIP section, where the blonde he'd left waiting stood watching with a mix of curiosity and quiet suspicion. She had seen the entire scene unfold.

The Kid, always composed, offered a small, disarming smile. "Sorry about that—I had to say hello to an old friend I haven't seen in thirty years." His charm, as always, was effortless.

A few days later, he reached out to see if Angela was free for lunch. At a table in an Italian restaurant in Manhattan, they lost themselves in conversation for hours, effortlessly revisiting the tender, carefree days of their youth. Every laugh, every whispered memory of stolen moments seemed to transport them back to a time when the world was simpler and their hearts beat in unison.

During that lunch, Angela opened up with a vulnerability both raw and beautiful. She confided how heartbroken she had been when he left—a parting that shattered the delicate world they'd built together during those early, secret years. "It took me years to pick up the pieces," she admitted softly, her eyes glistening with a mixture of pain and hope. "But I never ever forgot you."

They had first met in school when they were barely thirteen—two wide-eyed kids drawn together by a potent, undefinable connection.

For two precious years, they saw each other almost daily. In school, after school, and on weekends, they sneaked around like conspirators in a secret romance. Each meeting was a rebellion against the ordinary, a small victory of the heart amidst the strict rules of grown-up disapproval.

Angela's father—a hardworking, steadfast man, much like Dominic's own father—had strictly forbidden her from seeing him—well aware of the dark shadow cast by Dominic's grandfather, a man whose name carried weight and notoriety.

He feared that any association with someone connected to that notorious world would drag his daughter into dangerous territory.

Yet, despite the disapproval and the constant warnings, Angela's heart remained stubbornly true. She always found subtle, ingenious ways to be near him—quietly defiant moments in which love triumphed over fear—believing that what they had was worth the risk. By the time they were fifteen, they had become each other's first love, sharing secret smiles, hushed words, true intimacy, and memories that, even in innocence, hinted at the depth of what was possible.

I recalled how the Kid had once mentioned leaving a girl behind in New York when he first moved to LA—a remark I had dismissed as yet another fleeting encounter in his tumultuous life. I never imagined then that beneath that casual tone lay a connection so profound with Angela that her memory would linger like a bittersweet refrain.

Now, reflecting on their reminiscent conversation, it was as if the years melted away; every soft laugh and lingering glance spoke of a love that had survived time, distance, and the harshness of separation. In that moment, their words wove a tapestry of a shared past, the resilient beauty of their connection. It was a love that had borne the scars of forbidden passion, yet still managed to shine—a reminder that even in the shadows of hardship, the heart remembers its truest desires.

As the weeks went on, it became evident that their reunion was no mere coincidence. Angela, with her Italian heritage and fluent command of the language, was a marketing director for a prestigious Italian fashion magazine based in NYC. Her life was polished, cultured, graceful—an elegant contrast to the Kid's streetwise past. And yet, somehow, they fit. Together, they formed a portrait of balance: her refinement softening his hard edges; his depth, strength, and history grounding her grace.

In reconnecting with Angela, the Kid wasn't just rekindling old memories or revisiting the past. He was opening the door to something new—a second chance. A quiet possibility that maybe, after all he'd been through, his heart might still find healing.

Angela must have really caught his eye—sparked something inside him I had never noticed before Teresa. In the months that followed that fateful night at Opal & Onyx, whispers began circulating throughout the New Jersey office.

People noticed how often he disappeared for lunches, usually not returning to the office; how frequently he laughed with Angela on the phone; how long he lingered in conversations that stretched past the end of the workday.

Naturally, I couldn't help but ask him about it. Whenever I brought it up, his answers came with a measured tone—just enough to close the door without slamming it. "Oh, I'm just enjoying talking and spending time with her. We've known each other for so many years—it's just friendship."

If this had been twenty-five years earlier, I might have spotted the truth flickering behind his words—that subtle spark when Angela's name crossed his lips. But the Kid had changed since meeting and marrying Teresa. In the depths of that transformation—and especially after losing Teresa—something inside him hardened, like steel cooling after the forge. His demeanor had taken on a new weight, a guarded quality that made it hard to read his true feelings. He carried himself with a quiet gravity now, and whatever he was feeling about Angela was locked behind walls I couldn't easily read. So I accepted what he said at face value, convincing myself that what he claimed was probably the truth—or at least some version of it.

Then came a moment—one quiet afternoon with rain drumming against the office window—when his guard slipped. His voice softened, almost as if he were speaking to himself. "Angela had a difficult time after I left for LA. I like talking with her about it. In some ways, her story mirrors mine." He didn't explain further, but the meaning lingered in the air—shared pain, missed chances, a thread of longing neither of them had cut loose.

He told me he'd opened up to her about Teresa and the kids; about the grief that hollowed him out when he lost her; about the fight it took to keep going. He told her about growing up in LA, about the road that eventually brought him back east. Angela had never married, never had children, and she admitted—quietly, almost wistfully—"That might have been different if you hadn't left for LA." She confessed that nothing—no relationship, no connection—had ever matched the bond they'd shared when they were just kids.

The day before, the Kid had gone into the city to have lunch with her. He described it as if it had happened just minutes before. She saw him, smiled like she'd been waiting a lifetime, and wrapped him in a hug that lingered.

Then she kissed him—soft, familiar—and whispered, almost breathless, "You want to hear something crazy? I haven't seen you since we were fifteen, and now I can't go a week without seeing you. I think about you all the time. You're always on my mind. I don't even know how to explain it."

He'd smiled back, a touch of wonder in his voice. "I know—it's crazy. I look forward to seeing you too."

Over lunch, she said it all felt like a dream. And then, as if the universe wanted to prove her point, she reached up and unfastened the top two buttons of her silk blouse—just enough to reveal a small gold heart necklace. The same one he'd given her three months before leaving for LA. She had kept it all these years—a piece of the past resting just over her heart. In that moment, no words were needed. The meaning was as clear as the rain streaking the windows.

"She told me she'd been talking about me to her sister Maria—a woman I'd always liked," the Kid said. "Maria was five years older, sharp as a blade, and well-connected in politics. Back in the day, she'd been Angela's cover on many occasions, slipping her out of the house to see me, no questions asked. Angela said Maria had told her, 'Maybe it was fate.' She'd confessed that in all the years Angela dated and brought men home, something had always been missing. But now? Now, Maria said she had never seen her sister look as happy—or as alive—as she did when she was fifteen, sneaking around with me."

He explained to me that being intimate with other girls was simply a physical act, devoid of any deeper feelings. "For me, it was always just raw lust, a fleeting encounter that left me empty once it was over," the Kid said. "But when the opportunity arose to be intimate with Angela again, I found myself gripped by an unexpected fear—hard to believe, I know, Philly. Yet when we were together, all that doubt melted away, and it felt as if we were transported back to our teens, fresh with innocence and wonder. The emotions surged through me like a tidal wave, enveloping me in passion that felt so familiar, so intoxicating. I made love to her with the same tenderness and intensity that I once shared with Teresa. But later that night, when solitude wrapped around me like a dark cloud, the weight of guilt crashed over me, heavy and suffocating. I fought to bury that remorse deep within, pushing forward as if it could somehow be forgotten."

As the months passed, the talk about Angela grew louder, and it became clear that something had shifted in the Kid's life. Despite being thousands of miles away, I could sense the change every time we spoke. His tone softened when he mentioned her, and the way he described her carried warmth I hadn't heard since he spoke about Teresa.

Though he had been telling me he started going out a little, about six months before, it just wasn't the same. When we were in LA, he reveled in the constant shower of female attention. Now, he said, "the attention means nothing." When he talked about Angela, this was different. Angela wasn't just another name in a long list; she was very special.

I asked him, "Are you seeing anyone else besides Angela?"
He became silent.
I said, "Kid, it's all right. I'm on your side. You know that."
"I know, Philly, and no, I'm not."
I said, "Hang in there; maybe it will work."

And for the first time in a long while, it felt like the Kid was rediscovering joy, like his spark was reigniting after the darkness of Teresa's passing.

I told him I couldn't wait to meet Angela, and I asked him to send me some pictures. Amy was curious too—she wanted to see the woman who had managed to bring the Kid back to life. When the pictures arrived, I understood immediately. Angela was stunning, the kind of beauty that stops you in your tracks. But beyond her looks, there was something about the way the Kid spoke about her that made me feel like I already knew her. She had sparked something in him that hadn't been touched since Teresa—a connection that ran deeper than appearances.

One day, JJ shared a story with me that revealed just how much Angela had been through. She had recently broken up with an abusive, controlling ex-boyfriend named Gary—a man she was physically afraid of.

One evening, Angela was supposed to meet the Kid for dinner, but at the last minute, she canceled. Concerned, the Kid pressed her for answers. When she wouldn't say much, he went to her apartment.

She hesitated to open the door, but the Kid told her, "If you don't open the door, I'm going to open it from the outside." When she finally opened the door, she wouldn't look at him. Sensing something was wrong, he gently turned her face toward him—and that's when he saw it. A massive bruise darkened her left eye, a painful reminder of the violence she had endured.

Angela tried to reassure him, saying, "Please, just let me handle this. I have already called the police and filed a report. I told them it was my ex-boyfriend, Gary, who did it. They said they'd pick him up for questioning, but without his confession or proof, there's nothing they can do. It's just my word against his." Her voice trembled as she explained the situation, revealing the years of fear and manipulation she had endured.

"Dom," she said softly, "I don't want to get you involved in this. I dated Gary on and off for years. He's abusive sometimes, and every time I tried to break away, he'd find a way to make me change my mind. I guess it was my weakness—my fear of being alone. I know I need to get away from him, but I've been so scared."

She went on to explain that about a year ago, he was in some type of gunfight, and he was almost killed. "I know this sounds terrible," she admitted, "but I remember lying in bed after I found out, thinking how much better my life would be if he were dead."

I could only imagine the storm brewing inside the Kid as he listened to her story. He wasn't the type to stand by and let someone he cared about suffer. Angela's vulnerability—her courage in sharing her story—must have struck a chord deep within him. And while I didn't know exactly how he planned to handle the situation, one thing was certain: the Kid wouldn't let her face this alone. Angela had found someone who would fight for her, someone who understood the weight of her fears and the strength it took to confront them. And in doing so, she had unknowingly reignited a part of the Kid that had been dormant for far too long.

Angela told him more. "He has threatened to harm me if I don't let him back in my life. He said, 'No one will ever have me except him.' Since reconnecting with you, I've discovered something within myself that I hadn't recognized since we were kids—something I've been searching for my entire life. But now I feel scared and alone, and I don't want you to get involved.

"Gary warned me that he knows who you are, and if I didn't end things with you, he would kill you. I'm terrified, Dom, and I don't know what to do."

She looked at him with trembling eyes. "You know I'm falling in love with you again—deeper than I could have ever imagined—but I want to protect you from all this. You have your kids to think about. What would happen to them if something happened to you? I know you have a team of tough guys around you. I know who your grandfather was. But Gary is unstable and unpredictable. He's connected to the mob—today's mob—and that terrifies me. My father is probably rolling over in his grave, knowing who I got involved with. It's ironic; he never wanted me to be with you because of who your grandfather was. And what do I do? I go and get involved with an actual mobster."

"Angela, what's his full name?" the Kid asked.

She looked confused. "Why?"

"Because when someone threatens me," he said calmly, "I like to know who they are, just in case. I want to run a background check on him."

Angela hesitated. "Dom, he's very dangerous. I'm afraid of what he would do if he learned you were looking into him."

"Don't worry," the Kid said. "He won't find out. I'll be discreet. My people are very good at this; everything will be fine. Just tell me his name."

She finally relented. "Gary Guccini, but remember, he has mob ties. He's affiliated with the Barbieri family. I know you probably still have a lot of connections in that world, but I don't want you involved. You know what they're capable of, and I'm afraid of what he's capable of. He wouldn't think twice about killing you."

The Kid gave her a steady look. "Believe me, Angela, things aren't that different in LA. Like you said, I know exactly what these people are capable of, but I need you to promise me something: don't think or worry about this again. And don't mention our conversation to anyone, ever."

Angela looked taken aback.

"Do you understand?" he asked again.

She nodded. "Yes."

"He is never going to bother you again," the Kid said. Then he told her he would be back shortly and asked her to make them a drink. "I know you could use one," he added, kissing her gently on the lips before leaving her apartment.

Once outside, he got into his car and immediately called JJ. "JJ, find Gary Guccini, an associate with the Barbieri family. I want him now, and I want him breathing. Call me as soon as you have him."

JJ didn't ask questions. "I'll get back to you," he said.

Early the next morning, while he and Angela were still in bed, the Kid received a call from JJ. "We found him."

"Where?" the Kid asked.

"Number 2."

"I'm on my way," the Kid replied. He got up, got dressed quickly, and told Angela he had to go.

"Please be careful," she said.

He smiled, kissed her gently, and replied, "I'll call you later."

After that day, no one ever saw or heard from Gary Guccini again. As it turned out, he was a wannabe with the Barbieri family—not a made guy. I suspect the Kid made the appropriate calls, because no one ever inquired about Gary again.

I later learned from JJ that when the Kid arrived at house number 2—our code for one of the safe houses we used for various operations—Gary was already tied to a chair with plastic restraints. He told JJ to cut him loose.

When JJ released him, Gary stood and met the Kid's stare.
"You know who I am, right?" the Kid asked.
Gary nodded.
"I understand you're a tough guy with connections to the Barbieri family who likes to smack around women. Well, now it's time to prove just how tough you are."
What followed was a brutal beating—merciless, nearly to the point of death—until JJ stepped in.
"Let me handle this, Kid," JJ said firmly. "This isn't your thing anymore."
The Kid paused, considering his words, and said, "I don't want to see him again."
JJ nodded. "I'll take care of it."
No one ever saw Gary again.
Later that day, the Kid called Angela. He reassured her everything was fine, and he would take her out for dinner and explain. During dinner, he explained that he had some people talk to Gary, and he agreed to never contact her again, and to leave the state immediately and not return. He added that those who had spoken to Gary were quite persuasive. The Kid smiled and said, "You see, Gary is not the only one with connections in that world."
Angela accepted this explanation, or at least she didn't ask any questions or press the issue, and Gary's name never came up again. This marked the beginning of a new chapter for the Kid, who eventually introduced Angela to his children, his sister, and his mom, and things appeared to be going wonderfully. The Kid included Angela in almost everything, especially family gatherings. She got along great with his mom, sister, and the kids—who grew to really like her.
Just before Amy and I were due to head back home from Germany for good, I learned that the Kid and Angela had called it quits. I didn't get all the details; he simply said, "It wasn't going to work out. I still haven't gotten over Teresa. I just can't deal with all this grief and guilt."

Every time we spoke about Angela, there was a tenderness in his voice that told me she had once meant so much to him. I tried to encourage him, telling him to hang in there, that maybe this relationship could bring some stability to his life, and that it might be good for his kids to see their father in a steady, loving relationship. But no matter how much I pressed, he simply wouldn't listen.

"It's over," he kept saying, leaving no room for further discussion.

Deep inside, I hoped for his sake and the sake of his children, that it wasn't the end of it.

While I was in Germany, the Kid managed to take a few trips back to California—mini vacations that, over time, evolved into something more meaningful. During these trips, he always took Angela, and they spent a lot of time with Jimmy and Beth. Somehow, with each encounter, Beth and Angela began to get closer, and they kept in touch. Beth, who had always been like a big sister to the Kid, saw something in Angela that reminded her of the connection he once had with Teresa. She would often remark that Angela possessed many of the qualities the Kid had cherished in the past, and she wanted nothing more than to see him settle down in a stable, happy relationship.

But now, more than a month had passed since the Kid had last seen or spoken with Angela. He went out occasionally, but those at the office noticed he never seemed truly happy. Whatever female companionship he sought was nothing more than passing the time. It was clear that his heart was aching again—only this time, it was for Angela. And still, he couldn't shake the guilt.

CHAPTER TWENTY-FOUR
ANGELA WALKS IN

So, imagine my shock when I saw Angela walk into the ballroom at the Waldorf. She was almost three hours late from when the function began. The Kid's fate had taken a surprising turn. She was assigned a seat at Table 7, right next to the Kid's seat. At first, while sitting with us at Table 17, the Kid had his back turned to Table 7, and I couldn't help myself. I nudged him and said, "Turn around . . . Is that, Angela?"

With genuine surprise playing across his face, he replied, "Yes, and I see Beth's fingerprints all over this." Without a moment's hesitation, he got up and walked over to her. After a brief, warm exchange, he brought her back to our table and introduced her to everyone. I'd seen her photos before, and while they hinted at her beauty, nothing compared to meeting her in person. She was exquisite—every bit as stunning as they said, with a natural radiance and a sweetness that seemed to flow effortlessly.

The chemistry between the Kid and Angela was palpable the

moment she sat down. Everyone at our table could sense it. The conversation quickly turned lively as we continued to reminisce about the old days—stories of the Kid and me growing up, of misadventures and shared memories that filled the room with laughter and an easy camaraderie.

As Angela heard us refer to Dominic as the Kid, she finally asked, "What's with the Kid name?"

We all smiled. Thessaly, utterly absorbed in the stories, gave a light chuckle and said, "You're late for that one." Laughter rippled around the table.

The Kid leaned in and said, "I'll explain it later, but no one from LA calls me Dominic. They all know me as the Kid."

The Kid went on to share a few stories about him and Angela before he left for LA—their secret rendezvous and shared experiences. Our table, bathed in warm ambient light and attended by two waiters who hovered nearby with an almost ritualistic dedication, became the epicenter of attention in the room.

At one point, while one of the waiters was refilling wine glasses, the Kid asked, "What's your name?"

The waiter replied, "Russ."

With a mischievous glint in his eye, and pointing toward Angela, the Kid said, "Russ, you know she really loves fine wine. Do you think you could find us a special bottle of a top Red Grand Cru Burgundy?"

Although Russ's face betrayed his uncertainty, he quickly got to work, calling someone in charge, and within minutes, a sommelier arrived at our table.

The sommelier inquired politely, "Do you have any particular Red Grand Cru Burgundy in mind, sir?"

"Surprise us," the Kid said. "Bring something top shelf that you think she'll enjoy."

In less than five minutes, a bottle arrived. Initially, the Kid reached for his own glass, which the sommelier had filled for a taste, but then, with a decisive gesture, he swiveled and said, "No, let her try it."

The sommelier immediately poured a taste for Angela. She sampled the wine, closed her eyes for a heartbeat, and then smiled softly, declaring it was perfect.

The moment was contagious, as I said, "Well, if it's that good, I want to taste it." Soon everyone around joined in the levity of the toasted atmosphere. The Kid promptly ordered a few more bottles, setting the stage for a night that was as celebratory as it was transformative.

For the rest of the evening, we talked, reminisced, and savored the wines, until around midnight. When the Kid danced with Angela, you could see the love flowing. Despite the buoyant mood at the table, there were moments when the Kid briefly left to dance with Joanne, and then Natalie, who both insisted. And each time I glanced up, I could see Angela's sparkling face watching the Kid intently on the dance floor—I wasn't sure if it was jealousy, or sorrow, or a combination of both. One thing was for sure: despite past chapters closing, there was still something very much alive between him and Angela.

The next day, around noon, I picked up the phone and called the Kid. I wasn't sure where he was—or more importantly, if he was alone—but my gut told me he wasn't. Sure enough, when he answered, I asked, "Can you talk?" and he simply replied, "No, I'm still sleeping."

"Call me when you can," I said, and he murmured, "Talk later."

That afternoon, his call finally came through. My anticipation got the better of me, and I said, "Okay, now what the hell is going on?" He chuckled, and I pressed him further. "Come on, give me some details. I assume you were with Angela last night?"

To my surprise, he casually admitted he'd been with Natalie. "It just happened," he said, as if it were nothing.

I couldn't hide my shock: "How did that happen? What about Angela?"

His response was almost dismissive. "Hey, Angela is not going to work."

I was stunned. "Are you nuts? Were you drunk last night? Didn't you see the chemistry between the two of you? Everyone at the table saw it. A blind man could've seen it."

But the Kid's tone turned resigned. "Too much has happened. I have been through too much, losing Teresa. I can't do this again. The guilt and fear I feel is enormous. Like I told you, when I left Angela to come to LA, I broke her heart, and she carried that pain so many years. I probably screwed up her life, and that's how she wound up with an asshole like Gary.

"I can't do this again; I can't risk it. My insides are in a knot. I just don't think there's any future with her anymore. I don't think there's a future with anyone for me anymore."

I couldn't believe what I was hearing. "Wow, I never thought I'd see this. The Kid—in total denial." I tried to make him understand. "Look, I don't care about the details of what went down, or what she did or didn't do. I do know that after listening to you talk about Angela these last months, and seeing you both together last night, there's no mistaking how she feels about you—and how you feel about her. You can't let her go, Kid; you're going to regret that decision." I pressed on. "And how the hell did you wind up with Natalie last night?" Somehow, the story was muddled in my mind.

"I took Angela home. She pleaded with me to stay, but I couldn't. I was overwhelmed with guilt and fear. I ended the conversation with her feeling totally confused. Yes, I have deep feelings for Angela, but I feel crushed inside with guilt and regret."

In that raw moment, I realized the Kid was deeply conflicted. Was it the unbearable guilt from Teresa's passing? A haunting reminder that he hadn't been able to save her? Was he still too afraid to let go of her memory fully? Or was he simply regressing to his old habits—the wild ways of his youth back in LA? Was Angela just nostalgia? I didn't have the answers; only time would reveal the truth.

The Kid continued. "When I left Angela's apartment, feeling isolated and alone by the weight of the conversation and my decision, I knew I needed to talk to someone who truly understood me on that intimate level.

"I got in the car and called Natalie. My voice cracked when she answered. I'd woken her, but she told me to come over anyway. When I arrived at her hotel room, the air felt heavy, like it somehow knew I was bringing a storm with me. We sat on the couch, quiet at first. Then, over the gentle clink of wine glasses and the slow unraveling of the night, I just . . . broke open.

I cried—more than I expected to. I vented. I stumbled over my words, trying to untangle the chaos inside me. I talked about Teresa—about the guilt that wouldn't let me breathe. About how every time I was with Angela, I could feel the guilt from Teresa's absence, like I was cheating on her. I didn't know what I wanted anymore. I feel like I'm chasing ghosts, trying to love someone through a hole in my own heart.

"At some point, Natalie reached for me, and I let her. Maybe I needed comfort. Maybe I just wanted to feel something that didn't ache. We ended up in each other's arms. For a few fleeting moments, I thought maybe this was what I needed—someone to pull me out of myself, to silence the voices in my head. But even as we lay there, tangled in the quiet after, I could feel the guilt tightening around my chest like a belt.

"My mind was a war zone—regret clashing with shame, and the worst part was that I didn't even know who I was trying to make feel better. Her? Me? Teresa's memory? Was I just running away from Angela? I don't know.

"Just after sunup, I left. I couldn't sit in that room any longer without drowning in it. I drove home on autopilot, every red light feeling like a judgment. When I finally got home, I didn't even bother to undress. I collapsed into bed, stared at the ceiling, and let the silence wrap around me like punishment. I didn't sleep. I just existed, alone, unsure of what I'd just done—or why.

"Let's talk more on Monday," the Kid said. "I need to relax my brain and think. I'm mentally exhausted."

I managed a weary, "See you on Monday. Have a good

weekend." And with that, our conversation fell into an uneasy silence, leaving me with even more questions than answers about loyalty, love, and the complexities of moving on.

It was clear that Angela had ignited something in the Kid that I hadn't seen from him in years. I understood then that Angela had sparked a light within him that had been missing since Teresa. Her influence was subtle but profound; even Beth had observed that the connection between the Kid and Angela echoed the deep bond he once shared with Teresa.

Monday morning, the air in the office felt heavier than usual as the Kid walked in. I caught his eye, and without a word, I followed him into his office and closed the door behind us. I needed answers, so I asked, "What's going on?"

He paused, his gaze distant for a moment before he spoke quietly. "I'm not really sure. I've been thinking a lot about what you said Saturday about Angela. Maybe you're right—I just can't stop thinking about her." Then, with a mix of vulnerability and bewilderment, he added, "You want to hear something crazy? When I left Natalie on Saturday morning, she told me she loved me, as she always has, and she told me to patch things up with Angela. She said even she saw the chemistry between us."

I couldn't help but laugh, half in disbelief and half in empathy. "The only one not reading the tea leaves here is you, Kid."

He simply nodded, troubled yet contemplative, and murmured, "Maybe everyone is right. I need to think about it."

Over the next few days, I noticed a change in him. He worked, yes, but his focus was fragmented, as if a storm raged behind his eyes every time he tried to concentrate.

Then, on Thursday, around 11:00 a.m., as I was deep in conversation with JJ in my office, the Kid walked in. His mood was pensive yet determined.

"JJ, do me a favor," he ordered. "Find out where Angela is right now if you could."

JJ never questioned the Kid's requests. Without hesitation, he headed off to make the calls and returned within thirty minutes with the information: Angela was on her way to lunch with a client at La Grand Brasserie on 43rd Street, between 2nd and 3rd Ave. I looked at the Kid and said, "Good choice."

He just smiled.

"JJ, come on, you drive me, so I don't have to park," the Kid joked lightly before heading out with JJ, disappearing for the rest of the day.

The next day, as JJ recounted the drive, he mentioned the gridlocked traffic along 43rd Street and how, when they finally neared the restaurant, the Kid had gotten out with a terse, "I will call you. Stick around."

I could almost picture him, standing on the busy sidewalk, scanning for that one familiar figure.

Sure enough, as the Kid approached the restaurant—partly open to the beautiful sunlight that day—he spotted Angela. She was sitting, engaged in conversation with another woman. Angela, poised and radiant, was facing 43rd Street, from where he was emerging. The moment their eyes met, she excused herself from her conversation and stood up. In one fluid motion, she walked toward him and, without hesitation, threw her arms around him and kissed him. It wasn't subtle or secretive. Right there in front of onlookers, their reunion was an unspoken declaration.

"Come, meet my client—she's a friend," she announced lightly, introducing the stranger as Sally.

The Kid, never one to let a moment pass without charm, greeted Sally with his trademark easy smile. "It's a pleasure to meet you, though I don't want to interrupt anything."

Sally, ever gracious, replied, "It's great to finally meet you. I've heard so much about you." And with that, she excused herself, leaving them to bask in the charged intimacy that had suddenly reclaimed the day.

For the next two hours, the Kid and Angela remained together at their table, as if everything else had faded away.

Other patrons at the restaurant would catch snippets of laughter, tender glances, hand holding, and a sense of the deep connection that defied the Kid's earlier hesitations.

Finally, breaking the hush of their private world, the Kid leaned in and said softly, "Call your office and tell them you're not coming back—ever."

Angela's eyes sparkled as she considered his words, and after a brief, thoughtful pause, she smiled and murmured, "What a wonderful idea. I love you. I think I have been waiting for you since you left for LA."

Minutes later, the Kid called JJ on his phone. "Where are you?" he asked.

"Sitting on 3rd Ave," JJ replied without missing a beat.

"Stay there. We're coming to you," the Kid said, and JJ soon drove them back to Angela's apartment in Brooklyn. The Kid stayed there until 8:00 a.m. the following morning—hours that I can only imagine were spent in the quiet intimacy of long conversation, shared dreams, passionate lovemaking, and perhaps the healing that comes from finally embracing a new love.

In the early light, JJ picked him up, drove him home to change, and later, he returned to the office. When he walked in that day, I simply looked at him and knew. Our eyes met, and we both smiled—the unspoken understanding passing between us was clear. From that day forward, the Kid was never without Angela.

I sat there, reflecting on the tumult of the last few weeks—the turmoil, the heartbreak, the restless nights, and the sudden, breathtaking reconnection with feelings that he had long since buried under grief. It was as though, in Angela, the Kid had rediscovered a part of himself that had been dormant since Teresa's passing—a spark that now promised new beginnings, hope, and the potential for healing. And in that quiet moment, surrounded by the hum of our busy office life, I knew that the Kid's heart had finally found something worth fighting for.

After a few months of building a fragile yet hopeful life with Angela and his kids, the Kid decided it was time to embrace a fresh start—a new beginning that he called simply "a fresh start."

He said, "Even though a part of me could never fully move past Teresa, I eventually realized that she would have wanted me to be happy—to see the kids happy—with someone who could provide the nurturing guidance our kids so desperately need. Angela did that in her own gentle way."

I remember a conversation we had one quiet afternoon in the office. The Kid confided in me about how much he still loved and missed Teresa. His voice carried the weight of both devotion and grief—a raw, unguarded moment that laid bare the depth of his loss.

"She was so incredible," he said, his eyes distant with memory.

It was clear that no amount of time would ever erase her from his heart.

But then, almost seamlessly, he shifted to speaking about Angela—the way she had stepped into his life with grace, how she cared for his children as if they were her own, and how she brought a steady warmth that had slowly filled the emptiness he'd carried for so long.

"At first," he admitted, "I wondered if what I felt was just the echo of old emotions—some kind of youthful infatuation rekindled. Maybe just puppy love for the first girl I ever loved."

He paused, then added with quiet certainty, "But now I know. What Angela and I have is something deeper, something real. It's stronger than what we remembered from our younger days. I love her for who she is, for everything we're building together. In some strange way, it feels like this was always meant to be—like destiny finally caught up to us."

About two weeks earlier, the Kid had had a long conversation with his mother. She spoke with deep affection about Teresa, and then—perhaps more surprisingly—about Angela. She told him she had come to love Angela just as much, and she wondered aloud if maybe God had always intended for his life to be shared with both women.

When he admitted he was thinking about marrying Angela, but still wrestled with guilt, his mother asked gently, "Do you want to marry her because you love her and want to spend your life with her, or because she's perfect for the situation—with the kids and all?"

The question gave him pause. "Maybe both," he replied.

She nodded. "Then figure out which one is stronger."

He took a week to reflect. In the end, he knew the answer. He loved Angela deeply—enough that if there had never been Teresa, never been children, he would marry Angela without a second thought.

When he told his mother that, she smiled and said, "Then I have just one question: What are you waiting for?"

He smiled back. "Thanks, Mom. I love you."

The Kid later shared this story with me. "There are only a few people I really listen to when it comes to matters of the heart—my mother, Jimmy, Beth, and you. I know what the others think, especially after the Waldorf. Now I want to know what you think."

I gave him a knowing smile. "You know what I think. Stop looking for a reason not to do what your heart already knows it wants."

The Kid smiled and nodded. "Thank you."

That same afternoon, he called Misak, his trusted diamond merchant, and said, "I want a three-carat—or so—round natural blue diamond. Let me know when you have something I should see."

Three days later, we were on our way into the city. Misak presented three stones, all round natural blues. The standout was a three-and-a-half-carat round, D color, flawless clarity, excellent cut—a truly rare find. Misak called it the most perfect stone he'd ever sourced.

"But it's super expensive," he warned. "$275,000 with GIA documentation."

He also offered a four-carat stone that appeared perfect to the naked eye for $75,000 less. The Kid didn't hesitate.

"Let's see a setting for the 3.5."

A week later, the ring was delivered to the office. It was spectacular. When I asked when he planned to give it to Angela, the Kid just said, "Soon. But I want it simple—no fanfare, no restaurants."

That Saturday, the kids were all out—little Teresa had plans, and the others were with friends—leaving the house unusually quiet. Angela suggested going out for dinner, but the Kid proposed staying in.

"Let's grill some steaks, open a great bottle of wine."

Angela smiled. "That sounds perfectly romantic."

After dinner, they sat together on the couch. The lights were dim, the music low. The Kid turned to her and said, "I have something to ask you. It's something I knew I wanted to do all the way back in Brooklyn but never got the chance."

Angela's eyes widened.

"Will you marry me?" he asked, revealing the ring box.

Angela gasped, covering her face with both hands as tears poured down her cheeks. She took the box but didn't open it right away.

"Yes. Yes. Yes! I've wanted this my whole life." She threw her arms around him, the unopened box still clutched in one hand. "You have no idea how much I love you," she whispered.

"I think I do," the Kid replied. "Because that's how much I love you. I know it was a long road for me to get here, but I thank God you waited."

She opened the box, saw the diamond, and gasped again. "Oh my God. It's gorgeous."

She slid the ring onto her finger—it fit perfectly. "I'm never taking it off."

The Kid grinned.

Angela jumped up. "I have to call my sister."

She dialed Maria, and as soon as she answered, Angela shouted through happy tears, "You were right. It's on my finger."

They both cried and laughed, and Maria promised to come see it the next day.

"And tell the Kid I love him," she added.

In the days that followed, Angela and the Kid discussed the wedding. He asked what she truly wanted.

"We can go big or small, destination, New Jersey, New York, church—you name it. Whatever you want, we'll make it happen."

After weighing all the options, Angela made her wish clear. She wanted to be married in church, dressed in white, believing with all her heart that her late father would be smiling down on her that day.

For the reception, they chose Ninety Acres in Somerset County, New Jersey—a breathtaking venue, renowned not only for its cuisine but for its old-world charm and intimate elegance. With its stone architecture, expansive grounds, and timeless ambiance, it felt like something lifted from the pages of a classic French novel.

The Kid didn't hesitate. He bought out the entire property for the day, ensuring the event would feel private, personal, and flawless, with seating for up to 120 guests, ensuring the day would be theirs alone.

The wedding day arrived, and it was everything they had hoped for. The ceremony at Assumption of the Blessed Virgin Mary Church was deeply moving—emotional, beautiful, and full of reverence. Angela looked radiant walking down the aisle, and the Kid—rarely one to be shaken—was visibly moved. The reception that followed was intimate and joyful, attended by the children, both mothers, Gloria, me as best man, Maria as maid of honor, the inner circle from STS Security, and a close-knit group of about seventy others made up of old friends and trusted business associates. The Kid even invited Blue Eyes this time.

The entire day flowed effortlessly, filled with laughter, misty eyes, and a joy that felt like a quiet, earned reward for everything the Kid and Angela had endured to finally reach this moment. It wasn't about showing off; it was about love, family, and gratitude.

After the wedding, it became clear that the Kid simply couldn't remain in the house he'd built with Teresa. That home, imbued with her dreams and memories, no longer felt like a place of forward movement—it was a monument to the past. To allow for a real, liberating change, the Kid decided to let Angela shape a new dream.

He mentioned, "I even called the architect, and soon we were set to sit down, sketches in hand, to design a new home that reflected our renewed hopes. This time, the kids would be involved in the conversations too, ensuring that every new corner of our future lived up to the dreams of tomorrow."

Soon after the happy occasion, everything had begun to fall into a promising rhythm. The Kid's new home was beginning to take shape, and STS Security was expanding, our profits growing steadily year by year. I found myself flying to Munich twice a year to check in and see how things were evolving—working closely with our new European president, who had taken over the reins of the Munich office. The Kid, it seemed, had returned to a semblance of his old self: more decisive, more driven, yet still marked by both his past grief and the new spark that Angela had ignited.

Back home, Amy and I eventually started joining the Kid and Angela for evenings out and family gatherings. It was heartwarming to see not only the Kid but also his children flourish under Angela's gentle care. She treated the kids with warmth and affection, seamlessly becoming a part of our extended family.

In time, even Amy and Angela found common ground. Over long conversations, Amy confided how close she had once been to Teresa—and how happy she was to witness the Kid's emerging joy. Amy believed that Teresa, with her profound love and commitment, would have wanted nothing more than for him to find stability and contentment in a new relationship.

In quiet moments, as I watched the Kid's tired eyes light up with hope, I saw the long-overdue healing in him. He was finally building a future that carried both the weight of his past and the promise of love—a future in which Angela wasn't a replacement for what he had lost but a partner in creating something entirely new and beautiful for everyone. The future was just beginning.

CHAPTER TWENTY-FIVE
THE PILL RETURNS

One Monday morning, a call came into the receptionist's desk that immediately set my nerves on edge. The caller insisted on speaking with the Kid, saying he had sensitive information about a federal investigation into Dominic Argianno—specifically involving Sammy the Pill.

Our receptionist, who by this time knew that Dominic was also sometimes called the Kid, didn't recognize the name Sammy the Pill, so she asked the caller to leave a number. He refused and warned that she was about to make a serious mistake if she didn't put the call through.

I happened to be walking by the reception desk just as she was asking, "You want me to tell him it's about Sammy the Pill?"

That stopped me cold. I asked, "Who's on the phone?"

She put the call on hold, looking flustered, and said, "He won't give his name, but he says it's about Sammy the Pill and something to do with the Kid."

Realizing this wasn't some routine call, I told her to transfer the call to my office—immediately.

I stepped inside, closed the door, and picked up the line. The voice on the other end was clearly disguised—digitally altered—and he demanded to speak directly with the Kid.

I said firmly, "You've got two options: either tell me what this is about, and if it's relevant, I'll make sure the Kid gets the message; or hang up now, and you can be assured your call won't get through—ever."

He paused and asked, "Who is this?"

I shot back, "I'm the person you're talking to."

Then he got to it: there was a confidential federal investigation currently underway. According to him, Sammy the Pill had confessed he was pressured into lying on the stand during the Philip Fiore trial. The caller claimed the Kid was behind the coercion and said the Feds were now stitching together a case that could tie him directly to it.

I pressed him. "If that's true, why are you being so generous with the information?"

His answer was chilling. "Simple—I want five million dollars in unmarked bills if you want to know where they're holding Sammy the Pill. "

I asked for a number where I could reach him. He flatly refused. "No numbers," he said. "I'll call you again on Friday. That should give you enough time to check out what I just told you." Then he hung up.

As soon as the line went dead, a wave of regret hit me. I couldn't shake the thought—I should've taken care of Sammy back in LA the moment the Kid told me to lose him. He was a problem then, and now he was a bigger one. One thing was certain: this would be the last time Sammy brought grief to our doorstep.

Without wasting a second, I marched straight into the Kid's office. He was in a meeting with Howard Cohen, our in-house CPA, and Jim Rodriguez, our IT guru. The Kid must've seen the storm brewing on my face because he immediately asked them to excuse us. Howard and Jim gathered their papers and left. I shut the door behind them.

"What's going on?" he asked.

"You're not going to fucking believe it," I said, and then I laid out everything—the call, the demand, the threat. When I finished, a long silence filled the room.

Finally, the Kid asked, "Do you believe it?"

"Yes," I said without hesitation. "Why else would someone make that kind of call unless it was real?"

He sighed. "All right, let's see if we can get out ahead of this."

I nodded. Then, with a seriousness that chilled even me, I said, "If this is true, and Sammy's in play, there's no room for negotiation. This time, the Pill is dead."

The Kid's eyes met mine, and he gave a single nod. In that moment, we were on the same page. That day marked a turning point. The Kid and I both knew that if Sammy's scandal—or even the hint of it—got any closer to home, we'd be out of options. I told myself then, for the last time: Sammy would never cause us trouble again.

We had to figure out if this story was legit, a setup to force us into trying to cover it up, or just a scam for a fast five million dollars. The Kid wasted no time—he picked up the phone and called JJ into the office. He laid everything out and told him to dig—fast. JJ got to work immediately, while the Kid began calling in serious favors. His Rolodex ran deep—federal judges, congressmen, senators, DOD, DHS, FBI, CIA—even contacts in the White House.

It took nearly two days, but we finally started turning up intel. And what we found was unsettling. Apparently, it was all true. Cheryl Adams—the head prosecutor in the Southern District of New York and a rising political star—was running the investigation. The case was locked down so tightly that only she, her right hand, and three US marshals knew where Sammy was being held.

Friday finally arrived, and we hunkered down in the office. Our surveillance team was on full alert, tracking every incoming call, though we knew tracing the line would be a long shot. We had agreed in advance: neither the Kid nor I would take the call—this job fell to JJ. Sure enough, around 2:30 p.m., the phone rang. The same disguised voice from before, distorted and cold, demanded to speak directly with the Kid.

The call was routed to our conference room. JJ hit the speaker button and answered with a crisp, controlled, "Hello."

"I want to talk to the Kid directly," the voice repeated.

JJ didn't flinch. "Look, I know you want five million," he said, his tone firm as steel. "If I like what you have to say, that can happen. If not, you're wasting my time. And one more thing—under no circumstances are you going to talk to anyone but me. My name is Jeff."

He used a fake name, assuming the call was being recorded.

There was a brief pause before the voice replied, "I want five million in unmarked bills. I'll tell you where and when. You'll get the Pill's location only after the money is paid."

JJ pressed. "How do we know the information is real?"

"You'll just have to trust me."

JJ leaned in. "Listen, you're calling the shots, but we're only putting up two point five million up front. The rest comes after we verify the information."

The voice turned sharp. "This is nonnegotiable. I want all the money up front."

JJ didn't budge. "That's not going to happen. You can hang up if you want—we'll take our chances. Your call."

In our world, leverage was everything. We knew the guy wouldn't just disappear. But what was his endgame? He wanted five million in untraceable cash, but we still didn't know his endgame.

There was a long silence. Then finally, the voice said, "Fine. I'll call you Monday with instructions. Get the money ready." *Click.* The line went dead.

I immediately checked the trace. The call had bounced through multiple servers across Europe—no pattern, no origin, no digital trail.

Whoever we were dealing with knew exactly what they were doing.

Monday morning rolled around, and the tension in the air was thick enough to cut with a knife. Over the weekend, the Kid had pulled every string he could think of, calling in favors from some of the most powerful people he knew. But nothing—absolutely nothing—came back with any useful information. It was like trying to grab smoke.

The Kid, always prepared for the unexpected, had a private safe in his office with five million dollars in unmarked hundred-dollar bills—ready for situations just like this. Only four people knew the combination: the Kid, me, his late wife Teresa, and Alice, our office manager. I wasn't sure if he had given Angela the combination.

At 11:00 a.m., the call came in. We were all gathered in the conference room, waiting. JJ answered, and the disguised voice said, "Wire five million USD to:

Beneficiary Name: Zhao Ming
Bank Name: Guangdong Central Commerce Bank, Shenzhen Branch
Branch Address: 88 Lotus Road, Futian District, Shenzhen, China
Account Number: 3827-4169-2046
SWIFT Code: GDCNCNSZ
CNAPS Code: 123456789."

JJ, quick on his feet, replied, "I thought you wanted unmarked bills?"

The voice snapped back, "Change in plans."

We had a whole team of our people ready to monitor a physical drop, but this sudden shift threw us. JJ glanced at the Kid, who nodded and held up one finger—signaling to change the up-front offer to one million.

"You changed the deal," JJ said, "so now I'm changing it. You get one million wired. If it checks out, you get the rest."

The caller exploded. "You asshole! The Kid deserves to go to jail! It's either my way or no deal!"

Without missing a beat, JJ shot back, "Fuck off," and hung up.

For a moment, JJ looked uncertain—second-guessing if he'd gone too far.

But the Kid, calm as ever, said, "Exactly the way I would've handled it."

JJ exhaled. The Kid added, "Let's see if this prick calls back. In the meantime, we keep digging."

Less than five minutes later, the receptionist buzzed us. "The caller's back."

JJ picked up. "I'm listening."

The voice, now slightly more subdued, said, "Two point five million wired up front, and the rest after it checks out."

JJ didn't flinch. "That deal left when you changed the rules. You want the one million wired? Let's proceed. Otherwise, you're wasting my time."

A long silence. You could almost hear someone being consulted in the background.

Then: "Follow the wiring instructions I gave you by tomorrow morning, 10:00 a.m. sharp. No tricks. I'll call an hour after the funds clear."

As soon as JJ hung up, the Kid said, "I've got a bad feeling about this. Why switch from cash to wire? If they wanted the money to disappear, they'd stick with cash. Now they'll settle for one million wired, which has a trail. They could've insisted on two point five million. Think about it: once we wire the money, it confirms we want the info. If we want the info, that makes us look guilty."

He paused, then gave the order: "Hold off on the wire. We need information. Let's hit the phones again—hard."

That afternoon, and deep into the night, we worked every source we had. Finally, at 1:00 a.m., the Kid's phone rang. I don't know who was on the other end, but when he hung up, he looked at me and said, "We found him. Sammy's being held in an FBI safe house in New York—on 45th Street, just off Broadway."

We didn't know how long they'd keep him there, but we had to assume it would be until they brought charges against the Kid. Time was not on our side.

The Kid made the call. "No more talking to this mystery caller. If this is a setup, we're not giving them anything."

JJ, with the help of Jim, our IT guru, set up deeper, more advanced surveillance on incoming calls—hoping the caller would slip. Meanwhile, the Kid turned to me. "I want you to check out this safe house. Take a few dependable guys with you."

I nodded, grabbed a couple of hours of sleep, then met the team back at the office by 5:00 a.m. We headed into the city.

At the same time, the receptionist was given new instructions: stall the caller.

Sure enough, at 10:00 a.m., the phone rang. She put him on hold. He waited two minutes, then hung up. He called back immediately.

She told him Jeff was in a meeting but would be available soon. She put him on hold again—another minute.

When she went back and picked up to say Jeff was almost done—that's when he lost it. He started berating her, threatening her, ranting about how the Kid was going to jail.

In his fury, he forgot himself, lost track of time, and stayed on the line nearly four minutes. Long enough for our surveillance team to get a trace.

The call led us to a quiet residential neighborhood in Queens. JJ dispatched a team.

The next morning, two men walked out of the Queens house carrying large briefcases—gear used to mask digital calls. They got into a blue Ford pickup, and our team followed.

Photos and facial recognition confirmed it: they were undercover cops assigned to the assistant US attorney in the Southern District of New York. It had all been a setup—a sting to entrap the Kid.

Thank God we didn't wire the money. Without that, they had nothing. But that raised a new question: Was Sammy's testimony strong enough to bring the Kid down? If so, why the elaborate sting?

Back at the office, the Kid, JJ, and I regrouped. We kept surveillance on Sammy's safe house, waiting for a move. Weeks passed. Sammy stayed put—except for short walks, flanked by US marshals.

Then, one morning, the Kid called us into his office. "Pull the surveillance on Sammy," he said. "It's definitely a sting. I got a call from an old contact at the federal prosecutor's office in DC. They're using Sammy as bait. Trying to get us to make a move on him. If we do, they'll try to flip the shooters and use them to testify against me."

JJ shook his head. "Fucking prosecutors. She's more corrupt than La Cosa Nostra."

We laughed, but the Kid stayed serious. "I want to know who put her up to it. My contact said he didn't know, but he'd try to find out. This didn't come from her. It had to come from above."

We pushed every connection we had. Most of our usual sources were in the dark. This was high level.

Weeks turned into a month. Sammy was moved. We didn't try to find out where because we didn't care.

Then, out of nowhere, the Kid got a call—from someone in a senator's office. An insider on the intelligence committee. The voice on the other end told him what we feared: Senator Clayton Hargrave of Kentucky—chairman of the powerful intelligence committee—was the mastermind behind it all.

Hargrave had a grudge. The Kid had backed his rival in the last election, and Hargrave had warned him: switch sides, or face consequences.

The Kid, never one to respond well to threats, stood his ground and declined to withdraw his support. Unfortunately, Hargrave prevailed in the election and retained his seat. Now, this was his way of settling the score. The Kid realized he had made a powerful enemy—one who might need to be dealt with.

CHAPTER TWENTY-SIX
MEET THE PRESS

About six months later, everything was flourishing. The business was thriving, and the Kid and Angela couldn't have been happier. Amy and I were spending more and more time with them, and the children, who had once eyed this new family dynamic with caution, were settling in nicely—adjusting to their dad and Angela forming a truly loving marriage.

Then one ordinary Sunday morning, while watching the news, I saw NBC's *Meet the Press* run a shocking story. Unnamed sources claimed that Seal Team Six Security—owned by Dominic Argianno—was under investigation by the DOJ for alleged criminal activity. The report hinted that Argianno might have used threats or corrupt persuasion to influence a witness in a federal case in CA many years ago—a violation notably covered under federal law, specifically 18 U.S.C. §1512. With that detail firmly in place, the allegations took on an even graver tone.

Without hesitating, I grabbed my cell phone and called the Kid. "Are you watching *Meet the Press* this morning?" I asked.

He admitted he hadn't been awake yet.

"Well, get up—something is up," I insisted. I couldn't hide my disbelief as I continued. "I can't believe the BS they're running on these shows. NBC apparently has inside information that the DOJ is investigating you on criminal charges. I know it's all BS, but we might need to address it for PR purposes." I said all this just in case the phone lines were being monitored. "Do you want me to reach out to Sophia?"

"Not yet," the Kid said. "Let me see what's going on first."

Across town, the ripples of this scandal were already reaching political circles. Senator Clayton Hargrave of Kentucky, the chairman of the powerful intel committee, a figure known for his decisive and no-nonsense approach, was cornered by reporters about the allegations. In a live interview that afternoon, his face betrayed both shock and determination.

"If these allegations prove true," he declared, "we'll have no choice but to look into canceling Seal Team Six Security's government contracts." His statement was a stark reminder that the implications extended far beyond personal reputations. The integrity of multi-hundred-million-dollar contracts and political careers were at stake.

Monday morning started with an air of urgency. By 7:00 a.m., long before the rest of the staff arrived, certain senior members of the team were called in. Even Peter, who wasn't typically involved in these executive meetings, was summoned. The group—comprised of the Kid, myself, Peter, JJ, Alice, Sophia, Howard, and Frank—gathered in the conference room, the tension palpable.

The Kid wasted no time. "We need to find out how this BS info was leaked to NBC and who leaked it. Then we'll know who the enemy is. I suspect it was Senator Hargrave—he's still bitter about the Sammy the Pill entrapment case falling apart. Let's see if we can verify this."

The only people who knew the correct facts about the California case in question were the Kid, myself, JJ, and Peter.

Turning to Sophia, he asked, "How do you think we should handle this with the press? They'll be all over us."

Sophia, ever the voice of caution, replied, "Until we know more, I think you should avoid meeting with them."

The Kid's response was immediate and firm. "Sophia, you should know me better. I don't run and hide. I'll let them corner me, and I'll simply say the allegations are unfounded."

Peter interjected, his tone measured but concerned. "But if you do that, Kid, it could backfire if they produce any evidence—even if it's fraudulent evidence."

"I understand," the Kid replied, his voice steady. "But running and hiding is not how I think we should play this, Peter."

The Kid began delegating tasks with precision. "Sophia, draft a list of questions you think the press will throw at me, along with possible answers. Alice, make sure the reception staff knows to answer no questions other than no comment, and admit no one to the office without your personal clearance—no visitors, period. Peter, reach out to your contacts at the DOJ and see what you can dig up. Frank, you and Howard start going over the government contracts and see if we have any legal exposure. Let's all grab some coffee, and I want Philly and JJ in my office now. That's it, everybody."

As the meeting broke, JJ and I followed the Kid into his office. Once the door closed, his tone shifted, becoming sharper and more focused. "In the meantime, I want you both to start digging and find something we can use against Senator Hargrave. We need to find something on him, and it needs to be good. Reach out to everyone—disgruntled former staffers, anyone with dirt. Philly, find out who's controlling crime in Kentucky and get to them. Someone has to have something on this piece of shit, and we need to find it."

We nodded, understanding the gravity of the task, and left the office to get to work. The stakes had never felt higher.

By the end of the day, news crews were set up outside our building, like sentinels waiting for the Kid to emerge. He received a call from Angela—she'd seen on the security cameras that news trucks had also gathered on the street outside their home compound. The property, a sprawling twelve-acre estate in Convent Station just outside Morristown, was now part of the breaking story.

Although the Kid usually left the office by driving out of our underground private parking garage, today he decided to walk out and address the press head-on. Stepping into the glare of the flashing cameras, the Kid was instantly swarmed by reporters with microphones thrust forward. The onslaught began, and here's how it unfolded:

Reporter 1: "What do you think of the accusations from NBC News that the DOJ is investigating you for witness tampering?"

The Kid: "I think it's totally preposterous—simply false. I wish the press would wait until they've seen real evidence and stop using anonymous sources. It's beyond me how anyone could think I had anything to do with it."

Reporter 2: "Senator Hargrave mentioned canceling your government contracts. Is your company in trouble?"

The Kid: "Not at all. Our company is on solid footing. We operate fully above board and within the law. We can withstand any investigation thrown our way."

Reporter 3: "What evidence do you offer to refute the witness tampering claims?"

The Kid: "We comply with every law. There is simply no evidence to support these wild allegations. How can I offer evidence against false accusations?"

Reporter 4: "Why is NBC sensationalizing this story without any verified proof?"

The Kid: "NBC is chasing ratings, not facts. They're willing to air unverified rumors from anonymous sources if it means higher viewership."

Reporter 5: "Are you considering legal action against those responsible for these false claims, including NBC News?"

The Kid: "My focus is on setting the record straight here and now. Rest assured, if someone attempts to defame my name or the name of this fine company, we will pursue every legal avenue available."

Reporter 6: "Critics say your political ties might be compromising your business decisions. How do you respond?"

The Kid: "My decisions are based solely on what's best for STS Security and the country. Any political insinuations are mere distractions from the truth."

Reporter 7: "Some claim that the investigation is politically motivated because of your support for Senator Hargrave's opponent. Is that accurate?"

The Kid: "I support initiatives that strengthen my company and the nation. Political agendas aside, these allegations are baseless and designed to stir up trouble."

Reporter 8: "What assurances can you give government officials that these allegations won't disrupt your operations?"

The Kid: "Our operations have outlasted many storms. We have robust systems and deep-rooted support from staff and employees around the globe, ensuring that no investigation, however baseless, will derail us."

Reporter 9: "Will you cede any control or step down or step aside during this public controversy?"

The Kid: "Absolutely not. I stand firmly by my leadership, and I'll continue running STS Security with the same dedication and resolve I always have."

Reporter 10: "Do you fear that even fabricated evidence might someday tarnish your reputation?"

The Kid: "I trust that the truth will prevail. We're prepared to expose any fraudulent evidence and remain committed to complete transparency.

"Thank you very much, ladies and gentlemen, but I have to get back to work."

After fielding these ten rapid-fire questions, the Kid's authoritative tone and unwavering composure sent a clear message: the allegations were nothing more than a storm to weather. The press slowly dispersed, leaving behind a buzz of speculation and a deepening sense of urgency inside our organization.

Meanwhile, on Wednesday, in a move that underscored the escalating stakes, news had broken that Senator Hargrave announced the Senate Intelligence Committee would open its own investigation into the allegations. Given that those allegations implicated Dominic Argianno, CEO of Seal Team Six Security, the senator was now recommending to the Department of Defense that no new contracts be signed until the investigation was completed.

The Kid arranged for a high-level meeting with DOD officials scheduled for Friday in Washington, DC.

Early the next morning, he informed me, "I'm heading to DC tomorrow for this crucial meeting. Hold down the fort here."

Although I barely contained my disappointment at being left behind, I knew it was best. His presence in DC was vital. Along with JJ, Peter, Frank, Shelia, the Kid also asked Angela to join him to project an image of family unity and support. Their relationship had grown stronger over time, and she was always eager to be by his side, no matter the circumstances.

They flew our newly purchased company G550 out of Newark and touched down in DC around 8:00 a.m., where a stretch Suburban vehicle awaited their arrival at the airport.

Walking into the Pentagon was no stranger to the Kid. His high-level security clearance and years of experience meant that he navigated its halls with confidence. In a secured conference room, they met with Lt. General McNeill, in charge of government NGO procurements, along with two other military officers. After a brief round of introductions, a captain entered the room and asked the Kid to please follow him.

He was escorted to another room where the secretary of defense, Theodore Blackwood; the chairman of the joint chiefs,

General Edward Kingsley; and the CIA director, Evelyn Hawthorne, awaited him.

The secretary opened with, "What's going on, Dominic? These allegations are causing us a serious problem."

"I agree, Mr. Secretary. They're all BS, but I know that doesn't solve our issues. Senator Hargrave's targeting me, likely due to my support for his electoral opponent. I'm working on a strategy to manage this, but in the meantime, I need to absorb these punches."

Evelyn interjected. "We rely on your German contracts for ongoing CIA operations in Europe. How can we help deflect the senator's pressure?"

"I'm not sure yet, but I will keep you posted," was the response.

Ed added, "You're essential in providing protection details in Italy and Germany for the military, and that's nonnegotiable. We need that to continue."

The Kid nodded steadily.

Secretary Blackwood continued. "We'll do our best to resist canceling contracts based on these allegations, but until the dust settles, the president may halt any new signings—we have three pending. Work on a solution, and keep us posted." He then added, "Evelyn, if we need your intervention, we'll reach out."

The Kid nodded in the affirmative, and after a round of handshakes, the captain was called to escort the Kid back. Once he returned to the conference room, he shook Lt. General McNeill's hand and thanked him.

"It's time to head out," he announced, and soon after, all of them exchanged their farewells and departed.

On the way back to the airport, as they rode in the car, Peter asked, "What was the point of having all of us there, Kid?"

With a chuckle, the Kid replied, "Cover. I got exactly the meeting I needed the moment I stepped out of the room."

That night back at the office, the Kid gathered JJ, Peter, and me in his office. In a low, determined tone, he disclosed the high-stakes meeting results and stated, "We need to find something on Senator Hargrave and do it as soon as possible." Both JJ and I nodded.

Two weeks had passed, and Senator Hargrave's committee was still in the process of organizing. Peter had received no word from his DOJ contacts, and the media were growing increasingly bored with the story. It was a Tuesday morning, and I was sitting in the Kid's office chatting, when reception buzzed in with a peculiar call. The caller asked for me but wouldn't give a name, only claiming to be from Kentucky.

I glanced at the Kid; we both knew I should take the call. Reception put it through, and I hit the speaker button on the desk phone located on a table in the Kid's office.

"This is Philly," I said.

A measured voice responded, "I'm calling on behalf of Wyatt. He would like to schedule an in-person meeting with you."

I replied immediately, "I'm available as early as this evening."

After a pause, the voice returned: "Then, 7:00 p.m. tonight at the bar at the Manchester Hotel, in Lexington's Historic Distillery District."

"I will see him there tonight," I confirmed.

I then updated the Kid: earlier, when I had reached out to Fabrizio about Senator Hargrave, he mentioned he'd contact Wyatt on our behalf—his muscle in Kentucky.

The Kid's eyes widened. "That sounds promising." He immediately picked up the phone and dialed Alice. "Call Newark and have the G550 fueled and ready. Philly is flying to Lexington in a few hours." He hung up and said to me, "Take JJ with you for backup."

"Let me go home and change. I'll keep you posted," I replied.

The Kid nodded with a hopeful smile. This unexpected development felt like a turning point—a chance to uncover vital details that might finally shift the balance in our favor.

A car picked me up at home—JJ was already in the car—and we arrived at Newark by 4:00 p.m. The company's new Gulfstream G550, which the Kid had purchased just two months before, was simply amazing. We finally had our own company plane. The plane was waiting, and we were wheels up by 4:45 p.m.

We landed in Lexington at 6:00 p.m., and a car was waiting to drive us directly to the Manchester Hotel in Lexington's Historic Distillery District. We stepped into the hotel at 6:30 p.m.—always mindful of my days in La Cosa Nostra and the habit of being early for meetings.

We headed to the bar, and I ordered a Pellegrino with a lime; JJ ordered the same. Barely had we taken a sip when a striking blonde approached and asked, "Is one of you Philly?"

I smiled and nodded in the affirmative.

"Please follow me," she said, guiding us into the dining room.

There, I noticed a table at the back set aside from the others, where two gentlemen were seated. As soon as the tall, thin, distinguished man with glasses stood up, his large companion—whom I quickly recognized as the bodyguard—stepped aside. The distinguished gentleman extended his hand and said, "Philly, I presume."

I shook his hand and replied, "Yes, it's a pleasure to meet you, Wyatt."

Meanwhile, JJ positioned himself beside Wyatt's bodyguard, just far enough away to stay out of earshot of our conversation.

We sat, and Wyatt asked if I'd like a drink.

"I'm fine," I replied.

Then he began. "Fabrizio instructed me to help you out if I could. I understand you have a problem with Senator Hargrave—which, believe me, I understand. Ordinarily, he doesn't bother us and, in fact, occasionally, he assists us with special favors. Fabrizio knows how important Senator Hargrave is to us and that I'd hate to lose my leverage over him. However, Fabrizio has instructed me to share the leverage with you.

"It would be best for everyone if you simply use it without disclosing it publicly—because if you did, we'd lose our leverage."

I nodded in understanding.

Wyatt handed me a large envelope, its weight hinting at the volume of its contents. Without pausing to inspect it, I accepted it, and Wyatt began to explain.

"These papers," he said, "are copies of contracts, spreadsheets, bank statements, and correspondence between Hargrave's wife and her father—a highly influential figure in the Russian government. This is the main source of Senator Hargrave's wealth."

He continued, his tone steady but deliberate, each word like a stone dropped into still water. "The senator's wife owns 49 percent of a Russian container company—an interest she's never declared. On paper, her father holds the title. The profits stream quietly to a Bermuda LLC in his name, then slip into a Nassau firm, before surfacing in a US LLC registered to her. From there, the money filters into her consulting business in Kentucky. Together, these shells hide over a hundred million dollars." Wyatt set the documents down, the whisper of paper loud in the silence, and looked up long enough to see the shock take root. "These," he said, tapping the stack, "map every step—all the way to Senator Hargrave's wife."

My eyes lit up like a fire. Wyatt reiterated the utmost importance of keeping these papers out of the public domain if possible.

"It's vital for our leverage that none of this goes public," he stressed.

"I fully understand," I assured him. "We will do our best."

I thanked Wyatt for his time and promised to get back to him. When he asked if we'd join him for dinner, I declined, saying we needed to return to New Jersey to pass on the information as soon as possible. Wyatt understood my decision. After a firm handshake, I took the envelope, and JJ and I walked out of the hotel.

On the ride to the airport, we kept the conversation to basic chitchat. After all, we didn't know the driver. Once we were on board the plane, I said, "I think we have what we need." I made a mental note not to look at the papers until we reached the office with the Kid. Since it was late and we wouldn't be back at the office until around 11:00 p.m., I called the Kid and suggested that he meet us there, with Peter, Frank, and Howard joining as well.

The Kid replied, "That sounds promising."

I affirmed, "It is." Then he wished us a safe flight and hung up.

Once we got to the office, the Kid and everyone I had asked for were already waiting. The Kid gathered us in the conference room, but before joining the group, I pulled him aside. We stepped into his office and closed the door. Without mincing words, I explained what Wyatt had told me: it was imperative that these documents never become public, as they wanted to keep their leverage. I warned that although we had the backing of Fabrizio, using the papers openly would cost us our new relationship with Wyatt—a cost we wouldn't want to give up unless we had to.

The Kid nodded and said, "I got it. Let's go in the conference room."

Once we were all assembled, the Kid smiled and teased, "Philly, how long are you going to keep me in suspense?"

I stood up and took the floor, laying out the situation exactly as Wyatt had described it. I presented the envelope of documents—a collection of contracts, spreadsheets, bank statements, and secret correspondence meant to expose Senator Hargrave's financial dealings.

"This is why I wanted all of you here," I explained. "We need your expertise to sift through these papers and verify that they confirm the picture Wyatt painted. Then it's your call, Kid—how you want to play this?"

The Kid made it clear. "These papers do not leave this office." He then asked, "Are you all alert enough to dive into them now, or should we reconvene early in the morning?"

Peter was the first to answer; he'd prefer to catch a few hours of sleep and start fresh in the morning. Frank and Howard agreed, so the Kid instructed, "All right, put the papers back in the envelope. I'll lock them up in the safe. Let's meet again at 7:00 a.m. tomorrow."

Everyone nodded in acknowledgment.

The following morning, Wednesday, we reconvened at 7:00 a.m. Peter, Frank, and Howard immediately began their research, even calling in Jim to work his computer magic on the data. Meanwhile, the Kid, JJ, and I retreated to his office to strategize.

The Kid pondered aloud, "How do we show Senator Hargrave what we have without drawing too much attention? If we request a meeting with him directly, too many eyebrows will be raised. JJ, see if you can find someone—with the right connections—who can secure a private conversation with the senator."

JJ replied confidently, "I'm on it, boss."

The Kid then turned to me, adding, "You did good, Philly—really good."

I smiled appreciatively, recognizing the trust he had in me. By the end of the day, the research team confirmed that the documents were rock solid. Now it was all in JJ's court.

The next day, around 10:00 a.m., JJ passed my office with an eager look. "I think I got it," he said. As we walked into the Kid's office, JJ repeated, "I think I got it, boss."

The Kid, all ears, encouraged him to continue.

"Angela's sister, Maria, with all her political contacts, happens to be personal friends with Senator Hargrave's daughter, who works in the senator's office," JJ said. "Maybe Angela could ask Maria to arrange a meeting between Senator Hargrave's daughter and me, so I can explain the situation and have her review some of these documents."

A heavy silence fell over the room as everyone processed the suggestion. Finally, the Kid said, "I hear you, JJ. I like the find, but I'm not sure I want to pull Maria into this. Let me think on it."

About an hour later, the Kid called us back into his office. "Time isn't on our side," he admitted, "but something about this isn't sitting right with me. I need to speak with Angela and see what she thinks. I hate involving her family in these matters. We'll revisit this first thing in the morning. Thank you, guys."

That night, the Kid sat down with Angela to explain the situation and asked for her opinion on involving Maria. Angela responded immediately, "I think she'd love to help you. You're not asking her to do anything illegal."

"No, I'm not," the Kid replied sharply.

"Then why wouldn't she want to help? She thinks the world of you."

Pausing, the Kid continued. "I know exactly how highly I regard her—and that's exactly why I'm hesitant. There's nothing illegal here in her setting up a meeting, but if it ever gets out that she was instrumental in arranging a meeting where documents were uncovered that could sink Senator Hargrave, she might struggle to get new clients. And I know how much she loves politics."

"Let me call her and talk it over," Angela said.

Instantly, the Kid interjected. "No. Either call her and ask her to come over, or you go to her. I don't want this conversation over the phone."

Angela agreed and called her sister.

Later, in a quiet restaurant in Jersey City—just across the river from Manhattan—Angela met with Maria and laid out the situation. She asked if Maria would be willing to arrange an introduction between someone from the Kid's office and Senator Hargrave's daughter.

Maria replied warmly, "Tell the Kid that for you and him, I'd do anything. But why does he want this meeting?"

Angela gave a small smile. "It's really best if you don't know. What I can tell you is that it's a meeting that ultimately Senator Hargrave will be happy he had as opposed to the alternative. It's information he would want to know. Please, don't ask me to go further."

Maria studied her for a moment, then nodded slowly. "I can see how delicate this is. Just let me know when you want me to make the introduction."

They embraced briefly—an exchange of trust sealed with a hug and a kiss—before parting ways.

When Angela returned home, she relayed Maria's enthusiastic response to the Kid. He smiled and said, "Tell her I love her too. Ask her to arrange the introduction for tomorrow, if possible. Let her know that Peter will be in DC for meetings and has something very important that her father would be interested in."

Angela promptly made the call.

Senator Hargrave's daughter agreed to a Friday meeting, though she could only meet at 3:00 p.m. for a half hour. Peter was already en route on the company plane that Friday morning at 10:00 a.m. Upon meeting the senator's daughter at a local restaurant just outside the Capitol, Peter explained that he held no personal grievance against the senator—he was simply commissioned to deliver a message.

He showed her several copies of pages from the documents and explained, "The senator will recognize the source of these documents. All of these papers will be released unless both the Senate Intel Committee and the DOJ's investigations into Seal Team Six Security and Dominic Argianno are dropped."

"Are you blackmailing my father?" the senator's daughter asked sharply.

"I'm not," Peter replied calmly. "I'm just passing on a message. If the information I'm presenting you is false, simply ignore this conversation."

She excused herself, saying, "I have to go back to work," and took the copies before leaving.

After his meeting, Peter returned and briefed the Kid on what had transpired.

"Now it's a waiting game," the Kid remarked.

The following week brought the breakthrough we'd all been hoping for. The DOJ announced it was dropping the investigation into Seal Team Six Security and Dominic Argianno for lack of sufficient evidence, and just a few days later, the Senate Intelligence Committee followed suit, ending its inquiry as well.

Reflecting back, I was impressed with the Kid's hesitation about involving Maria, underscoring his integrity, even in the face of immense pressure.

The resolution, with both the DOJ and Senate Intel Committee dropping their investigations, felt like a hard-earned victory. It was a testament to the team's resourcefulness and the delicate balance of leveraging information without crossing ethical lines—almost.

CHAPTER TWENTY-SEVEN
ON THIN ICE

Over the next year, everything went rather smoothly. STS Security continued to grow. Amy and I began taking more vacations with the Kid and Angela—and sometimes their kids joined us too. The bonds we'd built over the years had only deepened.

However, as little Teresa grew older and began dating, she wasn't as available to vacation with us as she once was. She had her own life now—college, friends, and Ryan. The days of her always being around had grown fewer. We missed her but knew she was becoming her own woman.

One night after dinner, little Teresa went out with her friends—as did the twins—while the youngest headed over to the Kid's mother's guest house located on the property. Angela stood by the kitchen sink, rinsing the last of the dinner plates. "Let me finish up here," she said with a soft smile. "Then we can relax with our wine in the living room."

"I like the sound of that," the Kid replied, drying his hands with a dish towel. "I'll help. But just a little—I don't want to break my streak of domestic excellence." Angela chuckled.

They settled into the living room, the warm glow of a nearby lamp casting golden shadows across the walls. Outside, crickets chirped, and a gentle breeze stirred the curtains on a warm, beautiful, breezy night.

Angela swirled her wine slowly, staring into the glass like it held the words she couldn't quite find. The Kid noticed.

"Okay," he said, smiling faintly. "That look on your face? It's louder than anything you've said tonight."

Angela hesitated. "I'm not sure how to tell you this."

"You know me," the Kid said gently. "Straight up. No dancing around. Whatever it is, just lay it out, and we will deal with it."

Angela took a slow, measured breath. "You know how much I love you and how much I cherish our family now. The last thing I ever want is to upset that balance." She glanced toward the lightly lit hallway, as if checking for ghosts. "I've grown very close to Teresa—I even think of her as my daughter." Tears welled in her eyes as she added, "Dom, this is so hard."

The Kid leaned forward. "Angela, whatever this is, just say it," the Kid urged gently.

Angela nodded, swallowing hard. "You know I never had kids. But with Teresa, it's different. When I see her laugh, when she hugs me, when she asks me for advice—it fills something I didn't know was empty. I love her like I gave birth to her. Which is why what I'm about to say is so difficult. But I feel what I'm about to say might jeopardize my bond with Teresa—yet I know I have to tell you for her sake."

The Kid's smile faded. "Go on."

Angela hesitated, then asked quietly, "Are you happy with Ryan?"

There was a pause. "He's okay," the Kid answered, rubbing his jaw. "Not my first pick, but I tolerate him. I know he's trying to stay on my good side.

"Probably tries too hard, if I'm being honest."

Angela set down her glass and took his hand. "Please don't react the way I think you might."

He tensed. "Angela—"

"About six months ago," she began, her voice quieter now, "I walked into Teresa's room just after she got home from the mall with Ryan. She was standing in front of her mirror—not removing her makeup but adding more. That's when I saw it. A faint bruise on her cheekbone."

The Kid froze.

"She claimed she bumped into a door in a fitting room at the mall. But when I gave her that look—the one only women know how to give each other—she caved. Whispered, 'Please don't tell my dad. You know what he or Uncle Philly will do.' Then she told me the truth: they'd argued, and Ryan slapped her."

Angela's voice broke. "She said it was the first time. That he apologized right after and swore it would never happen again. She begged me to keep it between us."

The Kid sat motionless, jaw clenched.

"I told her about Gary. About the hell I went through. How your father stopped it—but not before I'd lost too many pieces of myself. I said, 'You're not weak, Teresa. You don't have to live like I did. And you have people who love you and will protect you.' She cried. Said she understood. But she made me promise."

"I agreed, because while I don't keep secrets from you—I love you with all my heart—protecting Teresa's trust is equally precious."

"I know this isn't the end of the story," the Kid said quietly.

"No, it isn't," Angela affirmed. Angela looked up. "I kept that promise. Until last night."

The Kid's voice was low. "What happened?"

Angela took another breath. "You remember the get-together? All the kids were hanging out in the rec room downstairs—music playing, games going on, dancing."

He nodded.

"You went upstairs to watch a movie. Before I came up, I went down to check if they wanted snacks. I couldn't find Teresa, so I started searching the rooms until I came to the soundproof theater. I didn't think she would be in there watching a movie, leaving her friends outside, but for some reason, I opened the door."

Angela's hands trembled slightly. "I saw Teresa pinned against the wall. Ryan's hand was gripping her face—tight. The moment he saw me, he let go. She ran past me in tears. I wanted to strangle him myself.

"Ryan tried to explain, 'It's not what you think. We just got into an argument, and maybe I had a little too much to drink.'

"I looked him straight in the eye and declared, 'If I go upstairs and tell Dominic what I just saw, you'll be waking up in a hospital bed if you're lucky.'

" 'Please don't say anything—it will never happen again,' Ryan pleaded.

" 'I'm done here, Ryan. It's time for you to go home—and I mean now.'

" 'Yes, ma'am,' he said as he quickly left."

"Dom, don't look at me like that. You waited until now to tell me this."

"Why didn't you tell me last night?" the Kid said abruptly.

Angela looked at him, pain in her eyes. "I've been struggling all night—I didn't sleep a wink. I was afraid that if I mentioned it last night, Ryan might end up like Gary."

The Kid's surprise was palpable. "What do you mean, 'like Gary'?"

Angela met his gaze steadily. "I know what happened with Gary—not because someone told me, but because I know you so well. I've known you long enough to trust that you would never let someone hurt me the way he did and walk away unscathed. I don't care if Gary is alive or not; he got what was coming to him. But I know you didn't just let him off by having someone talk to him—you made him pay a price."

The Kid offered a warm smile but remained silent.

She leaned in, her tone earnest. "I love that you'd protect me like that. But this time, you have to think. Teresa isn't me. If you handle Ryan the way I know you want to, she may never forgive you. Talk to her first, Dom. You're not the Kid in LA anymore. Let her decide before you make your decision."

Softening, the Kid looked at Angela and said earnestly, "I love you, Angela." They shared a warm, lingering hug. After a few moments, he stood up and picked up his phone. "JJ, find out where little Teresa is right now. I want to know," he instructed. For our protection, we all carry special trackers in our phones. Yes, it limits our privacy a bit, but in a pinch, it could save our lives.

JJ called back within five minutes. "She's at the Hollywood Movie Cinema in Morristown," he reported.

"Go pick her up and tell her I need her back at the house right now," the Kid said. "And JJ, make sure Ryan comes back too."

Within the hour, they were all home. Little Teresa asked, "What's up, Dad? Is everything okay?"

"Everything's fine, sweetheart. Let's head to the living room. I have something to say." Once seated, he continued. "I heard some disturbing news tonight." At that moment, Ryan shifted in his seat, already nervous, fear evident on his face.

"There's been a potential threat against the office," the Kid said smoothly. "Nothing serious yet, but we're taking precautions. I want everyone home until we know more. Why don't you hang out at the house until I'm sure it's safe."

After a half hour, the Kid glanced at his phone. "All clear. Ryan—your car's still at the theater. It's late. JJ will drive you to pick it up."

"I'll go with him," little Teresa offered.

"No, I prefer you to stay here tonight, sweetheart," the Kid said, voice even.

She looked at her dad for a long second and said, "Okay."

"Sure, Mr. A, whatever you say," Ryan replied.

The Kid looked at JJ and reiterated, "Take him to his car."

Once they left, little Teresa turned to her father. "What's really going on, Dad?"

The Kid smiled warmly. "You've always been so perceptive, Teresa—one of the many things I love about you."

Glancing at Angela, little Teresa added, "I have a feeling I already know. Is Ryan going to be okay tonight with JJ?"

"For now, he is." The Kid grinned.

"There's no sense having separate conversations when we're a family," the Kid continued. "We need to discuss this together."

Little Teresa reminded Angela, "You promised."

The Kid jumped in, "Teresa, you should be thanking Angela. If it weren't for her, Ryan might be in the hospital with tubes coming out of him right now. Let's stop the finger-pointing and get to the heart of the matter."

She crossed her arms. "Dad, he's not a bad guy. He treats me well most of the time—even if he occasionally flies off the handle after a few drinks," little Teresa protested.

The Kid leaned forward, his tone firm. "Listen, Teresa—God knows I've had my moments when I was young. But never—not once—have I raised a hand to a girl. Not your mother. Not Angela. Not anyone, ever. Once a guy raises his hands to a girl, that's not the end—it's only the beginning."

Taking a steady breath, he continued. "I know if I tell you not to see him, you'll only want him more. Angela can attest to that from our childhood."

Angela smiled and teased, "Isn't that the truth? Though, I wanted you anyway." They both smiled.

"So here's what I'm saying," the Kid declared. "You can do a lot better than Ryan. You deserve better. But if you choose to keep seeing him, that's on you. However, if he ever lays a hand on you again, a shove, a grab, a slap, anything—for any reason whatsoever—I will make sure he lives to regret it. Do you understand me?"

Little Teresa, looking a little nervous, replied, "Yes, Dad."

"You know I want nothing but the best for you and your siblings," he said. "But no guy will ever lay a hand on you, your sister, or Angela and walk away. Not as long as I'm breathing.

"Now that I know he's raised his hands to you, he's permanently on my shit list," the Kid warned. "I'll allow him into this house if you invite him, but remember, he's on thin ice."

Little Teresa frowned and said, "I know." She added, "I love you, Dad. I know you always have my back. And I love you too, Angela." At that, Angela immediately pulled little Teresa into a tight hug.

Later that night, as they were getting ready for bed, Angela spoke softly, "I think he knows—you know. I saw the fear in his eyes when he looked at you tonight."

"Good. I'm glad he knows," the Kid replied. After a brief pause, he added, "Now let's hope Teresa sees the light and moves on from him."

Angela smiled gently. "I have a feeling she will; just give her time. And by the way, I'm proud of how you handled it tonight with Ryan."

The Kid returned the smile. "We shall see."

CHAPTER TWENTY-EIGHT
LEGACY

Over the next few years, change quietly settled in like a long-anticipated season.

About two months after the basement incident, little Teresa called a family meeting. She sat across from the Kid and Angela in the sunroom, her expression calm but resolute. "I've decided to end things with Ryan," she said. "I've realized he's not the one for me." The Kid exchanged a knowing glance with Angela. It wasn't smug—just quiet relief. Little Teresa smiled faintly and added, "You were both right." Angela reached across and squeezed her hand.

The Kid gave a single nod. "Proud of you, sweetheart."

She'd already told Ryan. Despite his pleading—calls, texts, even a voice message that bordered on desperation—she stood firm. When he asked if he could swing by to collect a few things, she answered coldly: "I'll have them sent to you." It was final. Ryan was a chapter closed.

Maybe her clarity came from the time she'd been spending

with Christopher, a law school classmate with sharp suits and a sharper wit. Born and raised in South Jersey to Italian parents, Christopher spoke the language fluently—and often teased Teresa that her own Italian was "tourist-grade at best."

She gave as good as she got, but he had a point. Her grandmother and father rarely used Italian at home, and though little Teresa could manage simple conversations, deeper discussions escaped her. Angela, on the other hand, was fluent—and clearly delighted by Christopher's presence. She saw a spark between them that reminded her of her own beginnings with the Kid. Whenever she and little Teresa cooked together or drove to the market, she'd slip into Italian, coaching her stepdaughter with patient correction and playful challenges. It became a game—and maybe, a quiet blessing.

Meanwhile, the Kid had begun entertaining a different sort of shift. One afternoon, he called me into his office. The sun cut through the blinds in golden stripes, and he was leaning back in his chair with that look he always had when something big was about to drop. "Let's talk," he said.

I grinned. "Last time you said that, you ended up leaving LA."

He laughed. "Touché."

Then he got serious. "I've been thinking about stepping back. Not completely. Just semi-retirement. I want to travel more with Angela, play more golf, spend time with the family. Hell, maybe even learn how to cook something other than steak."

I nodded. "Sounds like you've thought this through."

"I have. But I want your thoughts. You've earned that."

I shrugged. "You mean about you retiring, or me retiring as well?"

The Kid laughed. "Both. It's hard for me to think about retiring and leaving you working every day. Who am I going to play golf with?"

He leaned forward. "Philly, you've got more money now than you'll ever spend. Don't you think it's time to start enjoying the good life a little?"

I considered it—and quickly realized the Kid was right. He usually was.

"Okay," I said. "How would this work?"

"I'm going to stay on as CEO," he said, "but I need someone to handle day-to-day operations. Someone I trust. You did an amazing job running our German division—hell, you built that team almost from scratch. But you're not going back to the grind, not unless you want to. If you want this, it's yours without question, but I would much rather be out on the golf course with you, not just reading about business in your group texts."

I laughed. "So, who's the pick?"

He hesitated. "Not decided yet. Assuming you semi-retire with me, I'm leaning toward promoting from within."

"JJ?"

"Exactly."

"You know I love that kid," I said. "Two reasons why he's a great choice: one, you can trust him without question. Two, he's young, hungry, and smart. I mean, we both know what it felt like to be given a real shot. You gave that to me when you put me in charge of Germany. JJ deserves the same chance. The only thing you have to decide is if he's ready."

The Kid sat back, nodded, and smiled. "Thanks, Philly. That's exactly what I needed to hear."

The next morning, he called JJ into his office. They spoke for three hours. When JJ finally stepped out, the expression on his face said it all. He looked like a man reborn—focused, energized, proud.

The following morning, the Kid called me and JJ into his office. The room felt still, charged with anticipation.

He started without fanfare. "JJ, I've been thinking a lot about our lengthy conversation yesterday. I told you I was leaning toward handing you the reins of STS Security's day-to-day operations. I needed to sleep on it. I had spoken with Philly before we met yesterday, and he was adamant—you're the guy. The only question we both had was if I thought you were ready.

"You know me, JJ—I don't pull punches. I think Philly's right. You're the right pick."

He paused, his tone shifting just slightly. "My only hesitation is your lack of business experience. But that's not stopping me. I've decided to name you president of STS Security. I want you to operate freely—within reasonable limits. Make decisions, grow the company. Some decisions you make will be solid, others will miss the mark, and that's okay. For now, run any major acquisitions or high-stakes choices by me. Think of that as a safety net, not a leash. I believe you've got what it takes."

The Kid glanced at Philly, then back to JJ. "Philly and I are just a call away if you need us. But don't use that phone like a crutch; it's there if you truly need it."

The Kid leaned back. "Your official start date as president is July 1st—two weeks from today. Your base salary will increase to 300K. You already know I don't operate with a fixed bonus structure; I reward based on performance—yours and the company's. I expect a lot from you." Then he smiled. "Now I'll shut up and let you speak."

JJ was visibly moved. "This means more than you know," he said. "Not just the title or the money, but the trust. I've worked for you for years, and you've always treated me with respect, like family. You and Philly are really close, and now I feel like I'm truly part of that circle. I won't let you down—either of you."

JJ turned to Philly, voice steady with conviction. "I want to build here what you built in Germany."

Philly nodded. "Thank you. I know you will, and whatever you need from me, I'm here for you."

The Kid stood. "Philly and I will keep our offices for now. You're free to operate the rest of the space as you see fit." The Kid looked JJ in the eye. "I believe in you. Now go prove me right."

That day, the future was sealed: JJ would become the next president of STS Security.

A week later, we held a leadership meeting—not in our usual glass-walled boardroom but in a private ballroom at the Hyatt

Regency in Morristown. We'd outgrown the old space, and the moment demanded something bigger. No staff, no waiters—just our core team and trusted managers.

At 10:00 a.m., after a hearty breakfast, we moved to the ballroom, and the Kid stepped up to the mic. "Let's begin."

His voice was clear, confident, but carried a new kind of weight. A sense of finality.

"We're here today because some big changes are coming. First, I want to thank all of you, many of whom have been with me for years, some since day one. We've built something extraordinary together. None of this"—he gestured around the room—"none of this happens without your hard work, your loyalty, and your belief in what we do." He paused, then smiled as the applause continued.

"I'm stepping down as president to pursue semi-retirement. It's time for more golf, more travel, and more time with my family. Philly will be joining me on that journey. But this company still needs leadership—vision, hunger, and energy." He looked over at JJ.

"That's why I've chosen JJ to be our new president. I trust him completely, and I know he's ready to take us into the future. I'll remain CEO, and Philly will continue to serve as our Senior Executive VP and is available to consult for as long as JJ needs." A hush fell over the room—then came the applause.

When the Kid handed JJ the mic, I saw something in his eyes I'd never seen before: not just pride but peace. He'd built something that could stand without him.

The years that followed were nothing short of golden. The Kid and I found our rhythm on the golf course, teeing off once or twice a week—sometimes at our home course, Baltusrol Golf Club, and other times at renowned courses across the country. We traveled often, almost always with Angela and Amy by our sides, sharing bottles of fine wine and trading jabs over missed putts and awkward swings. Eventually, Angela and Amy picked up the game themselves, and before long, the four of us were playing together regularly. What started as casual outings turned into spirited foursomes filled with laughter, light trash talk, and a shared love for the game. The competition never let up, but neither did the bond. With every round we played, the friendship—and the memories—grew stronger.

JJ proved himself. He ran the company with precision and passion, never needing a leash. Occasionally, the Kid flew to DC to introduce him to contacts in the Pentagon, but otherwise, his office collected dust. Mine too, mostly. We kept our names on the doors, but we were ghosts now—happy ones.

As for little Teresa, law school suited her. When she came home, she spent long afternoons shopping with Angela and Amy, laughing as they tried on shoes and exchanged recipes. And then there was Christopher—always there, always steady.

The Kid and Angela adored him. One evening, Amy and I had dinner with him at their place. By the end of the meal, I leaned over to Amy and said quietly, "This is the guy." She nodded in agreement.

Compared to Ryan, Christopher was light-years ahead. Confident, kind, and fluent in both law and love. He wasn't trying to impress anyone. He just fit.

And me? I look back now and marvel.

From the Grill in LA to the Gulfstream G550, from facing prison to retiring a wealthy man with a family and peace of mind—I owe it all to one person.

The Kid.

He changed everything. Pulled me out of a nosedive, gave me a second chance, and never once made me feel like I owed him for it.

I don't know what the future holds. Maybe we'll slow down more. Maybe the next generation will bring surprises of their own.

But I do know this: as long as the Kid and I are side by side, everything's going to be just fine.

D.J. Vella

www.ingramcontent.com/pod-product-compliance
Lightning Source LLC
Chambersburg PA
CBHW060453030426
42337CB00015B/1579